A Theory of Thrills, Sublime and Epiphany in Literature

A Theory of Thrills, Sublime and Epiphany in Literature

Nigel Fabb

ANTHEM PRESS

Anthem Press
An imprint of Wimbledon Publishing Company
www.anthempress.com

This edition first published in UK and USA 2025
by ANTHEM PRESS
75–76 Blackfriars Road, London SE1 8HA, UK
or PO Box 9779, London SW19 7ZG, UK
and
244 Madison Ave #116, New York, NY 10016, USA

First published in the UK and USA by Anthem Press in 2022

Copyright © Nigel Fabb 2025

The author asserts the moral right to be identified as the author of this work.

All rights reserved. Without limiting the rights under copyright reserved above, no part of this publication may be reproduced, stored or introduced into a retrieval system, or transmitted, in any form or by any means (electronic, mechanical, photocopying, recording or otherwise), without the prior written permission of both the copyright owner and the above publisher of this book.

British Library Cataloguing-in-Publication Data
A catalogue record for this book is available from the British Library.

Library of Congress Control Number: 2024946866

ISBN-13: 978-1-83999-415-9 (Pbk)
ISBN-10: 1-83999-415-0 (Pbk)

Cover image: Cover painting by Anna H. Geerdes, 'Incoming Tide'. Reproduced with kind permission of the artist and Compass Gallery.

This title is also available as an e-book.

CONTENTS

Acknowledgements		vi
Dedication		viii
1.	Introduction: Strong experiences and what causes them	1
2.	The study of strong experiences	21
3.	Epistemic feelings and knowledge	45
4.	Arousal, emotion and strong experiences	79
5.	The psychological background	99
6.	How literature triggers strong experiences	141
7.	Conclusions	179
Bibliography		183
Index		211

ACKNOWLEDGEMENTS

The research for this book was supported by the Leverhulme Trust, with a Leverhulme Major Research Fellowship titled 'Epiphanies in Literature: A Psychological and Literary Linguistic Account' (2014–2017).

I thank the readers of part or all of this book manuscript and associated materials for their invaluable advice: Stefan Blohm, Lizann Bonnar, Janet Fabb, Faye Hammill, Elspeth Jajdelska, Christine Knoop, Joanna McPake, Esperanza Miyake, Willie van Peer, Rob Sandler, Anna Thornell, Myfany Turpin, Stefano Versace, Eugen Wassiliwizky and Tim Wharton. Janet Fabb also helped format the bibliography and worked on other aspects of the manuscript. Over the longer term, Mark Aronoff, Deborah Cameron, Greg Currie, Félix Schoeller, Dan Sperber and Deirdre Wilson have all had an important role in bringing the project to fruition. I thank my colleagues in English Studies at the University of Strathclyde for their advice and comments on this project, and their practical support while I have been writing it, and I also thank my students, over many years, for contributing to helpful discussions around this project.

I thank Anna H. Geerdes for permitting the use of her painting on the cover, and Jill Gerber of Compass Gallery, Glasgow, for facilitating this.

Early versions of the material from this book have been presented as invited talks in many institutions, including talks in the Schools of Psychological Sciences and Health and my own School of Humanities at the University of Strathclyde. I thank those who invited me to give these talks. I have also benefited from talking to participants at various conferences in which some of this material has been presented. An early version of the project was presented at the Bangor Conference on Communication (1994). I returned to the project with a paper on 'the linguistics of surprise' at the CUNY Conference on the Word in Phonology (2010), followed by the AHRC workshop Method in Philosophical Aesthetics: The Challenge from the Sciences (Leeds 2012). During the 3-year period in which I was supported by Leverhulme, I gave talks on this material at Approaches to Text-Type-Specific Sentence Interpretation (Tübingen 2014), the Inaugural Conference of the International Society of

Literary Linguistics (Mainz 2015), Languages of Literature: Attridge at 70 (York 2015), Memory, an Interdisciplinary Conference in Arts and Science (Newry 2015), the Royal Society of Edinburgh workshop on verbal versus screen based narrative and episodic memory (Strathclyde 2016), ANU and the Sydney Conservatorium of Music (2016 and 2017), the Postgraduate Conference on Power (Stirling 2017), Meta-categories: Cross-disciplinary, Cross-cultural and Cross-temporal Perspectives (ANU 2017), Beyond Meaning (Athens 2017), the International Society for the Empirical Study of Literature (IGEL) special session 'What is Literariness?' (Paris 2017). And in the past few years I have benefited from presenting to the specialist audiences at IGEL (Stavanger 2018), Poetics and Linguistics Association (PALA, Nottingham 2021) and IGEL (Liverpool 2021). An earlier and somewhat different version of the argument presented in this book has been published as the chapter 'Experiences of Ineffable Significance' in *Beyond Meaning*, edited by Elly Ifantidou, Louis de Saussure and Tim Wharton (2021).

I thank Philip Davies for the invitation to submit this book to his series at Anthem, and I welcome the support from Megan Greiving at Anthem and the comments of three anonymous reviewers.

For Janet

Chapter 1

INTRODUCTION: STRONG EXPERIENCES AND WHAT CAUSES THEM

Strong Experiences

This book is about two kinds of experience, which I suggest have a common basis in surprise. One is an experience that we feel as a bodily thrill. This might be chills or tears or some other sudden arousal, usually pleasurable and fairly common for some people. The other is an experience of suddenly coming to know something very significant. It may be impossible to put into words what is known; that is, it is ineffable. This second kind of experience may be rarer and indeed can often be so rare as to be highly memorable. Experiences of the first kind can be called 'thrill', and I divide experiences of the second kind into two sub-kinds, namely 'sublime' and 'epiphany'. These kinds of experience can be combined: when a thrill accompanies a sense of suddenly coming to know something significant.

I group both kinds of experiences under a common heading of 'strong experiences' because I suggest that they have many characteristics in common, and I suggest that this is because they both begin as surprises. This explains many of their characteristics and incidentally means that strong experiences are variants of a very ordinary kind of experience and need no special psychology. The term 'strong experience' is borrowed from music psychologist Alf Gabrielsson's (2011) analysis of a large number of elicited reports of strong, intense and profound experiences of music. Strong experiences can be triggered when we are reading literary texts, and Chapter 6 explores why literature surprises us in these ways; I will show that all the ordinary characteristics of literature provide the materials that in the right combination and context can trigger a strong experience.

The strong experience of 'thrill' is a sudden arousal, such as chills or tears or some other bodily response, in response to some perception or thought. I take this generic term 'thrill' from the psychologist John Sloboda (1991), who uses the term to describe various arousals in response to music. Thrills were described by one of the pioneers of modern psychology, William James:

> In listening to poetry, drama, or heroic narrative, we are often surprised at the cutaneous [skin] shiver which like a sudden wave flows over us, and at the heart-swelling and the lachrymal effusion [tears] that unexpectedly catch us at intervals. In listening to music, the same is even more strikingly true. (James 1884: 196)

A second kind of strong experience is the experience of the 'sublime', which has many manifestations but is generally a strong experience involving a perception of something which is extreme and often very large. It is described here by the philosopher Immanuel Kant:

> Bold, overhanging, and, as it were, threatening rocks, thunderclouds piled up in the vault of heaven, borne along with flashes and peals, volcanoes in all their violence of destruction, hurricanes leaving desolation in their track, the boundless ocean rising with rebellious force, the high waterfall of some mighty river, and the like, make power of resistance of trifling moment in comparison with their might. But, provided our own position is secure, their aspect is all the more attractive for its fearfulness; and we readily call these objects sublime. (Kant 1952: 110)

A third kind of strong experience is what I call 'epiphany', but it has other names and, like the sublime, a variety of manifestations. It is often an intense feeling of significance derived from a perception of something ordinary. For the art historian Kenneth Clark it is a 'moment of vision':

> We can all remember those flashes when the object at which we are gazing seems to detach itself from the habitual flux of impressions and becomes intensely clear and important to us. [...] Mr. Graham Sutherland has described how on his country walks objects which he has passed a hundred times – a root, a thorn bush, a dead tree – will suddenly detach themselves and demand a separate existence; but why or when this should happen he cannot tell us. (Clark 1981: 6)

The epiphany appears frequently in fiction, particularly in modernist texts; the term itself is borrowed from the novelist James Joyce (1944).

> He told Cranly that the clock of the Ballast Office was capable of an epiphany. Cranly questioned the inscrutable dial of the Ballast Office with his no less inscrutable countenance.

— Yes, said Stephen. I will pass it time after time, allude to it, refer to it, catch a glimpse of it. It is only an item in the catalogue of Dublin's street furniture. Then all at once I see it and I know at once what it is: epiphany (Joyce 1944: 188)

The literary theorist Morris Beja (1971) uses the term 'literary epiphany' to describe a range of narrated experiences like this in modern writing. Another example comes from the novelist Virginia Woolf, who represents what she calls a 'moment of being' (Woolf 1928) or 'moment of vision' in many places in her fiction and nonfiction, and I take these terms to describe a strong experience that belongs to the same family of experiences as Joyce's 'epiphany'. Here are two descriptions, the first from a review and the second from her 1927 novel *To the Lighthouse*.

To catch and enclose certain moments which break off from the mass, in which without bidding things come together in a combination of inexplicable significance, to arrest those thoughts which suddenly, to the thinker at least, are almost menacing without meaning. (Woolf 1918)

The great revelation had never come. The great revelation perhaps never did come. Instead there were little daily miracles, illuminations, matches struck unexpectedly in the dark; here was one. (Woolf 2006: 132)

The distinction between the kinds of strong experience is not always very clear. Sometimes the kinds are combined. The psychologists Dacher Keltner and Jonathan Haidt (2003) suggest that the sublime and epiphany are related experiences of vastness; literary theorist Sharon Kim (2012: 68) says that 'in *Middlemarch*, a series of epiphanies gives Dorothea her ascent into the human sublime'; and the literary theorist Robert Langbaum (1999: 54) says that literary epiphanies produce in readers 'the modern sublime'. From a psychological perspective there may just be one general kind of strong experience, and the apparent sub-kinds are just experiences in which one or another aspect is prominent.

We can identify various other named kinds of experiences as 'strong experiences', because they share the strong feeling of significance, often ineffable, and they can also involve sudden arousal. They include what William James, in his psychological study of religion, called 'mystical experience' (James 1982). Marghanita Laski conducted an extensive evidence-based study of the type of strong experience which she called 'ecstasy' (Laski 1961). Psychologists in the positive psychology tradition who focus on how our experiences are positively enhanced have written about these experiences; they include Abraham Maslow's 'peak experience' (Maslow 1976), William

R. Miller's 'quantum change' (Miller 2004) and Keltner and Haidt's 'awe' (Keltner and Haidt 2003). The psychiatrist Graziella Magherini identified an extreme response to art which she called 'Stendhal's syndrome' (Magherini 1995). Sigmund Freud discussed the uncanny (Freud 1919), which I treat as a type of strong experience. The strangeness we feel as a result of the memory error which we call déjà vu is also related to strong experience (Brown 2004).

These experiences do not feel like the same experience; they are about different sorts of things and may vary in their epistemic feelings of significance and ineffability. Furthermore they are theorized and described at different historical moments and understood in different ways. The reason that I put them all together as strong experiences is that I suggest that they all begin as surprise. Their origin in surprise correlates with their being sudden and brief: two common features of surprise. The arousal component, particularly the goosebumps or chills feeling, can be understood as a response to surprise, as the psychologist David Huron (2006) argues in his extended account of surprise in response to music. And the feeling of knowing something significant can also be understood as originating in surprise, which arises when we come to know something which was not known before. I discuss in Chapter 5 how surprise can be theorized.

Strong experiences can have interesting characteristics which I explore and seek to explain in this book. First, it is interesting that the physical feelings are quite varied. Some involve feelings associated with cold or with fear such as chills, shivers or goosebumps, and others involve feelings which might normally be associated with sadness, such as tears or a lump in the throat; also there are various other feelings. All these are kinds of 'arousal' – the psychological term I use in this book – and specifically 'phasic arousal' because they arise suddenly and briefly. More specifically they are mostly kinds of (phasic) arousal in the autonomic nervous system, as discussed in Chapter 4. These arousals are shared with emotions, and emotion plays a role in strong experience. In strong experiences, the arousals are often mismatched with the trigger, in content, in intensity and in type. For example, we might expect to get a chill feeling when we are cold or perhaps when we are afraid, but it is less obvious why we get a chill in response to an artwork. The same can be said of a reader's tears in response to some fictional event which is not inherently sad, because it is not real and often not even sad within the fictional world. The mismatched nature of these responses also appears in the much-discussed problem of why we get emotional responses to literature.

Another important characteristic of strong experiences is that they can involve a feeling of coming to know something significant, which might be an insight into the nature of reality, of a deep truth or a supernatural experience. The feeling of knowledge can be life-changing. Often it is not possible to put into words what exactly is known, that is, what is known is 'ineffable'.

I introduce the phrase 'epistemic feeling' to name any feeling that seems to involve a kind of knowledge, and both the feeling of significance and the feeling of ineffability are kinds of epistemic feeling. There are many other types of well-studied epistemic feeling, including the feeling of knowing, the tip of the tongue experience, the feeling of déjà vu, the feeling of premonition, the feeling of fluency and so on. Chapter 3 explores the epistemic feelings that are part of strong experiences.

A third characteristic of strong experiences is that they have triggers, which are the real or imagined objects, people, events, sequences of events, thoughts, memories and so on, which, when perceived, cause strong experiences to happen. I borrow the term 'trigger' from Laski (1961), who cites a great variety of triggers. The following is one person's account of triggers of 'transcendent ecstasy' from the many examples that Laski solicited from the public.

> Aesthetic things suddenly – a Scotch folk-song – sudden *moments* like seeing a very well-turned sentence, or looking at the film 'The Member of the Wedding' – a curious sensation, a feeling of ecstasy induced by something that isn't physical, something creeping up your spine. (Laski 1961: 396)

It is worth noting that in this example, the epistemic feeling is 'induced by' the physiological feeling. Sloboda (1991) and many music psychologists after him have explored how various aspects of musical form can trigger thrills. Chapter 6 turns from the arts in general to literature, to look at the ways in which the characteristic and common forms and contents of literary texts can occasionally function to trigger strong experiences in readers.

A fourth notable characteristic of strong experiences is that they seem to be infectious. It is possible to 'catch a thrill' by hearing about someone else's thrill experience or remembering one's own. Gabrielsson (2011: 460) describes this infectiousness: 'Just the very act of reading these accounts [of strong experiences of music] has given me many strong experiences: now and then I have become totally absorbed and very moved, felt shivers, tears welling in my eyes, and recognized reactions in myself'. Writers can also try to cause a strong experience, including sublime and epiphany, in a reader, by representing the experience in the text. This is another kind of infectiousness. I explain it in terms of the role of metacognition and metarepresentation in strong experiences – notions introduced shortly.

Why This Book?

This book combines research areas which have not been combined before, but the individual parts have been very extensively studied, as I show in

Chapter 2. There is much research on the sublime in aesthetics and literary studies, including research which seeks to explain it in psychological or psychoanalytic terms. Literary epiphanies in novels and poems have been widely studied. Psychologists have written about various types of epiphanic experiences under various names. Popular psychology books describe strong experiences, including *Epiphany: True Stories of Sudden Insight to Inspire, Encourage and Transform* (Ballard 2014) or *Awake: Stories of Life-Changing Epiphanies* (Dyja2001) and the anthology *Epiphanies: Life Changing Encounters with Music* (Herrington 2015). Experimental psychologists have demonstrated how thrills arise, particularly in response to music, but also in response to literature.

The present book is the first to put together the thrill, sublime and epiphany experiences as the same overarching kind of 'strong experience'. The justification for doing so is that though they are different in many ways, I propose that the various experiences all arise from surprise and that some of their shared characteristics can be explained in terms of surprise. It is this shared origin that brings the experiences together as 'strong experiences'. By providing a rather simple account of how the experiences arise, it is possible to focus on what triggers them.

The book seeks a general, simple and unified account of a range of kinds of experience. The notion of 'strong experience' is not a natural kind of experience but a way of grouping different kinds of experience by suggesting that their characteristics can be explained by a shared origin in surprise. I have drawn the explanatory tools from the psychology of our everyday experience, and I assume that these aspects of psychology are shared by all humans. This has three implications. First, it suggests that our capacity to have strong experiences comes from our shared human psychology. Second, this approach is parsimonious because I propose no new psychological notions. Third, this approach assumes that that there are a finite number of aspects of psychology which might provide an explanation for these experiences, and I have chosen to focus on surprise. The idea that strong experiences are special kinds of experience which can nevertheless be understood in terms of our general psychology is borrowed from William James (1982) and Patrick McNamara (2009) who sought to explain religious and mystical experience without inventing a special psychology for them. Following these authors, I assume that an explanation of strong experiences in terms of general psychology is at the same time compatible with their being actual insights into another reality. This is important, because it means that the experiences might be entirely explainable in psychological terms, but nevertheless ontologically significant in a very special way.

If strong experiences arise from our shared human psychology then we might expect them to appear in all human cultures. They are attached to us as humans, and not as humans at a particular moment in history or place in culture: there is no reason to think for example that modernity has made strong experiences more or less available than in the past. However, though the principles which allow them to arise come from our common humanity as a species, nevertheless, it is hard to be sure that they do appear either in all other cultures now or in all cultures of the deeper past. Often, in the deeper past or elsewhere, there are no accounts of such experiences. To understand these gaps and to understand why strong experiences might not always appear, or not always be reported, we can refer to Robert Levy's (1973) account of cultural and experiential difference, which he observed in Tahiti. Levy says that a type of experience may be felt in one culture but not in another culture, even if it has a universal psychological basis. Levy suggests that feelings might be 'hypocognized' in a culture, which means that they are not discussed, have no name, and so on, even if they are felt. He says 'one "feels" considerably more than cultural forms may make culturally accessible'. For example, Enfield and Zuckerman (2024) discuss how déjà vu is an experience unrecognized in the Nam Noi valley of upland Central Laos: they say that déjà vu is hypocognized in Laos. The contrary situation can also arise because feelings can instead be hypercognized, which means that they are salient in the culture and are subject to extensive discussion, and this has been true of the sublime, and the epiphany in certain cultural contexts, such as Western culture since the eighteenth century.

Verbal art, which includes literature as its written manifestation, is capable of triggering strong experiences in us, and there is evidence that it has done so at least since Longinus described literature as a source of the sublime almost 2,000 years ago. Literature offers a case study by which we can examine in detail how an aesthetic practice can have inherent characteristics that are suited to the production of strong experience. After considering the various theoretical and psychological issues around strong experiences, I conclude the book in Chapter 6 with an exploration of some of the relevant features of literature as triggers of strong experience. I look at the forms of literature and how they can change and thereby trigger surprise, at the ways in which narratives manipulate our expectations, at how metaphor can produce complexities which trigger strong experience and at various other aspects which are part of the texture of literature. The chapter focuses specifically on literature, but the proposals in this book can also be applied to other aesthetic practices and to an understanding of our general experience.

Beyond academic considerations, I think it is generally worth looking for an explanation of why strong experiences arise. To make it personal, I have just pulled from my bookcase Jan Kott's *Shakespeare Our Contemporary*, in the Methuen University Paperback edition (Kott 1967). Inside the front cover it says, 'Nigel Fabb Autumn 1973'. I can remember reading it, sitting in the sun on the hill near my home, looking out at the sea. This is, incidentally, a typical location for strong experiences, as Laski noted. This book once communicated to me the intensely exciting power of a Shakespeare performance and first gave me a clear sense of how a literary text can suddenly produce a powerful moment, referred to here as a strong experience. In my memory, this was why I shifted from expecting to study science at university to studying English literature instead, and now, almost 50 years later I feel a personal obligation to try to explain what happened. I am not alone in this: many people I have talked to about this project have told me that they clearly remember such an experience happening to them. Perhaps as you read this book, this will happen to you too.

This book can only reflect on experiences that have already happened. Though we might find clues as to how to seek them out, it is not really possible to predict how to have strong experiences or to cause them in other people. This is because strong experiences are based in our ordinary psychology, and so they happen only when an unpredictable combination of circumstances boosts an ordinary surprise into something special. Our interest in our experiences is always personal, but I think the more general interest in this project is also that it is a reflection on other more ordinary aspects of aesthetic objects. In particular, I suggest that the same kinds of factor which enter into rare and special responses to aesthetic objects are also the factors which give aesthetic objects their general interest. This project offers one possible way of understanding more about literature and art and their effect on us. You may find that this book reminds you of your own strong experiences, and perhaps offers some routes into understanding why they arise. One of the fundamental claims of this book is that strong experiences are themselves surprising, and indeed thinking about them can trigger a strong experience; they have an inherent interest which draws us to try to understand them.

Strong experiences do not group together as a natural kind; grouping them under this term is a way of gathering experiences together to seek an explanation which connects them. In the many years that I have worked on this project, I have used other terms to name the experience, such as 'significant intense experience' and 'intense aesthetic experience', and one reader of this manuscript suggested 'profound experience'. My more neutral final choice of 'strong experience', borrowed from Gabrielsson, comes from the modesty of the adjective: 'strong' is an ordinary monosyllable with a general meaning which covers the range from the common thrill all the way to the life-changing epiphany.

Representation, Metarepresentation and Metacognition

In this section, I introduce some of the technical aspects of the psychology of knowledge and thought which are needed for the explanations in this book. This points forward to Chapter 5 on the central role of surprise in strong experiences. Surprise depends on a mismatch between our new perception and what we already know.

Mental states can have content. For example one kind of mental state is a mental concept, such as the concept 'cat' or the concept 'sleep' which can have a type of object (such as a cat) or a type of action (such as sleeping) as their content. Another kind of mental state is a thought, which can have a state of affairs or action or event as its content. Some of these mental states are propositional, meaning that their content can be expressed as a verifiable statement about a world. An example would be the thought 'It is raining right now' which at that moment expresses a proposition which is true or false. Mental states which have content are representations, and because these representations are held in the mind they are 'mental representations'. Following the philosopher and cognitive scientist Jerry Fodor (1975), I assume that perceptions, thoughts and memories can all take the form of mental representations. The assumption that these mental states are all representations enables them to be compared with one another, such that similar representations can be 'matched', for example if a perception is matched to a memory. This comparability will be important in understanding how a representation can be radically discrepant, or identical, relative to another representation: I will argue that these are two of the triggers of surprise, and so of a strong experience.

We can have a thought about a thought. This is an example of a representation of another representation and is called a metarepresentation. For example, 'I believe that Mary thinks it is getting late' is a metarepresentation that contains (and is about) the subordinate representation 'Mary thinks it is getting late'. Because this is a thought it is a mental metarepresentation, but metarepresentations also exist outside the mind; for example, if there is a representational photograph of a representational painting, then the photograph is a metarepresentation and the painting is the subordinate representation. It is worth noting that metarepresentation does not require a frame: if I repeat what someone else has said while making it clear that I am repeating another person, it is still a metarepresentation even though I have not framed it as 'he said that ...'.

The anthropologist and cognitive scientist Dan Sperber has studied metarepresentations in their role in the formation and transmission of culture (Sperber 2000). In a mental metarepresentation, the subordinate representation can be vague, not fully specified or not fully understood by the person who entertains the metarepresentation as their thought. These types of metarepresentation are particularly important in the spread of culture. Sperber (1985) calls this type of subordinate representation a 'semi-propositional representation' because its content is not fully specified and hence not verifiable. Semi-propositional representations are interesting for our purposes because they are inherently ineffable, and it is possible that some of the kinds of ineffability in strong experiences involve semi-propositional representations. Sperber argues that semi-propositional representations can be the basis of strongly held religious beliefs, precisely because they are not fully understood; thus, it is possible that the feeling of significance also relates to semi-propositional representations. This is discussed further in Chapter 3.

A mental metarepresentation is one example of 'metacognition', which is cognitive activity about cognitive activity. Not all metacognition is metarepresentational. For example, an emotion about an emotion is an example of metacognition but only in part involves metarepresentation, because emotions have nonrepresentational (e.g., valence and arousal) components in addition to their representational components, such as when emotions are about events. Another type of metacognition which may be only partly metarepresentational is empathy, where we have thoughts and feelings about another's thoughts and feelings. It is worth emphasizing that there is no technical distinction between a representation and a metarepresentation: they are both representations. Similarly, metacognition and cognition are both cognition. The meta- elements in these do not distinguish a different kind of mental state or activity but are ways of characterizing the rather special kind of content of these mental states or activities.

Our capacity to think about our own thoughts, including thoughts which we ourselves do not fully understand, may have a role in generating some of the strong experiences, caused when we are surprised at our own thoughts.

Schema

An important notion in the psychological study of mental content is 'schema'. A schema (plural schemata) is what we know in general terms about objects and events. For example what we know about cats is part of our schema for 'cat', which can be matched to perceptions and thoughts about specific cats, such as the cat currently sleeping on my windowsill. It is possible to think about schemata and the things they are matched to in terms of types and tokens. The schema is the type, such as the cat as a type of animal, and the tokens are the actual cats which can be matched to the type 'cat'. A schema is represented by words such as common nouns, verbs, adjectives and adverbs.

There are schemata for objects and for events and sequences of events (sometimes the term 'script' is used for schematic sequences). Perceptions and new thoughts are matched to schemata, and in this way, we understand our ongoing experience by matching it to the schemata which represent what we already know. Schemata may also be used to predict what we will perceive, given an expectation that the world will generally be roughly as we expect it to be. I return later to the issue of prediction and its role in these experiences. The definition of surprise used in this book depends on the notion of schema: 'surprise is elicited by events that deviate from a schema'.

In matching perceptions to schemata, a certain degree of discrepancy must be tolerated. I have a single schema for 'cat', but the actual animals which are tokens of this type vary from the schematic cat because they each have idiosyncratic characteristics. Actual entities in the world are rarely perfect instantiations of their type. Similarly, actual entities in the world which belong to the same type are rarely identical to each other, though there are exceptions such as twins, doubles, multiples and so on. I will suggest that because it is unusual for perceived entities to be perfect manifestations of their type or identical to other entities, that these are causes of surprise, and so might cause a strong experience.

When we perceive objects or events which are discrepant relative to the schemata to which they are matched, we have the option of changing the schemata, a process also called 'learning'. The result is that the objects or events will now more closely match the revised schemata. This is why something which surprises us the first time may not surprise us again, because we have changed the schema to which that thing is matched. But sometimes schemata are not easy to change, no matter what we perceive. This is because some schemata are more deeply embedded in our knowledge than others, in the sense that they are hard to change. So perceptions which are discrepant relative to these deeply embedded schemata are discrepancies from which we cannot learn (Boyer 1996). These deeply embedded schemata include schemata about basic physics and biology: deeply embedded schemata include the knowledge that things fall downwards when we drop them or that dead people are not able to walk around. These schemata may be part of our evolutionary inheritance and so constitute knowledge of the world which we already have at the moment of birth. We can learn new schemata which contradict them, for example, schemata about objects in gravity-free environments on spacecraft or schemata about ghosts. But these newly learned schemata are less deeply embedded and are always in contradiction to the deeply embedded schemata which we were born with; and this is why we continue to be surprised by floating objects or by ghosts. The anthropologist Pascal Boyer (2001) argues that these irreconcilable discrepancies are the basis of religious belief.

We have schemata for objects and events in the external world. But we also have schemata for our own mental activity and for other people's mental activity. These schemata express what we know about thought, memory, emotion and so on, and they are metacognitive, because they are schemata (hence cognitions) about cognition. I suggest that many of these metacognitive schemata are deeply embedded schemata. They will prove important in understanding how some of the strong experiences arise, and why strong experiences can be infectious, because strong experiences are surprising relative to those deep schemata. In summary, schemata are what we know, and strong experiences all begin with a perception or thought which challenges what we know.

Surprise and How It Leads to a Strong Experience

In this book I argue that strong experiences start as surprises. The theory of surprise which I use comes from an article by Wulf-Uwe Meyer, Rainer Reisenzein and Achim Schützwohl (1991: 296). They say that 'surprise is elicited by events that deviate from a schema'. I add that surprise is elicited also by objects that deviate from a schema, noting that objects are always embedded within and contribute to events. Thus schemata are fundamental to surprise and hence to strong experiences. Each new mental representation, including new perceptions and new thoughts, can be matched to a schema. For example, we perceive an object or event, or sequence of events, and match these to our schemata which are our knowledge and expectations. It is normal for there to be some discrepancy, such that whatever we perceive is an approximate match to what we already know or expect. A mismatch of perception to schema within this normal range of discrepancy is not surprising. But if the discrepancy goes above some threshold, then surprise is triggered. One of the ordinary functions of surprise is that it stimulates us to change what we know, by making us modify the schema, thus learning from experience, so that what we know will in future correspond more closely to what we perceive. But in strong experiences, we do not always learn, and this is true particularly of strong experiences that involve our coming to know something which we cannot put into words: we cannot put it into words because we have not been able to learn from our experience to change the schemata by which we can express what we know.

In principle, any surprise could lead to a strong experience. That is, the strong experience may be triggered by a perception which is highly discrepant relative to a schema. Not all surprises lead to strong experiences, and other factors, both personal and contextual, will play a role in making a strong experience occur. In Chapter 6, I discuss how literature can produce major discrepancies, for example, by the literary technique of 'defamiliarization' in which ordinary things are made to be discrepant. The strong experience of the sublime may often be an experience of a high discrepancy, where the sublime is in a perception of something extreme. Huron (2006) and others have shown that many of the triggers of thrills in music involve surprise as a trigger, where the music is highly discrepant relative to expectations of form, which are violated. Inanimate objects which take on animate characteristics, like living dolls (a source of the uncanny for Freud) or statues of saints which can hear prayers or shed tears (a subject of religious belief as discussed by Boyer), are all discrepant relative to deeply embedded schemata about animacy, and for this reason they are a potential source of surprise and strong experience.

There are several reasons to treat strong experiences as types of surprise. Surprises are sudden and transient, and we can explain the suddenness and transience of strong experiences if they are types of surprise. Surprise comes from perceiving something we did not already know or expect, which makes surprise an epistemic event (an event involving knowing), and strong experiences are epistemic events. Surprise can also lead to some of the kinds of arousal which we find in strong experience. This is because we have an evolved tendency to treat any surprise as a potential danger and to react accordingly: 'Since surprise represents a biological failure to anticipate the future, all surprises are initially assessed as threatening or dangerous' (Huron 2006: 38). This explains why many of the strong experience arousals are also found in response to a threat, whether the arousal prepares the animal for flight, fight or freezing in place. Huron (2006) argues that these animal responses have become adapted to become part of how we respond to surprises in aesthetic objects.

All strong experiences begin as surprise, and this can be in response to perceptions of objects and events which are discrepant relative to expectations. But this is does not explain epiphanies which are triggered by ordinary objects, such as the clock which triggers Stephen's epiphany in Joyce's account or the familiar natural object which triggers Graham Sutherland's moment of vision in Clark's account (both quoted at the beginning of this chapter). One possible explanation is that there is still a surprise, but it is a surprise about cognition itself, that is, a metacognitive surprise, as I discuss in the next section.

Metacognitive Surprise

Surprise can come from a discrepancy between an object and its schema. In this section I draw on the fact that as well as perceiving the external world, we also perceive our own experiences. Like any perception, we match these perceptions of experience to schemata for experience. These are the schemata which constitute our knowledge of our own perception, cognition and experience of the world. Surprise can emerge if our own perceived experience is discrepant relative to the schema to which it belongs. Any actual experience can be discrepant relative to one of our schemata for experiences, and this might be a source of surprise, and hence, potentially of strong experience. The notion that surprise can arise via metacognition is implied by Christopher Miller's (2007) discussion of surprise in Wordsworth, where he notes that 'surprised by joy' both means that the speaker is 'struck by a sudden feeling of joy' and 'surprised that I could feel joy' (Miller 2007: 425). This is an example both of joyful surprise caused by a perception, and metacognitive surprise about the perception itself.

For example, one of our deeply embedded schemata is that an identical event never occurs twice. The experience of déjà vu, which is precisely this, an experience of an event happening exactly as it happened before, is highly discrepant relative to this schema. For this reason, the experience of déjà vu is surprising, and indeed, always surprising because it is impossible to learn that identical events can occur twice. The feeling of premonition, which Cleary and Claxton (2018) associate with déjà vu, is similarly discrepant relative to a deeply embedded schema which constitutes the knowledge that we cannot know the future. Déjà vu and premonition produce metacognitive surprises.

Another deeply embedded schema constitutes our knowledge that entities in the world are never perfect instantiations of their type. We know that tokens vary within a normal range of variation from their type, and do not exactly instantiate them. If we are confronted with an object which we take to be a perfect instance of its schema, then we are surprised. Our surprise does not come from the object, because the object is not in itself highly discrepant relative to its schema; in fact, it is the opposite because the object is identical to the schema. Instead the surprise comes from our general schematic knowledge of the imperfection of objects, the fact that they are never perfect versions of their types; this is part of our knowledge that the world is full of variety. There is a high discrepancy between the perception of an object as perfect and the deeply rooted schema which tells us that perfect objects are not possible. This leads me to suggest that some epiphanic experiences are triggered by our perception of objects as perfect. One way in which an object can be a perfect instantiation of its type is if that object is perceived as unique, and hence, the only tokening of its type, and so in principle token and type are identical. The Rosetta Stone is one such object, and I can report my own strong thrill experience of seeing the original object in a case in the British Museum; one component of the thrill came from the discrepant nature of the perception of the object as a unique and hence perfect tokening of its own type. This is a metacognitive surprise. This object itself is incidentally also discrepant in other ways, for example by being fragmentary, by being extremely old and so on: this is a reminder that a perception can be discrepant in many different ways at the same time.

A related schema about cognition is that we do not expect two entities to be perfect copies one of another. This is related to the schema telling us that perfection is impossible, because in this case we have two identical tokens which might imply that they are equally perfect instantiations of a type. This schema is violated by doubles, which are a trigger for strong experience. One such double is found in Hugo von Hoffmansthal's 1898 *Cavalry Story* where, faced with his double, 'the sergeant stared and recognized himself as the apparition' (Von Hoffmansthal 2005: 8). Of this moment, the literary scholar Karl Heinz Bohrer (1994: 54) says, '[w]hat is suddenly perceived or perceptible in that moment remains, however, pointedly unexplained and submerged in the sphere of enigma'. This is a good example of a strong experience. The schema that forbids perfect copies is also confronted by a discrepancy, in the perception of multiples, which the eighteenth-century philosopher Moses Mendelssohn (1997: 193–194) treats as a trigger of the sublime, produced by a series of identical objects, such as a series of columns, or monotone repetition of a single word at equal intervals. Both doubling and multiplication are also fundamental characteristics of literary form and give literary form a potential to trigger strong experiences. They are all sources of metacognitive surprise. All these kinds of metacognitive surprise can be grouped together because they involve perceptions which violate some general 'principle of variation' which governs our expectations of how the world is.

Metacognitive surprise may explain why we can 'catch a thrill' from reading or hearing about someone else getting a thrill or remembering our own thrill; this is the infectiousness of strong experiences. I suggest that this is because a strong experience, as we perceive it, is itself discrepant relative to more deeply embedded schemata for experience; we do not expect this level of intensity, insight or ineffability, and we are surprised that such an experience can occur. The strong experience is itself a source of metacognitive surprise, which in turn can trigger a strong experience; in this way, we catch a thrill.

In sum, metacognition allows us to be surprised by perceptions and experiences which deviate strongly from deeply embedded schemata for how the world is and how we perceive and experience it.

Emotion

Surprise is related to emotion. The arousals such as chills or tears are also found in emotions. And so strong experience has a relation to emotions. I briefly introduce the theory of emotions here and return to it in Chapter 4. An emotion is a psychological episode with a beginning and an ending. It involves some kind of arousal, such as tears, laughter, smiling, chills or blushing. It is also valenced, which means that it is experienced as positive or negative (or somewhere in between or sometimes in combination). It is, incidentally, the valence which suggests that surprise is not actually an emotion in itself, because surprise is not inherently positive or negative (this argument comes from Ortony et al. 1988, and is controversial in emotion theory; e.g., Noordewier and Breugelmans 2013 argue against it). An emotion is triggered by some perception or thought. Emotions are also characterised by having names, such as 'sadness' or 'fear'.

Emotions have a history, in the sense that the written record suggests that different named emotions exist at different times, or different places, that some are more dominant than others, and indeed that emotion varies in how much it is reported. The historians of emotion Peter Stearns and Carol Stearns (1985) explore the local variability of potentially general human emotions. They argue that these emotions are always psychologically possible, but not always culturally manifested and reported. Using Levy's (1973) terminology we can say that emotions are always felt but sometimes hypocognized by being below the level of conscious discussion, and sometimes hypercognized by being extensively discussed in the culture.

'Aesthetic emotions' have been extensively explored particularly in the philosophical literature, as well as in the psychology of emotions. Aesthetic emotions include emotional responses to contentless forms, as in music, and to fictional events and characters. They are anomalous, because there is a mismatch between the emotion and its apparent trigger. In particular, there is something odd about their positive or negative valence, for example, in some instances we are happy to view sad events in a fiction. This mismatch is similar to that which we find in some strong experiences, where we have what ought to be negatively valenced experiences – involving not-knowing, fear-type arousals, and so on – but experienced in a very positive way.

The Extended Experience

A strong experience is sudden and often brief, but our general experience is continuous, and aspects of the strong experience may begin to appear while approaching the striking moment, including both epistemic feelings and arousal. Huron (2006) discusses not only the specific moment of surprise, but also the 'feeling state' which both precedes and follows it. In this section I consider some aspects of our extended experience or feeling state, and how they relate to strong experience.

For example, sometimes we have an ongoing experience which feels 'not quite right', manifesting perhaps as a sense of unease or of the uncanny. This kind of experience might be triggered by the same factors that trigger a moment of surprise, including a sequence of perceptions which are schematically discrepant, but where these perceptions are sustained over a period of time without breaking through into a strong experience. We may not quite be able to match our perceptions to what we know or find that our perceptions are slightly discrepant with what we know, but the discrepancy is never clear or salient enough to suddenly trigger the moment of surprise. Huron (2006) discusses how the 'chill experience' has a 'pre-outcome phase' in which we begin to imagine certain outcomes of the current situation, and perhaps become aroused and more attentive in preparation for a possible outcome; thus, the pre-outcome phase has both epistemic and arousal elements, which at a lower level can resemble those in the strong experience. This can be extended over quite a while or can be seen in the immediate lead-up to a chill, where it is possible to experience (and experimentally observe) a 'pre-chill' phase which can involve increased arousal (Wassiliwizky et al. 2017a: 1231).

Empathy is another relevant aspect of our extended experience. We may develop an empathetic relation with a fictional character in the course of a fiction, and this may both give us a certain ongoing feeling and potentiate a strong experience. There is experimental evidence that in reading poetry, moments of empathy with a poem's narrator or character may produce a thrill experience (Wassiliwizky et al. 2017a). Perhaps empathy with a character boosts the arousal effect of a surprise which involves that character. Further, some theories of the sublime suggest that we respond with our bodies to the external object, as though we identify with that external object. Empathy with an object might be metacognitively surprising, because it violates deeply embedded schemata which allow for empathy only with animates.

Another aspect of our extended experience is processing effort, explored in Chapter 5. When we make sense of our perceptions, or when we are thinking, we are processing mental representations, which means that processing effort is a continuous aspect of our experience, and furthermore, we seem to have some consciousness of relative processing effort. An input may demand greater processing effort, which is measured by how much time is devoted to processing the input and by how much attention is focused on the input. We can also engage in more processing effort at a particular moment compared with other moments. Processing effort might be relevant to strong experience in several ways. Fluent processing, when processing effort is low, has side effects such as the feeling of truth (Reber et al. 2004a), and perhaps other epistemic feelings. In contrast, complexity can demand high processing effort. Complexity is a common characteristic of aesthetic objects, perhaps making a strong experience more likely and relating to the feelings of significance and ineffability. The shift between high- and low-processing effort may also trigger a strong experience. Thus, literary scholar Barbara Herrnstein Smith's (1968) account of 'poetic closure' can be interpreted as involving a change in processing effort and may be a type of strong experience. Similarly, the experimental psychological study of musical form has shown that musical form can trigger thrills when the form changes, perhaps because the level of processing effort changes.

In sum, we can find ways in which the intense characteristics of strong experience, both epistemic and arousal, can be extended at a lower level across a literary text, enabled by the characteristic types of form and content, including narrative content, of texts.

The Chapters of the Book

This first chapter offered an overview of the basic ideas of the book, and the notion that thrill, sublime and epiphany can all be understood as kinds of surprise. A strong experience of any kind – whether thrill, sublime or epiphany – begins as a surprise. Surprise, and hence strong experience, is triggered by a new perception or thought which is discrepant relative to a schema. Surprise can also be triggered by other violations of expectation, such as expectations which are generated by and specific to an aesthetic object, though schematic knowledge may here also be in play. Discrepancy relative to a schema can arise in basically one of two ways. First, the perceived thing or event may itself be discrepant relative to the schema to which it is matched: the experience of very large things as sublime is a discrepancy of this kind. Second, some other aspect of the experienced relation between the perceived thing or event and its schema is (metacognitively) surprising because the experience is discrepant relative to our schematic knowledge of experience. This I suggest is why a strong experience can be triggered by perfect and multiple objects; the experience is metacognitively surprising.

Chapter 2 briefly considers some of the strands of research on the various kinds of strong experience. I look at some of the early accounts of the sublime, at William James's account of mystical experience and some related work on religion, at the humanistic psychology of strong experiences after Marghanita Laski and Abraham Maslow, and finally what Morris Beja (following James Joyce) called the 'literary epiphany' as a feature particularly of modernist writing.

Chapter 3 explores the epistemic feelings in strong experiences and asks what it means to have a feeling of knowing something very significant, and why what is known is often felt to be ineffable. The philosopher Diana Raffman's work on ineffability in music is important here, extended to the general feeling of ineffability. I also draw extensively on the work of Dan Sperber and Deirdre Wilson, including relevance theory and Sperber's anthropological work. This chapter explains in greater detail the notions of schema, mental representation and metarepresentation, which have been introduced in the first chapter.

Chapter 4 discusses the relation between strong experience and emotion, and in particular the role of arousal in strong experiences. I distinguish between the cold-related arousals such as chills, which relate fairly clearly to surprise, and the sadness-related arousals such as tears, which may be related to empathy as a feature in strong experiences. The psychologist David Huron's work on surprise in musical experience is fundamental to the arguments in this chapter, and I also draw on the large amount of experimental psychological work on thrills in response to music, which can be carried over to other types of experience.

Chapter 5 explores in greater detail the basic idea of the book, that surprise is a key factor in strong experiences. The chapter also looks at why objects might be perceived in a distinctive way in epiphanies, and at the role of empathy in strong experiences. It ends by noting some problems with introspection, which raise questions about what we can know about strong experiences, and finally looks at why different people, including in different cultures, have varying relations to strong experiences.

Chapter 6 illustrates how strong experiences might be triggered by the forms and contents of literary texts. The triggers are also the general characteristics of literary texts, and this raises the possibility that the general experiential effect of reading literature might be a generalized and milder form of the experiential peaks which occasionally arise to form a strong experience. Topics briefly covered include the sequential structure of literary texts and how they generate expectations; boundaries in texts, and the related issue of liminality, which is important in strong experiences; how the regulated but varying nature of poetic form allows for surprising changes, including in the relation of metre to rhythm; how metaphor and parallelism produce uncertain meanings; why fragments are triggers; and why certain motifs recur, particularly water.

Chapter 7 briefly concludes the book by summarizing the answers for three questions which have arisen in the course of the book. (1) How is a strong experience triggered? (2) Why, if strong experiences are always surprises, are all surprises not also strong experiences? (3) What is the relation between a strong experience and general experience, including general aesthetic experience?

Chapter 2
THE STUDY OF STRONG EXPERIENCES

In this chapter I selectively and briefly discuss aspects of the critical, philosophical and psychological traditions relating in particular to the epistemic experiences of the sublime and epiphany and some other related feelings.

The Sublime

The experience of the sublime involves both an epistemic feeling and an arousal. This is an epistemic feeling of coming to know something significant, which is often ineffable. Writing in 1804, Thomas Moore brings out the ineffability of the sublime when he says about Niagara Falls, '[i]t is impossible by pen or pencil to convey even a faint idea of their magnificence [...] We must have new combinations of language to describe the Fall of Niagara' (Dowden 1964: 77).

The experience of the sublime is characteristically triggered by the perception of something extreme, such as something extremely large or deep, old, fast or slow. Kant cites as triggers, 'the broad ocean agitated by storms' (1952: 92), 'shapeless mountain masses towering one above the other in wild disorder, with their pyramids of ice' (1952: 104) or 'deep ravines' (1952: 121). Addison says that '[o]ur imagination loves to be filled with an object, or to grasp at any thing that is too big for its capacity. We are flung into a pleasing astonishment at such unbounded views, and feel a delightful stillness and amazement in the soul at the apprehension of them' (Spectator no.412, in Monk 1960: 57). Why might extreme objects be a trigger of a strong experience? One possibility is that the extremely large object is experienced as looming, and hence a threat to be feared like a predator, and so a source of the fight-flight-freeze arousals. Extreme objects might also be perceived as tokens that are very discrepant relative to their types, by virtue of their size. But it is alternatively possible that very large tokens might be seen as too close to their type, as an effect of the magnified scale; the component features that define the type are more emphasized in very large objects, and this perhaps makes the very large token uncannily close to the type. This can be seen for example in Marc Quinn's supersized but otherwise hyperrealistic sculptures. The idea that an extreme token is discrepant relative to type applies also to the very small, which can produce the sublime even though there is no looming effect that might provoke fear. As an example of a strong response to the small, Miceli and Castelfranchi (2003: 260) describe aesthetic crying in response to the sublime of 'even tiny and sweet things'. They interpret this, along with Kant, as an inability to grasp and express. It is worth noting that Burke (1987: 124) disagrees: 'For sublime objects are vast in their dimensions, beautiful ones comparatively small'.

Arousal often plays a role in the experience of the sublime, which connects the sublime to the thrill as types of strong experience. James Kirwan associates arousals with the sublime: 'the horripilation [goosebumps], the benumbing, the inexplicable tears; the calm that is, physically, like floating backward through oneself: the amazement, vertigo, and sudden rush of undirected yet palpable potency seeming to lift me above the accidentals of my life. This is what I have in mind when I say "sublime"' (Kirwan 2005: 161). John Dennis lists six 'enthusiastic passions' associated with the sublime: admiration, terror, horror, joy, sadness and desire (Dennis 1704, cited Monk 1960: 51). Bishop Lowth lists five emotions that accompany sublimity: admiration, joy, love, hatred and fear (Lowth 1753). Often there is a combination of responses in a sublime emotion. In Smith's translation of Longinus, Sappho's sublimity is such that '[s]he glows, she chills, she raves, she reasons; now she is in tumults, and now she is dying away. In a word, she seems not be attacked by one alone, but by a combination of the most violent passions' (Smith 1996: 27; see Longinus 1998: 154).

The sublime is a contested notion. Sircello (1993: 545) argues that a true theory of the sublime is impossible because it claims the existence of a reality to which we have no access. Forsey (2007) takes a similar position, but Deligiorgi (2014) disagrees and Richardson (2012) reinterprets the basic claim. There are many kinds of experience which have been called 'sublime'. Richardson (2012: 24) lists 'Gothic and Romantic, Egotistical and Sympathetic, American and Indian, Racial and Androgynous and still more', including the Cognitive Sublime and his proposed Neural Sublime. There are also disagreements about what counts as a sublime experience. For example, Brady (2013: 120) argues that nature is best at triggering the sublime and that artworks do not have the formal qualities which can elicit the emotional experience of the sublime. Richardson (2012: 22) argues that the experience of the sublime is a distinct psychological kind of experience, and Ishizu and Zeki (2014) argue that Burke's distinction between the experience of the beautiful and the experience of the sublime depends on two different brain systems.

I now consider selected authors on the sublime, beginning with Longinus, for whom the sublime 'exhibits the orator's whole power at a single blow' (Longinus 1998: 144). The notion of the sublime is often traced back to the Greek text *On the Sublime*, which is traditionally assigned to 'Longinus' and may have been composed in the first century CE and which became influential from the seventeenth century, after its translation into French by Boileau. Longinus describes sublimity as a type of 'height' which is specific to writing: 'Sublimity is a kind of eminence or excellence of discourse' (Longinus 1998: 143). For him, the sublime is a valued kind of experience, not produced by trivia. A text produces the effect of the sublime when it has the power to cause great thoughts and strong emotion; for example, the re-ordering of words in hyperbaton 'throws the hearer into a panic lest the sentence collapse altogether, and forces him in his excitement to share the speaker's peril'. The sublime style produces its effects by amazement and wonder which we might see as experiences related to surprise, and perhaps involving a perception which is schematically discrepant. Longinus presents certain formal devices which may cause the experience of the sublime. These include (with illustrative quotations from Longinus) (i) devices of parallelism, conjunction and juxtaposition, which include amplification: 'You wheel up one impressive unit after another to give a series of increasing importance', and produce 'the conjunction of several figures in one phrase', (ii) disruptions to language such as hyperbaton, (iii) manipulations of tense as when presenting past events as present, (iv) tropes such as metaphor, and (v) harmony in speech such as the use of dactylic rhythms, as he says in discussion of a prose piece in dactyls by Demosthenes. All of these devices can be understood as ways of making the text more difficult to process, and I suggest that increased difficulty of processing is a type of change which can produce surprise in a reader. As an illustration of Longinus's ideas, here are three lines by Homer (*Iliad* 5: 770-2) which Longinus quotes as sublime.

> As far as a man can peer through the mist,
> sitting on watch, looking over the wine-dark sea,
> so long is the stride of the gods' thundering horses.
>
> ὅσσον δ' ἠεροειδὲς ἀνὴρ ἴδεν ὀφθαλμοῖσιν
> ἥμενος ἐν σκοπιῇ, λεύσσων ἐπὶ οἴνοπα πόντον,
> τόσσον ἐπιθρῴσκουσι θεῶν ὑψηχέες ἵπποι.

Longinus says that it is the impressive image, and its meaning of vastness which produce sublimity. These lines illustrate all five of Longinus's types of stylistic device. There is (i) amplification, because the man peers, is on watch, and looking, which is the same gesture described three times. There is (ii) a type of hyperbaton, because the man on watch is introduced before it is clear that a simile for the horse's stride is being introduced, with 'horses' (*ἵπποι*) as the last word in the sentence. Tense is manipulated (iii), where present tense is surrounded in the (here omitted) previous and following lines by past tenses. There is a trope (iv), a simile containing two metaphors: the sea is 'wine-dark' and the horses 'thunder'. (v) The text is metrical, in dactylic hexameter: the first line manifests the mixture of dactylic and spondaic feet which is common in this metre, while the second line is an isorhythmic sequence of all dactyls. A final point to make about Longinus is that he is an extensive user of quotations, including famously citing the Hebrew Bible, as noted by Usher (2007). Perhaps his use of quotations functions not only to illustrate the sublime but also to produce the sublime by deploying a textual fragment, which is a common trigger of strong experiences.

The arousal aspects of the sublime are emphasized in Moses Mendelssohn's (1758) *On the Sublime and Naive in the Fine Sciences* (*Über das Erhabene und Naive in den schönen Wissenschaften*) where the sublime is a reaction to something immense, and involves 'shuddering' which runs over us ('*ein Schauern, das uns überlauft*'). Elsewhere the arousal is called 'a sweet shudder that rushes right through us' ('*einen süssen Schauer, der uns ganz durchströmt*'). And Mendelssohn also says that the sublime is close to laughter: 'and even while his lips are stirred to laugh, a shudder pours itself out through his heart, reducing this laughter to a reflection, filled with amazement' ('*ergiesst sich ein Schauer durch sein Herz*'). The triggers of the sublime are capable of inspiring awe (*Bewunderung*), which comes upon us like a lightning bolt; like Longinus, Mendelssohn emphasizes surprise as the core event of the sublime.

> The senses, which perceive things insofar as they are homogeneous, begin to ramble in an effort to comprehend the boundaries, and end up losing themselves in what is immense. The result, as was shown in the first essay, is initially a trembling or shudder that comes over us and then something similar to dizziness that often forces us to divert our eyes from the object. (Mendelssohn 1997: 193)

Extremity is thus one of the triggers of the sublime for Mendelssohn. I have suggested that this involves a great discrepancy in matching the perceived token to the schematic type, and thus, a source of surprise, and also perhaps fear in the looming effect. We can also find the perfect match of token to type, which equally surprises us because it is below the expected range of variation. Thus the sublime can be produced by a series of identical objects such as a series of columns. The sublime can also be produced by power, genius and virtue, as in the social vastness of an impressive person; I suggest that this is also a perfect match of token to type, because the impressive person constitutes their own unique type.

Edmund Burke's 1757 book *A Philosophical Enquiry into the Origin of Our Ideas of the Sublime and the Beautiful* (Burke 1987) explains the sublime in terms of psychophysiology, particularly focused on fear, and this makes him a predecessor of what Nadal and others now call neuroaesthetics (Nadal and Pearce 2011: 172; Nadal and Skov 2013: 3). Burke thought that the same general psychophysiology was at work in both aesthetic and non-aesthetic situations, and thus, that aesthetics is rooted in common emotions: this is a view shared by William James and also in the present book. Terror of any kind produces 'unnatural tension and certain violent emotions of the nerves', which can paradoxically produce pleasure or awe (Burke 1987: 287). As Monk notes, Burke reinforced the association between the sublime and the irrational by saying that fear has the power 'to rob the mind of all its powers of acting and reasoning' (Monk 1960: 92–93). Burke thought that obscurity is a source of the sublime:

> The mind is hurried out of itself, by a crowd of great and confused images; which affect because they are crowded and confused. For separate them, and you lose much of the greatness; and join them, and you infallibly lose the clearness. The images raised by poetry are always of this obscure kind. (Burke 1987: 62)

Language is able to play a particular role in producing the sublime, because, Burke thinks, poetry works by communicating not external images but passions; strong expressions describe a thing 'as it is felt' (Burke 1987: 175).

Immanuel Kant says of the sublime that though it is triggered by an object, the sublime does not reside just in the object: it requires a perceiving or cognizing subject for the sublime to arise. Emphasizing the metacognitive aspect of the sublime, Kant says that it is not the object itself which is sublime, but our feeling of a supersensible faculty and our awareness of the superiority of our powers of reason (Forsey 2007: 383). The following description is an example of Kant's sublime, where the experience is triggered by a perception of great size after crossing a threshold, and thus demonstrating the common motif of the liminal zone as a place of strong experience.

> The same explanation may also sufficiently account for the bewilderment, or sort of perplexity, which, it is said, seizes the visitor on first entering St. Peter's in Rome. For here a feeling comes home to him of the inadequacy of his imagination for presenting the idea of a whole

within which that imagination attains its maximum, and, in its fruitless efforts to extend this limit, recoils upon itself, but in so doing succumbs to an emotional delight. (Kant 1952: 100)

We might interpret this in terms of a perception which is discrepant relative to a schema, because the object is too big for its schema, and this schematic discrepancy is one trigger of the experience of the sublime. For Kant, '[t]he sublime is that, the mere capacity of thinking which evinces a faculty of mind transcending every standard of sense' (Kant 1952: 98). Following Kant, David Miall says that the sublime is 'an extreme mode of defamiliarization', a type of schematic discrepancy that overwhelms the subject (Miall 2007: 155). The response may also be a kind of fear as a response to a large object that suddenly appears (Kant 1952: 120). This is the 'looming effect' that triggers fear, because it might signal the approach of a predator.

Loss and associated negative emotions are commonly tied to the conception of the sublime and are described by Kant:

> Thus, too, delight in the sublime in nature is only *negative* (whereas that in the beautiful is positive): that is to say it is a feeling of imagination by its own act depriving itself of its freedom by receiving a final determination in accordance with a law other than that of its empirical employment. (Kant 1952: 120)

The sublime can lead to a loss of language, and the impossibility of expression, and perhaps this loss is associated with the sense that though something significant is known, it is not fully grasped because it cannot be put into words. Ferri (2012: 567) describes the Italian romantic playwright Vittorio Alfieri as experiencing an impasse in the contemplation of the sublime: 'Each description is tinged with a trace of regret hinting at the failure in communication: in Genoa he observes: "And if I had then known any language at all [...] I would have certainly composed some verses"'. Bloom defines the literary 'negative' sublime as 'being that mode in which the poet, while expressing previously repressed thought, desire, or emotion, is able to continue to defend himself against his own created image by disowning it, a defence of un-naming it rather than naming it' (Bloom 1981: 224). Lyotard says that 'the sublime is kindled by the threat of nothing further happening' and that the sublime feeling is 'the name of this privation' (Lyotard, quoted in Morley 2010: 40). For Žižek, 'the Sublime is an object whose positive body is just an embodiment of Nothing' (Žižek 1989, in Morley 2010: 61). For Richardson (2012: 32), the neural sublime is the experience of cognitive emptiness. An unusual cross-cultural application of the notion of the sublime comes from Dalton (1996), who offers an anthropologist's account of the creation and exchange of shell ornaments (*kunawo*), interpreted in terms of the Kantian sublime. The sublimity of these shell ornaments comes in part from their beauty which makes the 'eye rejoice'. But they also produce a feeling of loss, a 'sublime sense of absence', because the ornaments are received in exchange by someone who gives away a valuable animal, but they are never equivalent in value to what has been given away. Kuiken et al. (2012) think that the sublime is associated with the lack of a shared explication, which produces disquietude along with wonder. The association of the strong experience with loss is found also in other types. Thus, Panksepp (1995) discusses chills in response to music in terms of loss and separation, particularly the mother's separation from her child. And Chater and Loewenstein (2016: 146–147) treat Piaget's accommodation, triggered by schematic discrepancy, as a kind of loss.

Mystical Experience as a Type of Strong Experience

In his 1902 book *The Varieties of Religious Experience. A Study in Human Nature*, William James (1982: 380) identifies four marks of mystical experience, of which two, ineffability and a certain noetic quality, 'entitle any state to be called mystical', and the other two, transiency and passivity, are often found. The noetic quality is a feeling of significance, which combined with ineffability, means that what James calls a mystical experience counts as what I call a strong experience. James does not emphasize either suddenness or surprise and allows mystical experiences sometimes to be gradual, unlike most of the strong experiences discussed in the present book. In contrast, I take surprise to be fundamental to strong experience. This may mean that mystical experiences form an intersecting but differently defined group of experiences from the strong experiences as discussed here. Of the ineffability of the experience James says '[t]he subject of it immediately says that it defies expression, that no adequate report of its contents can be given in words'. On the noetic quality, he says that mystical experiences are experienced as states of knowledge: 'They are states of insight into depths of truth unplumbed by the discursive intellect. They are illuminations, revelations, full of significance and importance, all inarticulate though they remain; and as a rule they carry with them a curious sense of authority for after-time'.

> The simplest rudiment of mystical experience would seem to be that deepened sense of the significance of a maxim or formula which occasionally sweeps over one. 'I've heard that said all my life,' we exclaim, 'but I never realized its full meaning until now'. 'When a fellow-monk,'

said Luther, 'one day repeated the words of the Creed: "I believe in the forgiveness of sins," I saw the Scripture in an entirely new light; and straightway I felt as if I were born anew. It was as if I had found the door of paradise thrown wide open'. This sense of deeper significance is not confined to rational propositions. Single words, and conjunctions of words, effects of light on land and sea, odors and musical sounds, all bring it when the mind is tuned aright. Most of us can remember the strangely moving power of passages in certain poems read when we were young, irrational doorways as they were through which the mystery of fact, the wildness and the pang of life, stole into our hearts and thrilled them. (James 1982: 382)

Though James is not explicit about arousal, we can see here a trace of evidence that he saw arousal as part of the experience, for example in the 'thrilling' of the heart. James wrote elsewhere about thrill arousals (James 1884: 196, quoted earlier), when he said that 'a sudden wave flows over us', and this is parallel to the phrase used here, that the sense 'sweeps over one'. The quotation below exemplifies James's notion of 'religious mysticism pure and simple', which involves 'sudden realization of the immediate presence of God', as one of his types of mystical experience. This is a description by the German idealist Malwida von Meysenbug, who had previously been 'unable to pray, owing to materialist belief':

I was alone upon the seashore as all these thoughts flowed over me, liberating and reconciling; and now again, as once before in distant days in the Alps of Dauphiné, I was impelled to kneel down, this time before the illimitable ocean, symbol of the Infinite. I felt that I prayed as I had never prayed before, and knew now what prayer really is: to return from the solitude of individuation into the consciousness of unity with all that is, to kneel down as one that passes away, and to rise up as one imperishable. Earth, heaven, and sea resounded as in one vast world-encircling harmony. It was as if the chorus of all the great who had ever lived were about me. I felt myself one with them, and it appeared as if I heard their greeting: 'Thou too belongest to the company of those who overcome'. (James 1982: 395)

I have chosen this example from among the many offered by James, because it is so densely packed with characteristic motifs such as the liminal zone of the seashore, and the relation of individual to crowd where she is among the chorus of the great. Categories are mixed, hence discrepant relative to their schemata, and this may be what triggers the surprise leading to a strong experience.

Thus, '[e]arth, heaven, and sea resounded as in one vast world-encircling harmony'. The ocean is 'illimitable' which is a type of schematic anomaly, and its vastness along with the conventionally vast Alps recall the discrepantly large objects of the sublime.

Other accounts of mystical and religious experience sometimes fit into the broad category of strong experience: there is a feeling of knowing something profoundly important, but ineffable, which can be a noetic quality, insight, illumination or a sense of true reality. In the next few sentences I list some of the characteristics offered by James, as well as by other theorists of mystical and religious experience such as Stace (1960), Pahnke (1967) and Stange and Taylor (2008), as well as in the longer list of McNamara (2009). Many of these characteristics will be addressed in later chapters where I consider their psychological basis. The experience may be described as intense, which implies emotion, and as intensely joyful. 'Awe' and 'wonder' are English words sometimes used. The experience may result in lasting positive attitudes and behaviours. It is usually described as transient. Time is experienced differently, perceived differently or experienced as stopping. The experience may be 'unitive', involving unity or integration with the self or others. There may be an acceptance of normally incompatible opposites. The religious or mystical experience can involve a sense of an Other, which might be a spirit or God; for James, the subject submits passively to the Other. At the same time, the subject can feel that he or she has been assigned power by the Other. McNamara (2009) also lists various other features found in religious and mystical experience, including changes in visual perception, perception of music, changed sexual, artistic and authorial behaviours, ritualization, and an enhanced sense of empathy and mind reading. Some religions and spiritual practices emphasize the strong experience; for example, in modernist Buddhism there is a focus on a flash of insight or moment of enlightenment, a *satori* (Sharf 1995: 266; Ornstein 1977: 182; Beja 1971: 25).

In *The Idea of the Holy*, the scholar of religion Rudolph Otto (1923) theorized the numinous experience as an experience of a reality perceived as wholly other than the subject, as 'outside what can be thought'. Yandell (1993: 236) describes a numinous experience as an experience of a being which has the property of 'being awesome, being majestic, being overwhelmingly powerful, being fascinating but dangerous, and the like'. Smith (2013) says that Otto thought that the numinous was connected to the sublime, both 'mysterious and intensely compelling for the beholder'. Sundararajan (2002) says that the experience is a shock to the mind – a kind of surprise. The emotional reaction is not only a kind of fear but also a kind of interest, a 'dread and fascination'. Otto is an influence on humanist psychologists including Maslow. Elkins (2001: 180) lists the numinous as part of a collection of terms describing the experience of 'presence' in art, most of which can be allied with strong experience: numinous, empathy, aura, uncanny, de Chirico's enigma and the abject.

Freud (1919) discusses the 'uncanny feeling' triggered by certain perceptions. The uncanny has some elements in common with the strong experiences, because it involves a feeling of significance, though with a rather specific range of triggers, and can also involve arousal. Jentsch (1906) thought that the uncanny was associated with uncertainty, which makes it clearly an epistemic feeling, and Windsor (2019) offers a similar account. Characteristic triggers are a sense of the presence of ghosts or other supernatural beings, a perception of ordinary things as taking on strange characteristics, and an experience of doubles such as identical people. Freud suggests that these triggers are objects which are ordinary in the different psychological experience of the child, but are repressed as we develop an adult knowledge of the world. When they reappear to adults, they are the return of something which is repressed, and so what was 'canny' (*heimlich*) for the child becomes 'uncanny' (*unheimlich*) for the adult. From our perspective, we can see that the triggers fall into the two kinds of trigger for strong experiences, either being perceptions which are discrepant relative to our schematic knowledge (ghosts and strangely altered objects) and hence directly surprising, or being perceptions of a kind of impossible perfection (doubles) and hence metacognitively surprising. Keltner and Haidt (2003: 311) say that the uncanny is related to awe and that both lead to 'a massive need for accommodation'. For Otto, the uncanny is associated with the numinous (Yandell 1993: 16). Levy (1973: 151) describes a Tahitian concept close to the uncanny which is *mehameha* and which has both arousal and epistemic elements: 'the head begins to swell. You get gooseflesh and you think "there is a spirit"'; it can be triggered when a person is alone and hears a noise but does not know what is causing it. Again, we see the link to the strong experiences, based on fear from not knowing, which is an epistemic uncertainty.

I suggest furthermore that aesthetic practices are uncanny in a general sense, a suggestion I explore later in this book. This comes from their repetitiveness or doubling, and from the ways in which they take ordinary things and make them strange. Thus, literary language is a strange or uncanny version of ordinary language. As another example, dancing is an uncanny form of walking and jumping, uncanny because it is too regular and repetitive.

The Psychology of Strong Experiences

In a landmark study of strong experience, Marghanita Laski (1961) surveyed people's experiences of what she called 'ecstasy'. Ecstasy is 'being in a state of mind other than one's usual one', which is 'joyful, transitory, unexpected, rare, valued and extraordinary to the point of often seeming as derived from a praeternatural [beyond normal] source' (Laski 1961: 39). Ecstasy can have a lasting positive effect, generally 'improving mental organization' (Laski 1961: 371). It must involve some combination of feelings (listed in Laski 1961: 42), but the experience is not easily summarized. She says that many ecstasies involve some kind of statement of gain accompanied either by a quasi-physical feeling or, as in the sublime, a statement of loss. There can be an emotional reaction of the thrill type such as changes in heart rate and breathing and tingles. Ecstasies usually last a moment, like surprises. They can be religious or non-religious, and for Laski, ecstasy need not involve either of James's essential features of mystical experience, the noetic quality and ineffability. This makes Laski's ecstasy an experience in which feelings are more fundamental than the epistemic aspect. Laski's emphasis on feeling as the central characteristic fits with her description of ecstasies as suspending the faculty of reasoning (Laski 1961: 183). Laski focuses on experiences that have triggers, which are 'circumstances preceding ecstatic experiences and probably standing in a causal relationship to such experiences'. She notes that triggers have no single factor in common, but many of them resemble the phenomenology of the ecstasy experience, involving upward movement, rhythm, flow and light. This is an interesting meta issue, where our metacognitions about the experience itself are similar to our assumptions about what triggers the experience. She argues that ecstasy in her sense cannot arise where the experience is caused by drugs such as mescaline (Laski 1961: 261–266), because ecstasies differ from drug experiences in real and experienced duration, in emotional response, and so on. However, we might now want to disagree with Laski, given our better understanding of the neurochemistry of strong experiences, which can be influenced by drugs.

Laski undertook her research by asking people to fill in a questionnaire in which one of the questions was 'what has induced transcendent ecstasy in you?' She did not provide a definition of 'transcendent ecstasy' because she wanted people to work out for themselves what the phrase meant. Her published results offer us a rare set of descriptions from which we might be able to work out what is causing the strong experience. As an illustration, here are the full set of claimed triggers from three people, labelled Q6, Q50 and Q51, where I have added numbers for each of the sixteen items for later reference.

Q6 (1) Mathematics, (2) mountains, (3) poetry – Eliot's 'Prufrock', (4) Tennyson's 'Ulysses'.

Q50 (5) A line of poetry, often 'Loveliest of trees –' and (6) 'Look thy last on all things lovely – ' and, (7) I know it sounds corny, but 'Magic casements – ' (8) suddenly coming across an unexpected view that stretches for miles with the consciousness that you'll never recapture it, except in the mind. (9) Once eating thin bread with butter *and* jam as a child: I can recapture it in memory even now.

Q51 A really beautiful piece of music, (10) most Beethoven, (11) some Mozart, (12) the night I heard Kathleen Ferrier singing 'Chanson de Mer' (13) a really beautiful spring or autumn day, mostly autumn – a play beautifully acted and produced, Shakespeare, (14) Olivier's 'Richard III' and (15) 'Titus' at Stratford – and (16) ballet, the first I ever saw.' (Laski 1961: 377, 393)

These are what three people reported as triggers for ecstasy. As always, there is never enough information about the experience and its context to enable us to come to clear conclusions about how the experience is caused and what other factors were involved, whether contextual, individual or cultural. Several of these triggers are explicit about surprise, with the subject faced with something unexpected: (8) the sudden view, (9) the new combination of foods and (16) the first ballet. Some triggers involve vastness: (2) mountains (8) the view that stretches for miles. Others involve extremes: (5) 'loveliest of trees', (6) 'look thy last', (10) 'really beautiful music' and (13) 'really beautiful day'. Vastness and extremes are themes in the types of experience called 'sublime' or 'awe'. Some triggers relate to death and loss, often implicitly, as is true of (4) Tennyson's 'Ulysses'. (5) 'Loveliest of trees' is the first line of Housman's poem about the limited number of opportunities in a lifetime to see cherry blossom. (6) 'Look thy last on all things lovely' is from de la Mare's poem on a similar theme. (7) 'Magic casements' are windows that open on 'faery lands forlorn' in Keats's 'Ode to a Nightingale', and which offer another type of fantastic vision, associated with loss and the passing of time. Perhaps loss is behind the choice of autumn rather than spring in (13). (12) probably refers to Chausson's 'Poème de l'amour et de la mer' (Laski notes the possible error in the answer), which we might note is particularly associated with Ferrier's early death from cancer because she sang it first a few days before discovering the cancer, and sang it to Barbirolli in the hospital a few days before she died; perhaps subject Q51 is mixing in a memory of this biographical fact. It is possible to understand triggers of death and loss in three ways, and all three ways might contribute to strong experiences. First, these are emotionally arousing notions. Second, they may involve empathy. Third, they may involve discrepancies: a life at its end is a life outside the normal range of variation, and an example of liminality, a notion which is important in these experiences.

In the early 1960s, Abraham Maslow formulated a notion of 'peak experience' which is an experience of a deeper or greater or hidden reality, such as an experience in which 'the whole universe is perceived as an integrated and unified whole' (Maslow 1976: 59). This strong epistemic feeling suggests that the peak experience is a type of strong experience. Sloboda (1991) connects it to the thrill that he calls a 'peak emotional experience'. For Maslow the peak experience involves a special kind of cognition which can potentially lead to new knowledge, which he calls B-cognition (B for 'being') as opposed to everyday D-cognition (D for 'deficiency'). Maslow thought that it was possible to sustain the 'noetic and cognitive' component of the peak experience over a long period, constituting a 'high plateau' experience in which one remains 'turned on'. In his early account, Maslow says that peak experiences are rare and experienced only by certain people who are 'peakers' who have achieved the highest level of the 'hierarchy of needs', this being the other conceptual framework for which Maslow is widely known. In his later thinking, a much wider range of experiences are counted as peak experiences; here is a representative account of one of his own experiences, from an interview:

> Peak experiences come from love and sex, from aesthetic moments, from bursts of creativity, from moments of insight and discovery, or from fusion with nature. I had one such experience in a faculty procession here at Brandeis University. I saw the line stretching off into a dim future. At its head was Socrates. And in the line were the ones I love most. Thomas Jefferson was there. And Spinoza. And Alfred North Whitehead. I was in the same line. Behind me, that infinite line melted into the dimness. And there were all the people not yet born who were going to be in the same line. (Hoffman 1992)

Though this is not described as a surprise, the experience as described does have some of the schematic discrepancies that are characteristic of strong experiences, in particular the distortion of time, the indefiniteness of the boundaries of the line and the motif of the individual in the crowd. Stange and Taylor (2008) discuss the similarity between mystical and non-mystical types of experience, referring to Maslow, James, Laski and accounts of aesthetic experience. They undertook a study by questionnaire, in which 391 of 487 respondents mentioned a 'valid profound experience'. They found that whether this experience was interpreted as religious or aesthetic depended on personal religiosity or artistic engagement, which suggests that the core experience is interpreted in different ways, sometimes as religious and sometimes as aesthetic. Maslow's (1976: 20) view about mystical experience was similarly that it was not a distinct kind; instead 'these older reports, phrased in terms of supernatural revelation, were, in fact, perfectly natural, human peak experiences [...] phrased in terms of whatever conceptual, cultural, and linguistic framework the particular seer had available in his time'. Thus the basic psychological event is elaborated into specific ways of conceiving of strong experience.

Maslow's notion of peak experience was influenced by Laski and Otto (Maslow 1976: 54) and has influenced others, including Panzarella's (1980) 'aesthetic peak experiences' in the 'intense joyous experience' of listening to music or looking at visual art, or of remembering such an experience. He asked people to answer a questionnaire, and most of his respondents described permanent effects for their joyous experiences. Panzarella distinguishes four kinds of joyous experience based on different behaviours, qualities of experience and relations to the trigger. One type is renewal ecstasy, in which the experience of aesthetic objects is an experience of the world as better than thought, for example a sudden experience while looking at a painting, described as 'I found the colors as something great, profane'. Another type is motor-sensory ecstasy, involving physical phenomena including deliberate actions, dancing and feelings such as floating and including the usual kinds of arousal. A third type is a withdrawal ecstasy, where external attention is focused on the aesthetic object, and its surroundings no longer attended to. A fourth type is fusion-emotional ecstasy, such as 'being at one with the music'. Panzarella notes (1980: 83) that a fragment of a work may trigger the ecstasy, particularly in visual art, where a colour or a shape might trigger it, and this is an example of the fragment as a trigger of strong experience. All Panzarella's kinds of experience follow a rising and falling pattern, in three stages. Stage 1 involves 'disruptions of perceptual set, like surprise and amazement', which is similar to my proposal that strong experiences start with surprise. Stage 2 is the climax of the experience involving a motor response, with activity and either hyper-arousal or hypo-arousal, and reduced perception of time and spatial orientation, sometimes along with feelings of floating or transport. Stage 3 involves various kinds of lower intensity feeling, and while stage 1 was accompanied by loss of the self, stage 3 involves a self-transformation.

Another development of these humanistic psychology ideas is the 'quantum change' of Miller and C' de Baca (2001, also Miller 2004), which I take to be a kind of strong experience. The quantum change is a 'vivid, surprising, benevolent, and enduring personal transformation', though some quantum changes are malevolent (2001: 154). Quantum changes produce ineffable knowledge (2001: 75), and occasionally arousal such as goosebumps. People who undergo quantum change were explicitly surprised in four out of five of the reported experiences. Miller and C' de Baca suggest that there are two types of quantum change, insights and epiphanies, where epiphanies involve a mystical sense of being acted upon by something outside oneself such as God. Thus they retain a religious meaning for epiphany and they allow for the possibility that God might actually be causing some changes. They offer several possible explanations of why quantum changes occur. A major change may occur because a person cannot continue as they are or because they are aware of a deep discrepancy between the current and possible life. People may be undergoing a maturational change to a different life stage in Piagetian terms, and also it may be that only certain personalities are able to undergo quantum change. Though quantum changes can sometimes occur without any apparent external cause, there may be triggers: 'a profound loss, a fireplace, a broken neck, a mirror, and abortion, and a runaway daughter. Did these externals just happen to be there at the moment quantum change struck, or did they play some role?'(Miller and C' de Baca 2001: 180). They leave this question unanswered, but more can be said about this by examining the ten full narratives of quantum change included in the book. Many of these experiences involve a kind of liminality, either travel or a liminal zone: one experience is while driving, two more come at the end of a journey or as it is about to begin, four more are while away from home (three at a retreat, one at a hospital). The only two which are in the person's home involve one on the patio (the liminal zone between house and outside) and one by a fireplace (from which God speaks and a liminal zone). The role of representations and metarepresentations is clear from the presence of other narratives intertwined with these. At least two of the narratives have motifs which appear to be taken directly from the Bible: a voice speaking from a fireplace and an experience of being spoken to by God while driving, explicitly compared with Saul on the way to Damascus. Miller and de Baca's book begins with two fictional examples – Scrooge, and George Bailey (from the film *A Wonderful Life*) which assumes a relation between the real-life quantum changes and fictional ones, and Bidney (2004: 472) says that quantum changes overlap with literary epiphanies.

Keltner and Haidt (2003) propose that there is a group of life-changing awe experiences, which include experiences of threat, beauty, ability, virtue and the supernatural, and which I take to be strong experiences. Their examples of awe include conversion experiences such as Paul's conversion, awe in response to a charismatic leader, and awe as the experience of the sublime. They cite Maslow on peak experiences. They also include Joyce's epiphany as a variant of awe where awe arises because the trivial event is felt to be connected to something vast; it is the implied vastness that produces awe (Keltner and Haidt 2003: 311). Theirs is one of the few theories to explicitly suggest that epiphany and the sublime are part of the same broad category of experience, as I do in this book. They suggest that a disposition to awe is associated with an openness to experience, but does not require an individual need for cognitive closure (Bonner and Friedman 2011: 224). Keltner and

Haidt's theory of awe uses Piaget's notion of accommodation: awe involves a demand for accommodation, which may or may not be met.

This notion comes from Piaget's account of how children think and learn, which I briefly summarize now (adapted from Sutherland 1992). Children's representations of the world are in the form of schemata. The child adapts to a changing and new environment, for example when a new object appears, in one of two ways. The child can assimilate the new perceptions to existing schemata, which can involve learning how to control the new object. The other option is to change the schemata themselves, for example by categorizing the object and learning a new word for it thus making the object effable: this changing of a schema is accommodation. Keltner and Haidt suggest that awe is triggered by an experience that cannot be fitted into existing schemata, typically because it is vast in the sense of being greater than the self physically or socially, as when faced with a charismatic individual. Keltner and Haidt say that this failure to fit into a schema causes awe, as a type of emotion. This emotion facilitates the subject's attempt to accommodate to the experience, for example by changing schemata, but this accommodation may not occur. If accommodation succeeds, the experience is positive; if it fails it is negative. Like Keltner and Haidt, I argue in this book that one source of strong experiences is a large mismatch between perception and schema.

For Armstrong and Detweiler-Bedell (2008: 325), citing Keltner and Haidt, our representational capacities are strained by the vastness of the sublime, and we must make mental changes to accommodate to its demands, and when accommodation fails it produces terror. These can all be understood as moments of surprise where a new perception cannot fit the schemata of what we already know; in many of these theories, the subject is able to change by Piagetian accommodation so that they can come to know the new perception. Huron (2006) argues that awe is a type of 'freeze' response to a threat. Shurtz et al. (2012) tested part of Keltner and Haidt's account experimentally and found support for their account. They asked subjects to report on their experiences of goosebumps which they described as 'when the skin on your body tightens and your hair on your arms, neck, etc. becomes erect'. They found that in 13.5 per cent of reported cases the self-reports of goosebumps were accompanied by an experience of awe. Where awe is directed at a powerful or otherwise exceptional person, they found that there was a positive correlation with vastness, as expressed by a view such as 'the person seemed to have qualities that were beyond measure'. Piff et al. (2015) explore further the ways in which awe produces prosocial tendencies, and this links back to the important role of empathy as a prosocial emotion in strong experience.

Pelowski and Akiba (2011) discuss how artworks can trigger surprising and sudden transformative experiences that are both epistemic and emotional and which they call just 'aesthetic experience'. Pelowski and Akiba refer also to peak experiences, epiphany, aha-moments and the sublime. Developing a 1934 account by John Dewey (1958) they say that the subject normally assimilates novel aspects of the artwork to pre-existing knowledge. But in some cases there is an unresolvable discrepancy where we do not appear to have mastery over the aesthetic object, as though it has its own independent existence outside us. The experience of the schematic change which can be a result of being confronted with a discrepancy can produce tears – this being one of the characteristic kinds of arousal in strong experience and a link between arousal and the epistemic feeling (Pelowski 2015). Though Pelowski and Akiba do not use the term, we might say, using Gibson's (1979) term, that it is as though the object is stripped of its affordances (Chapter 5). It may also be that the object no longer appears as one token of a schematic type, but has its own unique type/schema. This problem of the unmastered object that cannot provide meaning for us is resolved when the viewer transforms her self-image and schematic knowledge via a metacognitive reassessment, which enables her to resolve the discrepancies presented by the artwork and understand them.

Tangerås (2020) interviews readers whose lives have been changed by reading, and he explores these 'Life-Changing Reading Experiences'. They can be sudden or gradual, and at least some of them can be characterized as a life-changing form of strong experience. He describes them as instances of 'being moved', he notes the similarity to Keltner and Haidt's notion of awe, and to Kuiken's expressive enactment. One of his readers, 'Esther describes the effect of her reading experience as "absolutely moving"; giving her "a profound insight"; "an instant illumination"; it "was enlightening". "A realisation went through me." "All this was revealed to me when I read the poem."' This is the kind of language familiar from strong experience, and Tangerås calls it an epiphany (2020: 187–188). Tangerås's readers tend to be in late adolescence or in mid-life and have all been prepared for this life-changing experience by a prior life-crisis and so this is a rather special form of strong experience in terms of the effects it brings about; nevertheless, we might ask whether the triggering factors are similar, with the personal context changing how the experience arises.

Effable Strong Experiences

Sometimes the epistemic feeling of coming to know something important can be effable: what is known can be put fully into words (Kim 2012: 155, who is the source of the next few examples). Albert Einstein reportedly described scientific discovery as 'a sudden illumination, almost a rapture'

(Maurois 1968: 35). Some types of psychoanalysis or psychoanalytically inspired therapies involve moments of sudden discovery. Gestalt theory has the 'aha experience', associated with Karl Bühler and important in Köhler's (1921) 'insight learning'. In Doris Laub's trauma theory the therapist gains sudden illuminations (Laub and Felman 1992: 63). The term 'epiphany' is sometimes used to describe these sudden, effable discoveries. It is used in this sense for example in *The Wire* magazine's monthly section in which someone recounts an epiphany relating to the experience of music where epiphanies 'recalibrate the world and illuminate routes to other ways of being [...] moments of insight or formative experience' (Herrington 2015: 13).

Schooler et al. (1993) discuss sudden effable insights of the kind found in scientific and personal discoveries and argue that they arise only because they are preceded by unverbalizable psychological processes. Einstein said, '[t]hese thoughts did not come in any verbal formulation. I very rarely think in words at all. A thought comes, and I may try to express it in words afterwards' (from Schlipp 1949: 228). Schooler et al. (1993: 168), citing Einstein's quote, discuss a theory of spreading activation in which there are sub-aware processes that activate memories critical for the solution of the problem, and these memories pop suddenly into awareness. Among the sub-aware processes are elaboration by adding information, re-encoding by changing the perceptual interpretation such as flipping figure and ground or constraint relaxation where apparently necessary features are abandoned. They find various kinds of pre-existing evidence that insight problems involve an unverbalizable stage. First, subjects may grow silent immediately before an insight; second, subjects are unable to say how close they are to solving an insight problem, unlike non-insight problems; third, while a verbal hint may help a subject solve a non-insight problem they are typically unaware that they were given the hint. They present experimental evidence that if in fact a subject is asked to verbalize their thought processes, this interferes with insight. This is part of a more general phenomenon of verbal overshadowing, where 'verbalization of nonverbal tasks can interfere with successful performance [...] verbalization focuses subjects on the verbally relevant information and thereby overshadows information that is not readily verbalized' (Schooler et al. 1993: 166).

Félix Schoeller (2015a) has argued that chills might accompany the effable insights which involve full understanding. He quotes Moritz Schlick's reference to 'the "shivers of knowledge" which coursed down his spine' and James W. Cronin on particle physics: 'you get shivers up and down your spine, especially when you find you understand it' (Schoeller 2015b: 26, 34). Schoeller cites experimental evidence to suggest that the chills arise when there is a significant cognitive dissonance – a kind of discrepancy – where two opposed cognitions are equally resistant to being dismissed; the only way to resolve the dissonance is to find some third or middle way of accepting or reinterpreting the situation so that the dissonance is reduced.

The Literary Epiphany

The term 'epiphany' comes from the Greek noun *epiphaneia* 'manifestation'. The Greek adjective *epiphanees* expresses the coming to light or appearing of gods and also means 'in full view' or evident or notable or remarkable (Liddell and Scott 1889: 306). These various meanings, including the religious meaning, are present in modern secular uses of the term, as used for example by Beja (1971: 71), Nichols (1987: 5), and Ziolkowski (2014: 2–3). McDonald (2008: 91) notes the wide range of disciplines which now use the term 'epiphany', and Amos (2019)describes a range of other terms used with a similar meaning, particularly in psychotherapy. Tangerås (2020) has a useful discussion of the literary epiphany in the context of a broader empirical study of the reader's life-changing experiences. The addition of the word 'literary' as in 'literary epiphany' comes from Morris Beja's (1971) book *Epiphany in the Modern Novel*, which is a key work establishing and exploring the theory of secular epiphany as it appears in literature. Beja takes the term 'epiphany' from Joyce's (1944) novel *Stephen Hero*, where Stephen says: 'By an epiphany he meant a sudden spiritual manifestation, whether in the vulgarity of speech or of gesture or in a memorable phase of the mind itself [...] they themselves are the most delicate and evanescent of moments'. Adapting Aquinas, Stephen says 'claritas is quidditas': the object has a radiance which enables it to be recognized in its 'whatness' (Nichols 1987: 12, Beja 1971: 81 citing. Joyce 1944: 213). Stephen says: 'The soul of the commonest object, the structure of which is so adjusted, seems to us radiant. The object achieves its epiphany'.

Under the heading of literary epiphany, Beja presents chapters on Joyce, Woolf, Wolfe, and Faulkner; he also cites as users of literary epiphany Baldwin, Styron, Wallant, Durrell, Sarraute (e.g., *Tropismes*) and Robbe-Grillet (e.g., *Instantanés*). Tigges's (1999) edited collection has articles on Wordsworth, Milton, Radcliffe, Emerson, Whitman, Moore, Yeats, D. G. Rossetti, Barrett, Pound, Joyce, Woolf, Bowen, Evans/Agee, Stevens, Beckett, Proust, Larkin, Kubrick, D. M. Thomas, Sean Deane, Pynchon and Heaney, among others. Though many of the writers discussed belong to the twentieth century, descriptions of similar experiences can be found in other writers' works, for example Wordsworth. George Eliot gives us another example: 'Here was a man who now for the first time found himself looking into the eyes of death – who was passing through one of those rare moments of experience when we feel the truth of a commonplace' (Eliot 1872, vol.II. xlii. 370, cited in the OED under 'moment').

These writers have a variety of names for the experience, and 'epiphany' is strictly just Joyce's term, but following Beja, the term 'epiphany' has been generalized to cover all of them in critical analyses, including Bidney (1997) and the anthology edited by Tigges (1999). For Beja, an epiphany is 'a feeling of new knowledge', which comes suddenly and lasts for a moment, and is caused indirectly and by a trivial incident: 'I would call it a sudden spiritual manifestation, whether from some object, scene, event or memorable phase of the mind – the manifestation being out of proportion to the significance or strictly logical relevance of whatever produces it' (Beja 1971: 18). In an echo of this definition, Bidney (2004: 472) in an article on Dostoevsky and Tolstoy, says: 'A literary epiphany, as I define it, is a depicted moment that affects the reader as emotionally intense, unexpectedly resonant or expansive (appearing to signify more than such a transient moment would have any right to mean), and mysterious – seeming not fully accountable by reason'. The list of criteria as to what counts as an epiphany divides authors. Maltby pushes epiphany back to seventeenth-century moments of vision in Vaughan and Bunyan, because he allows for spiritual rebirth to be a type of epiphany. Langbaum (1999: 43) defines the literary epiphany as a modern phenomenon, claiming that Vaughan's moments are visions rather than epiphanies triggered by sensory perception of objects. Barfoot (1999: 66) takes a different view, allowing Donne and Marvell to have epiphanies because 'the mundane has opened to reveal the transcendent', and he also treats Imagist poems as 'short epiphanies'. On the other hand Tigges (1999: 21) thinks that Imagist poems are not epiphanies because in these poems the triviality of the image is not set against a wider context.

Virginia Woolf (1918), in a review titled 'Moments of Vision', discusses Logan Pearsall Smith's collection of anecdotes, *Trivia* (Smith 1917). This a key account of Woolf's notion of moments where things come together 'in a combination of inexplicable significance'. Smith himself, in an extract quoted by Woolf, talks of 'little moments that shine for me curiously in the past'. To illustrate, here is a complete example of one of Smith's trivia, called 'Bligh House', an example which is not mentioned by Woolf, but fits her account.

Bligh House

To the West, in riding past the walls of Bligh, I remembered an incident in the well-known siege of that house, during the Civil Wars: How, among Waller's invading Roundhead troops, there happened to be a young scholar, a poet, and lover of the Muses, fighting for the cause, as he thought, of ancient Freedom, who, one day, when the siege was being more hotly urged, pressing forward and climbing a wall, suddenly found himself in a quiet garden by the house. And here, for a time forgetting, as it would seem, the battle, and heedless of the bullets that now and then flew past him like peevish wasps, the young Officer stayed, gathering roses – old-fashioned damask roses, streaked with red and white – which, for the sake of a Court Beauty, there besieged with her father, he carried to the house; falling, however, struck by a chance bullet, or shot perhaps by one of his own party. A few of the young Officer's verses, written in the stilted fashion of the time, and almost unreadable now, have been preserved. The lady's portrait hangs in the white drawing-room at Bligh; a simpering, faded figure, with ringlets and drop-pearls, and a dress of amber-coloured silk.

The text describes two sudden incidents, where the man finds himself in the garden and is perhaps himself surprised, and where he is shot dead. But it is the effect on the reader which interests Woolf. Each of the sudden moments occurs at a liminality, and I suggest a liminality is inherently a schematic discrepancy. The scene in the garden is cut off from the surrounding events, hence, a schematic anomaly. The texts of the officer's verses are 'almost unreadable now', a characteristic transformation of a text into something not fully a text, unreadable and ineffable. Thus the text as described has various factors that might trigger strong experience.

In her review of Conrad's *Lord Jim* on its 1917 reprinting, Woolf quotes the following passage in which the narrator Marlow describes drinking with a French naval officer.

> ... as if the appointed time had arrived for his moderate and husky voice to come out of his immobility, he pronounced, '*Mon Dieu*, how the time passes!' Nothing could have been more commonplace than this remark; but its utterance coincided for me with a moment of vision. It's extraordinary how we go through life with eyes half shut, with dull ears, with dormant thoughts [...] Nevertheless, there can be but few of us who had never known one of those rare moments of awakening, when we see, hear, understand ever so much – everything – in a flash – before we fall back again into our agreeable somnolence. I raised my eyes when he spoke, and I saw him as though I had never seen him before. (Woolf 1917: 142; source in Conrad 1986: 148)

Woolf says, 'he expounds his vision and we see it too'. Here, strong experience is caught by the reader. The event is surprising, has significance, and apparently is ineffable. It has a characteristic trigger, which is a brief heard utterance. In the novel, while this is the only moment which Conrad called a 'moment of vision' there are other similar moments. Jim, for example, is called 'a gifted poor devil with the faculty of swift and forestalling vision. The sights it showed him had turned him into cold stone from the soles of his feet to the nape of his neck' (Conrad 1986: 114). Similarly, Marlow 'felt a creepy sensation down my backbone' (Conrad 1986: 110) in response to the peculiarity of Jim's story. In the narratively crucial scene where the boat is abandoned, Jim's 'brain and his heart together were pierced as with daggers' (Conrad 1986: 123), while later he says that 'I've thought more than once the top of my head would fly off' (Conrad 1986: 179). A person can trigger surprise if they are schematically anomalous, and this seems to be true of Jim as a trigger; when Marlow sees Jim for the last time, 'that white figure in the stillness of coast and sea seemed to stand at the heart of a vast enigma'. The narrator says that 'perhaps it is that feeling which has incited me to tell you the story, to try to hand over to you, as it were its very existence, its reality – the truth disclosed in a moment of illusion' (Conrad 1986: 281). The experience itself is not only caused by schematic anomaly, it is itself a schematic anomaly, and for this reason the description of the experience is able to trigger a metacognitive surprise and so a strong experience in a reader.

Nichols's 1987 *Poetics of Epiphany. Nineteenth Century Origins of the Modern Literary Moment* argues, as its title suggests, that the literary epiphany is a historically circumscribed literary technique, 'producing significance in poems' but with different kinds of significance for different writers, and playing a structural role in organizing narratives. Nichols traces a history of ideas about experience and time, with an important change relating to the 'moment' in the eighteenth century, and the momentariness of literary epiphanies arises from this. Losey (1999) argues that as postmodernists, Heaney and Larkin stress 'being' rather than the 'knowing' of modernism and that these historically varying circumstances mean that the epiphany is sometimes thought of as delivering a true revelation, sometimes an uncertain meaning. Zemka (2012) takes a similarly historicized view and critiques the use in fiction of epiphanies as ways of evading the historical circumstances of modernity, either by magically enabling moments of empathy between people or more radically by rupturing history to allow messianic liberation. Maltby (1997: 122) suggests that though 'visionary moments' are enabled in principle by human psychology, nevertheless people have learned through reading literary and religious texts to actually have these visionary moments. The view I take in this book is that literary epiphanies are examples of strong experiences, which can be explained entirely in terms of ordinary psychology and are not themselves historically specific; in principle they should be able to happen to anyone anywhere and at any time. However, whether someone will appraise the event which we call a 'strong experience' as a distinct experience, and further of a named kind such as 'moment of vision', and which is worth reporting, or writing about in a fiction: these are all dependent on historical circumstance.

One way of understanding this is to use Levy's (1973) notions of hypocognition and hypercognition.

> 'Feeling' becomes associated with cultural understandings which designate the cause of the feeling and what should be done about it. Feelings are halfway stations to action and are amenable to considerable cultural manipulation. I have suggested that some sets of feelings are relatively 'hypercognated', controlled, so to speak, by discrimination whereas others are 'hypocognated' and controlled by cultural invisibility or at least by difficulty of access to communication. (Levy 1973: 323–324)

The hypocognition of these experiences is when they are not attended to, named, or understood within the culture enough to be subject to much discussion or representation; so cultures in which strong experiences are fairly invisible are cultures in which the experience is hypocognized. In contrast, the hypercognition of these experiences is when they are so persistently attended to, named and understood within the culture that we perhaps make more of them than we might, finding structure and characteristics in the experience which we are perhaps putting into it; this is partly what postmodern and other critics of the epiphany have claimed, that the literary tradition helps to create the experience. I have also argued that metacognition, where we think about our own experience using the historically and culturally specific tools available to us, may play an important role in the generation of strong experience.

Summary of Chapter

This chapter has focused on strong experiences which include epistemic feelings of suddenly coming to know something significant and has selectively reviewed accounts of experiences with this characteristic in the Western tradition from the past few hundred years. Experiences of this kind have been theorized under various names, including the pre-Romantic and Romantic sublime, James's mystical experience, Otto's numinous, Laski's ecstasy, Maslow's peak experience, Panzarella's aesthetic peak experience, Miller's quantum change, Keltner and Haidt's awe, Pelowski and Akiba's aesthetic experience, the aha experience, the eureka moment, Schoeller's shivers of knowledge, Woolf's moment of vision and moment of being, Joyce's epiphany and Beja's literary epiphany and other intended meanings of the term 'epiphany'. In some cases, the experience is life-changing, but this is not a defining feature of strong experience. Sometimes it is triggered by something extraordinary and sometimes by something trivial, and I have suggested in other chapters that this difference is significant; the former is a surprise produced by a mismatch of perception and schema, and the second a surprise which emerges metacognitively. The differently named experiences share the crucial components of being sudden and feeling significant, but they can differ in other ways, not all of which are discussed here. The desire to talk about them, and name them, and put them into literary texts, is historically and culturally specific.

Chapter 3

EPISTEMIC FEELINGS AND KNOWLEDGE

In this chapter I explore the epistemic aspects of strong experience. I discuss schemata, and how metarepresentation plays an important role in generating certain strong experiences. I seek explanations for the epistemic feelings, including the feeling of strong significance and the feeling of ineffability.

Representations and Metarepresentations

Our thoughts have content, and we have introspective access to that content. In other words, we know what we are thinking about. This makes our thoughts representational, and they are one type of mental representation. Other types of mental representation include perceptions, schemata and so on. The various different kinds of mental representation can be matched to one another if they share content or have the same content; for example a perception of a chair can be matched to a schema for a chair. This is a matching of representations at different levels of generality. The matching of mental representations is important for the present project, because a discrepancy in the matching of mental representations, for example the match between a perception and a schema, can be a trigger of surprise, and hence sometimes of a strong experience.

We can sometimes introspectively examine the content of mental representations, but not always. And we have no introspective access to the structure of mental representations; we cannot introspectively know if they are formed like sentences in the language of thought which Fodor (1975) hypothesises. Similarly, though our memory is partly in the form of schemata, we cannot introspectively examine what a schema is. The same is true of many kinds of mental representation, including for example representations of sound or visual material, which may involve types of representation to which we have no introspective access. And while our ability to speak depends on our having mental representations of linguistic structure, again these are inaccessible to introspection. The same applies to our musical abilities, which depend on representations of musical structure which are themselves inaccessible to introspection. Raffman (1993) uses the term 'structural ineffability' to describe our inability to introspectively know about the structure of mental representations.

Metacognition is the ability to have cognition about cognition. This is an ability that may be specific to humans and allows us to think about our own thoughts or other cognitive processes and about other people's thoughts and cognitive processes. The ability to have metacognition includes the ability to have metarepresentations, which are representations of representations and include thoughts about thoughts. Jerry Fodor (1975) argues that some mental representations are articulated from component parts and that these thoughts are in the form of sentences, containing words. If thoughts are structured like sentences, then this allows a thought to structurally contain another thought, like a subclause inside a larger sentence. A thought [John believes [that Mary is happy]] is about (and contains) the thought [(that) Mary is happy], which is attributed to John. The mental representation [John believes [that Mary is happy]] is a metarepresentation, which metarepresents the representation [(that) Mary is happy].

We have definite knowledge of the content of some of our thoughts, by introspection and by explicitly verbalizing them. But there is another kind of knowledge in strong experiences, particularly in the sublime and epiphany, in the form of 'epistemic feelings', a term I use because they are feelings relating to knowledge. One of the epistemic feelings is the feeling of coming to know something significant, some deep truth. Another epistemic feeling is the feeling that something is known which cannot be put into words, that what is known is ineffable. William James (1890: 259) distinguished between definite images or thoughts in the mind and the 'psychic overtone, suffusion, or fringe, to designate the influence of a faint brain-process upon our thought, as it makes it aware of relations and objects but dimly perceived'. Mangan (1993) describes James's fringe of consciousness as 'that vague region of experience that surrounds what we now call focal attention' and quotes James:

> Every definite image in the mind is steeped and dyed in the free water that flows around it. With it goes the sense of its relations, near and remote, the dying echo of whence it came to us, the drawing sense of whither it will lead. The significance, the value, the image is all in this halo or penumbra that surrounds and escorts it. (James 1890: 255)

James elsewhere uses Crichton-Browne's (1895) term 'dreamy mental states' for 'these sudden invasions of vaguely reminiscent consciousness' including what would later be called déjà vu and describes other experiences that might also count as dreamy mental states, including feelings of awe and trances. Mangan divides the fringe feelings into feelings of rightness, feelings of wrongness and feelings of familiarity. Other fringe feelings include the tip of the tongue state that is related to the feeling of rightness, feelings of knowing of various kinds and the feeling of perceptual fluency (Reber, Wurtz and Zimmermann 2004a). Tulving's (1983) autonoetic feeling of personal involvement in remembered events is probably a kind of fringe feeling. When Kant says that the sublime arises when 'a feeling comes home to him of the inadequacy of his imagination', this is another fringe feeling. Many of these fringe feelings are what I call epistemic feelings, because they involve feelings about knowledge. Some of the fringe feelings are accurate insights into mental states and processes, and this can be shown experimentally. For example, the tip of the tongue feeling is often shortly followed by our being able to speak the missing word. However, we can also be misled by our fringe feelings. The feeling of fluency misleads us to attributing greater truth to what we are reading. And crucially for our purposes, the feeling of significance may not be accurate. In fact, because the feeling of significance is often accompanied by a feeling of ineffability, it may be impossible to verify whether what is known is actually significant.

William James makes a distinction between thoughts whose content we can clearly establish and the fringe experiences which for us include the epistemic feelings. However, there are overlapping cases. Proust and Fortier (2018: 6, citing Koriat and Levy-Sadot 1999) discuss metacognitive processing in which we think about our own thoughts and other cognitive activities. They suggest that both epistemic ('noetic') feelings and metarepresentation can be involved. The epistemic feelings are innate and universal to humans, and may be shared by animals, but metarepresentations are learned by humans in their cultural context. This may be one reason why strong experiences vary between cultures; the epistemic feelings may be the same for everyone, but how those epistemic feelings are taken into account in understanding one's own cognition will vary. Furthermore, some of the more complex fringe feelings such as déjà vu perhaps involve both epistemic feelings and metacognition, and it is the presence of metacognition which might explain why feelings such as déjà vu are not universally reported, even if the underlying mechanisms are common to all humans.

Schemata

I use the term 'schema' for our generalized knowledge of events and objects. The term 'schema' comes from Bartlett's (1932) work on memory. He showed that people's memories are not copies of their original perceptions, but are structured according to generalizations that we have derived from our experience of the world; these generalizations are schemata. Some schemata might also be part of our evolutionary genetic inheritance, such as those which form our basic knowledge of physics and biology. Rumelhart (1980) says that schemata are 'the building blocks of cognition', the packets of knowledge that constitute what we know. In this book I use the term 'schema' to mean a representation of the 'generalized concepts underlying objects, situations, events, sequences of events, actions and sequences of actions' (Rumelhart and Ortony 1977: 101). Thus a 'schema' can be what we know of an object, a type of action, a large event structure (sometimes called a script) or a complex concept. Schemata are held in our long-term semantic memory. Schemata relate to our vocabulary. For most words, including all common nouns, verbs, adjectives and adverbs, the meaning of the word corresponds to a schema. Schemata are important for this book in two specific ways. First, the strong experience may arise when perceptions have an abnormal relation to schemata, either by being too discrepant relative to schemata in classic 'surprise' or by being too close to schemata, which I argue has an uncanny or epiphanic effect. Second, if we know something ineffable, then what we know is unlikely to be schematic; schemata are capable of being expressed in words, because this is one of the purposes of words. There may, however, be unverbalized schemata; for example perhaps we have a variety of schemata for distinct smells, but these smells are not normally separately named with a vocabulary specifically for smell.

Schemata are mental representations of generalized objects and events. Perceptions are mental representations of specific objects and events, whose contents are matched to the schemata. Perceptions, however, also have non-schematic characteristics, that is, characteristics which are unlikely to be found in the schemata. One such non-schematic characteristic of perceptions might be a degree of granularity or fine detail in what is perceived. This is non-schematic if it is more specific than the level of generality expressed by the schema. For a similar reason it might be too fine-grained for linguistic distinction, so that the perception might be finer than can be expressed: this is a type of ordinary ineffability. We can for example distinguish perceptually between two shades of blue without having separate words for them, and it may be that our perceptual distinction is not based on a distinction at the schematic level. One of the ways in which ordinary objects can produce a mismatch between a perception and a schema is as a consequence of our attending to the fine detail of the object. This might be one source of epiphany, where ordinary objects appear to take on distinctive properties.

Cook (1990) and Semino (1995), amongst others, have argued that we can usefully understand our reading of literary texts in terms of schemata.

Literary texts are able to present situations that diverge from the schemata we already have, and thereby challenge the reader's schematic knowledge, potentially thereby changing the reader. Semino also notes that literary texts are also able to reinforce the schemata that readers already have. These are characteristics in general of literary texts as well as non-literary texts and need not produce a strong experience. However, strong experiences may arise when the discrepancies are too great. And strong experiences may arise when the match is too close, as when Jeffries (2001: 334) suggests that when a text matches our schemata we have a 'thrill of recognition'.

For our purposes, a really important point about schemata is that they are normative. Rumelhart (1980: 34) says '[a] schema theory embodies a prototype theory of meaning. That is, inasmuch as a schema underlying a concept stored in memory corresponds to the *meaning* of that concept, meanings are encoded in terms of the typical or normal situations or events that instantiate that concept'. For Rumelhart and Ortony (1977) schemata are more like encyclopaedic descriptions than strict dictionary definitions 'and even essential characteristics are represented in most cases as characteristics which normally or typically pertain'. Rumelhart and Ortony say that 'schemata attempt to represent knowledge in the kind of flexible way which reflects human tolerance for vagueness, imprecision and quasi-inconsistencies'. For example, 'knowledge has to be structured in such a way as to allow that dead animals are nevertheless animals, and that one-eyed faces can still be faces' (Rumelhart and Ortony 1977: 111). It is very important for my argument that schemata allow for variation in the objects or events which match them. In fact, I argue that when there is no variation, because the object or event exactly matches the schema or is imagined to exactly match the schema, then this is metacognitively surprising and can produce strong experience.

'Surprise is elicited by events that deviate from a schema' say Meyer et al. (1991: 296). I treat objects as matching to schemata, noting that objects are always contained within events. And so I extend Meyer's definition to say that surprise is also elicited by an object which is perceived such that it deviates from a schema. The perceived object or event can be called a 'token' and the schema called the 'type' to which it is matched. I sometimes use the terms 'token and type' and sometimes 'perception and schema', with similar meanings, and to capture the fact that we perceive tokens and schematize types. Perceptions of events and objects are matched to the schemata for those events and objects, but the matching is somewhat loose, because there is a normal range of variation in the matching; that is, schemata are normative. I propose that matches that fall either above or below this normal range of variation are surprising, for different reasons, and a potential trigger of a strong experience. A variation that is greater than the norm might arise when an object is extreme, for example extremely large, and thereby outside the normal range of variation for its schema. The sublime arises from a discrepancy of this kind. Another possible discrepancy is that the object has a faulty component part that makes it a bad match to the schema; Boyer's (2001) religious objects or Douglas's (1966) impure objects may be of this kind. These discrepancies trigger surprise because they are deviations from a schema.

The judgment that something is beautiful is sometimes seen as related to, but milder than, the strong experience of the sublime. The normativity of schemata is relevant in connecting these experiences. Patrick Hogan points out that experimental subjects find "averaged cases of categories preferable to actual instances", but more specifically that we experience beauty when specific features of the category (i.e., schema) are exaggerated; thus beauty comes from a shifting slightly away from the norm (Hogan 2013: 320, developing ideas from Ramachandran 2011). The strong experience, which includes the sublime – often contrasted with the beautiful – pushes the features much further from the norm so as to surprise us.

I propose that there is also surprise when there is a variation that is below the normal range. The normative status of a schema means that the schema is not exactly or perfectly instantiated by a perception. Thus, if the schema and perception exactly match, this is also a deviation from the norm, which I call 'perfection'. Here, the deviation arises between the perception and the schema, and the experience of a deviation depends on the metacognitive assumption of a normative expectation of some difference between perception and schema, which means that an exact match is deviant. This is important, because it allows various kinds of perfect match to produce surprise, and hence strong emotion, though the surprise is not immediately perceptual and instead based on a metacognitive assessment of a perfect match as falling outside the norm. The perfect match might include objects which are perceived as unique because something which is unique exactly matches its schema as a result of there being only one tokening of the type. We can extend this also to include doubles and multiples, because all the tokens are identical, thus show no variation from the type, and thus again produce a discrepancy. The multiple is a trigger of the sublime, and the double is a trigger of the uncanny (another type of strong experience). The idea that strong experience might arise from a perception-to-schema match which falls outside the normal range of variation, but either above or below that range, finds an echo in an account of the musical sublime by Christian Friedrich Michaelis (cited Korstvedt 2000: 58). Writing in 1805, he says that sublime transcendence in music arises when 'emotions are aroused as either completely prevent the integration of one's impressions into a coherent whole or, when at any rate they make it very difficult'. He then says that these emotions arise from 'entrancing uniformity and repetition, or from musical diversity and complexity so great as to dazzle the ear', which includes both perfection and discrepancy as possible triggers.

The theoretical basis for the notion that perfection is metacognitively surprising comes from Sperber's (1996) article on symbolic thinking about perfect animals and about anomalous animals. Sperber's focus is on group thinking which is the aggregate of thoughts and thinkers within a culture, rather than on individual thoughts and responses as here, but I extend his ideas to individual experience. Sperber notes and criticizes Mary Douglas's (1966) theory that symbolic treatment is a way of removing anomalies from taxonomic schemata, as in her famous proposal that the animals that the *Torah* prohibits as food are prohibited because they are anomalous relative to a taxonomy. Sperber argues that a taxonomy is a classification of animals in terms of their intrinsic features and that in principle any actual animal can be put into any taxonomy. This is because the features that define a species or genus in the taxonomy need not be manifest in an animal, but can also be virtual in an actual animal or in a type of animal. For example, a bird is defined as having feathers, but there are featherless birds, so these birds are said to have 'virtual feathers'. Similarly a cat which has lost a leg has a 'virtual' fourth leg, whose manifest absence does not prevent the animal being a four-legged animal such as a cat. These are not taxonomic anomalies, and so symbolic thought is not necessary in order to manage them.

However, he agrees with Lévi-Strauss (1962) that certain animals are good to think about as well as being good to eat. This goodness relates to their characteristics relative to the taxonomic classification. Animals must first be subject to taxonomic classification and identification, and once this is done they can be symbolically conceptualized as non-ordinary in one of two ways, either being above or below that normal range of variation that holds between a type and a token. They are non-ordinary because they are perfect relative to their type: 'That's a real horse!' is a claim that the animal is a perfect example of its species. But there is something wrong with this because '[p]erfect animals or a paradigmatic species are also statistical exceptions', because we expect tokenings of a type to vary within a normal range. This wrongness produces one way of thinking symbolically about an animal. Alternatively animals are non-ordinary because they are bad tokens relative to their type: 'You call that a horse?'. This can be scaled up to types of animals (species) that are anomalous relative to a higher classification (genre), such as those which the *Torah* says are unfit to eat. An example would be the eel as a species which is an anomalous match to the genus of fish to which it belongs. Sperber's 'hypothesis is that symbolism occurs when a judgment of normality is put forward as modifying a taxonomic identification, i.e., when the ideal norm is considered as an encyclopaedic component of the taxonomic definition'. Such a judgement leads to statements or beliefs which are not coherent. One such incoherent statement is a judgement of perfection, such as that a horse is true or real as opposed to other horses which by implication are not. Another incoherent statement is a statement of radical discrepancy, such as that a type of fish is not really a type of fish. Sperber describes these as paradoxes and says, 'here is the paradox that causes the representation of an animal or of a species to be processed symbolically'. Sperber argues that a culture collectively thinks symbolically about these outliers which are highly discrepant or perfect tokenings of a type. By this he means that we formulate mental representations about them which are semi-propositional, being incoherent, paradoxical or having missing parts. Symbolic thinking for Sperber thus involves various kinds of semi-propositional mental representation. We will return to his theory of semi-propositional mental metarepresentation. But the key thing to take from this discussion is that Sperber says that perfect matchings of token to type, or subtype to higher type, are as odd as very discrepant matchings, because they both fall outside the normal range of variation.

Before moving on, I briefly explore and then reject the alternative approach taken in Fabb (2021) to understanding why perfection is surprising. In that chapter, I take a different approach to the match between perceptions and schemata. There, as in my present approach I take variation to be the norm, but instead interpret this to treat any perception which falls either above or below a normal range of variation as 'discrepant'. This means that both too divergent a match and too close a match count as discrepant. In contrast, the theory of the present book treats only 'too divergent' a match as discrepant. The approach in Fabb (2021) now seems to me incorrect for three reasons. First, it is just odd to say that a close match between token and type (perception and schema) is discrepant, because the term does not have that meaning. Second, the strong experience of the divergent and the strong experience of the perfect are not normally treated as exactly the same. This roughly corresponds to the distinction between the sublime and the epiphany, and though I bracket them together as strong experiences, they are not identical. Third, my current approach uses metacognition as a way of understanding the strong experience of perfect things, and metacognition also has a role to play in explaining the infectiousness of strong experiences.

The Distinction between Episodic Memory and Semantic Memory

Semantic memory is the type of long-term memory in which we hold general knowledge in the form of schemata and scripts. Tulving (1972) distinguished between general semantic memories and the episodic memories for specific events. He treated the two types of memory as operating in distinct systems, with different characteristics. Suddendorf et al. (2009: 1317) offer experimental evidence to justify this distinction, showing that each type of memory can be impaired, for example by brain injury, while leaving the other type of memory intact. The evidence we have about strong experiences comes largely from episodic memories, as they are reported to us. We will shortly be looking at Wordsworth's 'Daffodils' poem, in which he reproduces a strong experience by remembering it later. This poem suggests that memory of episodes that lead to strong experiences can in turn produce strong experiences. When we have an episodic memory of something that happened to us, we experience the feeling of having been there, of having experienced the past event or episode which is remembered. The remembered event is attached to us personally. Tulving (1985) called this an 'autonoetic consciousness'. He described it as 'the characteristic phenomenal flavor of the experience of remembering' episodes. It belongs with James's fringe experiences. This phenomenal flavour that is attached to a remembered experience might be one of the routes by which an experience comes to be seen as significant, particularly since the self is involved. Referring to Suddendorf & Corballis (1997), Zentall (2005: 209) says, 'inherent in the idea of autonoetic memory is a concept of self in the past that is dissociated from the present self, a form of metarepresentation or perspective taking'. Metarepresentation is, I argue, one of the triggers of strong experience. The metarepresentational component of episodic memory thus links episodic memory to strong experience.

Episodes that we read in fictions can form remembered episodes that we did not experience. This means that they have no autonoetic aspect and so are not like episodic memories of real events. So what kind of memory are they? This problem is discussed by Rubin and Umanath (2015):

> In general, recall of events from an oral tradition, or of any fictional narrative, is not a good fit for semantic or episodic memory. It can be considered semantic memory in that it is the stable shared knowledge of a culture, but it is episodic memory in that the recall is of specific events that are perceived and reacted to as events.

Their solution is to treat episodic memories and as semantic memories not as distinct kinds but instead as made from component parts which can be combined in various ways to produce different kinds of memory. These include memories for represented events in fictions. Rubin and Umanath's approach is shared by Tinti et al. (2014) who propose a type of memory called 'event memory', which is a memory for the factual details of an event and can be separated off from autobiographical memory of the experience of that event. Another related kind is a non-believed memory, when a person has a memory but does not believe it to be true (Clark et al. 2012).

There is a literary angle on this, involving the common literary practice of intertextuality, which I suggest may be another contributing factor in strong experience. Intertextuality arises when a text makes us remember some specific aspect of another text, and thereby exploits the ambiguous status of represented and fictional events. An event in one narrative is both the same as, and different from, an event in another narrative if they are intertextual, or one alludes to the other. This 'is/is not' relation is found in Paul Ricoeur's (1977) account of metaphor and is a discrepancy which can trigger a strong experience. We might also think of memories for fictional events as experientially anomalous, and hence discrepant relative to our deeply embedded schemata which describe what a memory is. This is one of the kinds of mild strangeness that may be pervasive in literature and other aesthetic objects, and which can peak sometimes as strong experiences. When we remember episodes from a book, though this may feel like an episodic memory it perhaps cannot be as detailed as a real episodic memory, because narrated episodes are always thin in terms of what information they include when compared with the density of reality. Because the memories are based on events that are constructed from the words on the page, the events as remembered depend on the schemata which correspond to the words, and so they are also somewhat like semantic memories, memories which have a general rather than specific feel to them. So it is possible that memories of events in a book have an uncertain status when we reflect upon them, because they have the shape of episodic memories, but they are also like semantic memories. Thus we produce a discrepancy by engaging in this type of metacognition, and as I have suggested before, discrepancies produced by metacognition have the potential to trigger strong experiences.

A flashbulb memory (Brown and Kulik 1977) is an episodic memory which is a perceptually vivid memory of an unexpected and emotionally strong event. This might be a major historic event such as 9/11 or the assassination of President Kennedy or it might be a personal event. The strength of the memory correlates with the feeling of significance of the event and the strength of emotion felt at that time (Allen et al. 2008: 124). Flashbulb memories are thus memories of an event that might have triggered a strong experience. These actual events have a distinctive status relative to the general historical sequence, and some have argued that an epiphany is likewise a specific and localized moment that contrasts with the general historical sequence, and which disrupts it, transforms it or stops it (Wolf 1999: 177). Flashbulb memories are memories of something unique, and they are specific to an individual in a time and place, which makes them like epiphanies. They have an epistemological flavour, which is that they are characterized by subjective certainty, though not necessarily accurate, as Talarico and Rubin (2007) show. The potential for inaccuracy in flashbulb memories comes from the fact that the event may be initially recalled as vivid fragments, which are constructed into whole memories of the event by rehearsing the memory frequently. Each rehearsal may alter the overall structure of the event, leading to it becoming inaccurate. The notion of vivid fragments reminds us that the fragment is a trigger for epiphanic experience. Flashbulb memories can be enhanced by interest and by prior knowledge, which enables better processing of incoming information; the enhancement by prior knowledge correlates with the role of expertise that has been shown to enhance thrill experiences. I will later discuss a 'flashbulb' moment in Robert Browning's poem 'Childe Roland to the Dark Tower Came', as a moment of strong experience.

Traumatic memories share with flashbulb memories the memory of a strongly significant event. Zemka (2012: 216) quotes Brison (1993) on how a survivor of a trauma experiences 'a shrinking of time to the immediate present' until the episode is integrated into narrative, and she compares this to Woolf's type of strong experience, the 'moment of being', whose 'original is a ruthless shrinking of time in the present, but the writer's practice transforms that compressed shock into its opposite, tranquility'. Holmes et al. (2005: 4) suggest that memory at moments of extreme arousal, as in trauma, is encoded primarily in a sensory-perceptual manner, rather than as a verbal narrative; this would make the memory ineffable. This raises the question of whether a strong emotional reaction might generally lead to processing that is not verbalizable, and so lead to a more general connection between strong emotion and ineffability. The fragmentariness and unclarity and incompleteness of the memory in trauma gives it a particular staying power. Perhaps strong experiences gain their memorability in a similar way, by being made from components that are incomplete and unintegrated into a coherent narrative.

Tulving's episodic-semantic memory distinction resonates with various cultural practices and cultural notions. For example, in Aboriginal Australia it might correlate with a distinction between the now and the eternal or more specifically between the everyday world and the everywhen or 'dreaming' of the Ancestors where 'country itself is known only in and through the repetitions – the marks, rituals, songs, stories – that contemporary people tell of it' (Biddle 2007: 70). Perhaps it is realized in T. S. Eliot's (1972: 49) distinction between tradition and the individual talent: 'This historical sense, which is a sense of the timeless as well as of the temporal and of the timeless and of the temporal together, is what makes a writer traditional'. Harvey Whitehouse uses Tulving's distinction to distinguish between two anthropological modes in religion, found in different cultures (Laidlaw 2004). One of these is the 'doctrinal mode', which is based on the memory of religious doctrine, reiterated in verbal form by religious leaders. Whitehouse suggests that this is a kind of religion that favours semantic memory. In contrast, episodic memory is favoured by the 'imagistic mode', where individuals reflect on their own experiences and meanings which are not part of generally shared knowledge. Whitehouse further suggests that the imagistic mode can depend on flashbulb memories formed in traumatic initiation ceremonies. Whitehouse is not claiming that a particular religion depends only on one kind of memory but rather that there is a distinction between the two modes, each of which favours a particular kind of memory over the other. He suggests that in the imagistic mode, episodic memories tend to produce meanings that are not shared and less verbalized; this connects with the ineffability of our experiences. McNamara (2009: 224) looks at the association of the imagistic mode with the experience of timelessness. He suggests that it arises because the witnessing of ritual 'requires suspension of, or displacement of, the immediate intentional states of participants' in which thoughts become less clear and that this experience of empty time intervals is a result of witnessing meaningless acts, and that this produces an experience of timelessness. Further, Whitehouse (2004: 195) suggests that in ritual, it is no longer clear who is speaking: the priest actually speaks but his speaking is the same as his predecessors. Note that though Whitehouse does not say so, this is another situation, like memory for fiction, in which episodic and semantic memory becomes blurred. The search for the original speaker in the original episode that underlies the semantic-episodic memory produces a 'haunting presence of Another Agent at work' (Whitehouse 2004: 199). In these various ways, the imagistic mode as associated with episodic memory also resembles strong experience.

Whitehouse suggests that ritual performance is both specific and generic. This combination is true of most aesthetic practices as well, where the text has both individual characteristics and also generic characteristics. For example, Charlotte Brontë's novel *Jane Eyre* (1847) is both a story about specific events and individuals, but also a text that has generic characteristics. These generic characteristics, which can be expressed as schemata, mean that the events of the story have a certain characteristic shape and sequence, derived not from the imagined reality in which the characters live, but more from the conventions of novels. But at the same time they are specific imagined incidents, and so they are both generic and specific at the same time. Similarly, characters such as Grace Poole or St. John Rivers are individuals but also symbolic types, as demonstrated by how their names draw on the religious and earth-air-fire-water imagery found in the names of many of the characters. The generic aspects of a specific represented event can be realized in different ways in a literary text. As already noted, the event can have generic characteristics – the hero and heroine get married at the end or the family is restored. Symbols can be individualized, as happens with the naming of characters in Jane Eyre, and in particular with Jane herself, whose name recalls not only 'air', but also the narrative themes of 'err' and so 'error' or wandering, 'heir', and perhaps an eagle's eyrie which is mentioned in the novel and related to its bird imagery. And as part of her name, her initials J.E. ('are there any letters for J.E., I asked') via the French references in the novel become the *je* ('I') of the narration. In these ways, an individual character is a mix of the specific and the general. Perhaps this mixture is itself recognizable as a type of discrepancy, when reflected on metacognitively, and so the ordinary workings of fiction are potentially a source of strong experience.

There are other mixings of the specific and the generic. What Whittier-Ferguson (2011) characterizes as Woolf's shift towards greater repetition and cliché in her later novels may also be a way of producing moments of being via the contrast between the specific and the generic. Furthermore, texts may be intertextual, and this can include texts which represent epiphanies. Joyce's overheard talking, which is the first epiphany in *Stephen Hero*, may be intertextual with the song overheard by Augustine in his strong experience during conversion. Wordsworth's 'Daffodils' is reimagined in Seamus Heaney's epiphanic poem 'Postscript' (1996) about a flock of swans by a lakeside. Lamb's (1997) account of the sublime brings up a similar dichotomy between episodes (episodic memories) and facts (semantic memories). Thus Wordsworth's spots of time offer

> heterogeneous particulars as the bare historical contingencies of passion at the same time as rehearsing them as the most compelling forms in which passion may be re-presented:
>
> > The single sheep, and the one blasted tree,
> > And the bleak music of that old stone wall
>
> > > (Lamb 1997: 416, quoting Wordsworth
> > > *The Prelude* 11.378-9)

Lamb cites Addison on 'a dual response to phenomena as both singular and representative, as free-standing impressions and as signs of universals. The intensity generated by this mutual relation of particle and form is experienced variously as awe, power and belief, and it is assigned by some of the more notable scriptural critics as the cause of the sublime in poetic language' (Lamb 1997: 413). The mixing of the specific and the generic may thus characterize not only ritual but also strong experience.

Communication and Indirectness

The proposal that thoughts are mental representations is the basis of relevance theory, the theory of communication proposed by Sperber and

Wilson (1995). I use this theory because it is useful for conceptualizing how the feeling of significance might arise, and it also gives us a way of thinking about metaphors, which are a potential trigger of strong experience. The next paragraph offers a brief summary.

Communication involves a speaker and a hearer. The speaker seeks to get the hearer to construct specific thoughts and to attribute those thoughts back to the speaker, as the thoughts which the speaker is attempting to communicate. Language is a good way of providing evidence for thoughts, because the vocabulary and syntax of language offer a very rich way of coding meaning into form. In principle, many mental representations can be directly encoded in language, that is, many thoughts can be put directly into utterances. However, though utterances *can* encode thoughts, the hearer can never be certain that the encoded meaning of an utterance *is* the intended meaning of an utterance. As Sperber and Wilson say, 'communication takes place at a risk'. As a hearer we cannot be certain whether the words used directly or literally encode the thoughts. This is because the speaker can never offer an explicit and reliable guarantee that they are speaking literally or nonliterally. There are also reasons why the speaker should not want to put their thoughts directly into words, one of which involves the advantages of metaphor.

Metaphors exploit the potential indirectness of all communication. In a metaphor, the communicated meaning is radically different from the encoded meaning of the words. This means that in a metaphor the meaning encoded in the utterance can be incoherent or untrue, while at the same time the meaning communicated by the utterance is both coherent and potentially true. One of the advantages of metaphors is that because the communicated meaning is separated off from the literal meaning, it is possible for one utterance to communicate many different meanings at the same time. Sperber and Wilson use the term 'poetic effects' to describe one of the possible effects of a metaphor. They say that the poetic effects of a communication 'marginally increase the manifestness of a great many weakly manifest assumptions', and this results 'from the accessing of a large array of very weak implicatures in the otherwise ordinary pursuit of relevance' (Sperber and Wilson 1995: 224). The feeling of poetic effects is the feeling of having access to a large number of thoughts at the same time, but without necessarily bringing those thoughts to consciousness, or fully formulating those thoughts. The feeling that there are poetic effects is an epistemic feeling. This epistemic feeling may perhaps contribute to the feeling of significance.

Relevance theory is appropriate to describe communicative events (Sperber and Wilson 1995). These are events in which a hearer seeks to maximize the cognitive effects of the utterances they hear, and where cognitive effects are contributions to knowledge. But there are other situations in which speakers and hearers may deliberately seek non-understanding, where nothing new is learned, and where verbal and other apparently communicative behaviour is not understood, either fully or partially. These are not communicative situations, and so relevance theory does not apply to them. For example, in some ritual contexts, only some of the participants can understand the language used, as when for example Latin is used in church services attended by participants who cannot understand it.

Some of the accounts of strong experiences emphasize ways in which not understanding is a good thing. In his discussion of the sublime, Longinus says that 'he admires what passes his understanding'. John Dennis describes as 'enthusiasm' the passions aroused 'when their cause is not clearly comprehended by him who feels them' (Dennis 1701, cited Monk 1960: 48). William Crotch, lecturing on music around 1800, said that '[t]he sublime is founded on principles of vastness and incomprehensibility' (quoted Korstvedt 2000: 58). Keats associated aesthetic ability with being 'capable of being in uncertainties, Mysteries, doubts, without any irritable reaching after fact & reason' (Rollins 1958: 193). Laski (1961: 359) describes the incomprehensibility of experience in ecstasies as a warrant for belief, based on a belief 'that rational explanation destroys the numinous'. Lewis (2002: 61) says about Goethe's response to Strasbourg cathedral that what excited him was its very incomprehensibility: 'An impression of oneness, wholeness and greatness filled my soul – an impression which, because it consisted of a thousand harmonizing details, I could savour and enjoy, but by no means understand or explain'. Elkins (2001: 28) suggests that crying in front of paintings is a kind of emotional experience which 'is always at least a little mysterious' and should not be understood, thus explicitly formulating a stance of not-understanding, or 'becoming acclimated to not knowing, to never knowing'. He says, 'I do not *want* to understand these wonderful phenomena'. Juslin (2013: 261) suggests that our experience of music improves when '[i]n listening to music, there is a strong sense that something "highly structured" and "meaningful" is being said, but our brain cannot make out what it is. The resulting feeling might be construed as "mild excitement" mixed with "confusion" as our brain is continuously "hooked" by this subtle yet inexplicable language-like structure that we call "music"'. Sperber (2010: 587) argues that in religious belief, 'impenetrability indicates profundity'. He adds, '[b]ecause of the authority they grant religion, believers are convinced that the content of mysteries would be extraordinarily relevant to them if only they could grasp it [...] The existence of barely glimpsed hyper-relevant content is yet another confirmation of the supreme authority of religion'.

Psychologists have explored why the failure to understand might be a positive experience. Wilson et al. (2005: 6) show that in pleasurable circumstances the pleasure derived from events lasts longer when it is difficult to make sense of the events. They offer experimental evidence that if we know a story has a positive outcome, 'some uncertainty about its dénouement would prolong people's pleasure'. They cite Pennebaker's (1997) general finding that 'romantic infatuations last longer when they involve a degree of uncertainty and lack of understanding', and Clore and Colcombe's (2003) finding that 'uncertainty about the source of positive affect leads to a general sense of well-being'. Tolerance for uncertainty and ambiguity are necessary for health, and failure to do so can lead to generalized anxiety disorder (Grenier et al. 2005), which also suggests that uncertainty should bring rewards. These are all reasons for thinking that if strong experiences have a component that involves not understanding what is happening, then this may be experienced positively and sought out.

Metarepresentation and strong experience

A metarepresentation is a representation of another representation. Many aesthetic practices use metarepresentation (Trentini 2014). As Iser notes, this includes literature: 'The ability to perceive oneself during the process of participation is an essential quality of the aesthetic experience. . . [the reader] is involved, and he watches himself being involved' (Iser 1978: 134, quoted Sundararajan 2002: 176). Metarepresentation is relevant for strong experience, and particularly mental metarepresentation, that is, thought about thought. Mental metarepresentations are a kind of metacognition (cognition about cognition).

Metacognition is manifested in Kant's proposal that we experience the sublime by reflecting on our own perceptions and cognition, and in particular by recognizing that our cognitive abilities are greater than our perceptual abilities: 'The sublime is that, the mere capacity of thinking which evinces a faculty of mind transcending every standard of sense' (Kant 1952: 98). Similarly Richardson (2012: 32) says that what he calls the 'neural sublime' arises from the judgment, which again we can call metacognitive, 'that conscious perception is unreliable and that the vivid and apparently stable object world it presents to us is illusory and marked by a kind of emptiness'. Tangerås (2020: 96) describes how one of his interviewees, Veronica achieves a turning point, in effect a strong experience, by metacognition: 'it is a turning point: Veronica reads her own reading, and then interprets what implications this meta-cognitive act must have for how she relates to herself.'

I now offer four suggestions about why metarepresentation might lead to strong experience.

The first suggestion has already been presented in Chapter 1, in the discussion of metacognitive surprise. I suggest that we are able to compare our actual experience with our schemata for experience and to be surprised by a discrepancy between them. Metacognitive surprise is set off by perceptions of doubles and multiples, and by tokenings which perfectly match their type.

My second suggestion is that we can understand the 'catching' of strong experiences by metarepresentation. There is good evidence that we are able to experience a thrill by remembering a thrill or by hearing someone else describe a thrill. Here the original trigger may no longer exist, but just thinking about a thrill can cause a thrill. This may be because we match the perceived thrill experience to our schemata for experience, and find it discrepant relative to those schemata, because the thrill experience is anomalous in various ways.

My third suggestion relates to the possibility of mistaking a subordinate representation for a primary representation, and suddenly realizing the error, which is a surprise which can trigger a strong experience. Some terminology is needed to explain this. Any representation that is contained in another is a 'subordinate representation' and any representation that is not contained in another is a 'primary representation'. A metarepresentation is a representation which contains another representation, and it is worth noting that a metarepresentation might itself be a subordinate representation within a higher-level metarepresentation. To illustrate how a subordinate representation can be mistaken for a primary representation, consider the beginning of Jane Austen's 1815 novel *Emma*, where at first we take the representations of the fictional world to be primary representations and only realize half way down the first page that we are reading secondary representations, which are subordinated under Emma's own perceptions. What is being said is not what the narrator tells us on her own behalf, but what the narrator represents Emma as telling us. This novelistic blurring of the status of representations is a general characteristic of fiction.

As an example of how the shift in perceived status can produce a strong experience, I offer a personal example of how such a shift produced in me a strong thrill experience. This was in the course of watching the *Star Trek Voyager* television episode 'Living Witness' (1998), a science fiction narrative set in the future. When the episode begins, we see events which, after a few minutes, we realize are not primary representations as though they are actually happening in front of our eyes, but in fact are subordinate representations within a metarepresentational frame. This realization comes when we discover that the events we see are a holographic reproduction of an imagined past set of events, in a museum, being watched by other characters. The metarepresentational frame was initially concealed from us but is now revealed: what appeared to be a primary representation was suddenly revealed to be a subordinate representation. Then, almost at the end of the episode we discover that everything that has happened so far is itself a hologram, watched by yet other characters in a more distant future. Again, what appeared to be a primary representation was suddenly revealed to be a subordinate representation. The revelation that there is a metarepresentational frame around the events, was quite unexpected and gave me a strong chill experience.

These examples of anomalous shifts between representation and metarepresentation have a psychological analogue. Frith (1992) discusses the pathological experience of thought-insertion in which we have a thought that feels like someone else's thought, inserted into our minds. He suggests that this is a situation in which we experience a subordinate representation without its metarepresentational frame, as though it is a primary representation. For example, if I have a thought such as 'it is raining' then I can metarepresent this thought to myself as 'I think that it is raining'. Thought insertions are in fact our own thoughts but we fail to metarepresent them to ourselves as our own thoughts. We do recognize them as thoughts, though, and we engage in metacognition about them, for example attributing them to aliens or spiritual sources. Luhrmann et al. (2015) discuss the range of culturally influenced ways in which internal voices of this kind are interpreted. The experience of having a thought without being able to attribute it to ourself is metacognitively surprising.

Metarepresentation and Semi-propositional Thoughts

In this section, I explore Dan Sperber's notion that our 'meta-representational abilities allow humans to process representations which they do not fully understand' (Sperber 1996: 71). Sperber (1985: 51) notes that in a representational theory of mind, a thought can be a 'propositional representation', which means that it is a representation that has a proposition as its content. A proposition is a representation of the world which is in principle verifiable as either true or false. Sperber suggests that our thought can also be a 'semi-propositional representation', which is a representation that corresponds to a 'half-understood idea', and is not verifiable. We can entertain semi-propositional representations by embedding them inside metarepresentations. An example would be a metarepresentation with the structure 'I believe that P', where P stands for the semi-propositional representation. The metarepresentation itself is fully propositional and verifiable, and thus a fully understood thought, even though it contains a semi-propositional representation. This, Sperber argues, is why we can have 'apparently irrational beliefs' where the subordinated thought is in some sense irrational, but it is embedded within a fully rational state of belief. Thus, we can have unclear beliefs (Recanati 1997 calls these 'quasi-beliefs').

What characteristics does a semi-propositional representation have? One option is that it might contain a term whose meaning we do not know. Sperber (1996) gives as an example a child who believes 'that grandma is dead', but cannot explain what 'dead' means. Other types of semi-propositional representations include representations that are ambiguous or are metaphors or symbols without any determinate meaning.

There is a further possibility related to this, which is that the subordinate representation is propositional but is completely uninformative, hence minimally representational. For example we might have a metarepresentation 'I know that John saw something'. Here the subordinate thought is in fact propositional, since it has a truth value, but it is also very uninformative, and like a semi-propositional representation in having an uncertain meaning. The most uninformative version of this might be a thought such as 'I know something'. This is what Laski (1961: 346) is pointing to when she says that 'the most usual post-ecstatic feeling is that something new is known but it is not known what'. The subordinate representation might thus have no specific content but nevertheless we feel that it has substantial content, and it may be its lack of content which makes it feel significant.

So, we can have a thought that contains a semi-proposition or an uninformative proposition as its content. Further, we can think about that thought, thus metarepresenting at a higher level, and this further thinking can produce the conclusion that the representation is not able to fully express the significance of what is known, and hence that what we know is ineffable. Belief in an unclear thought is belief without understanding, and this is a type of ineffability: a belief cannot be put into words because some parts of it are missing.

Sperber suggests that the embedding of semi-propositional representations inside metarepresentations is typical of symbolic thinking. It can be important in religious belief because the gaps in the thoughts are interesting for people to explore, allowing an indefinite range of interpretations. Sperber suggests that these semi-propositional representations create 'the possibility of conceptual mysteries, which no amount of processing could ever clarify, invading human minds' and that these mysteries can spread to become central to a culture, for example in religions. Perhaps the power of conceptual mysteries relates to the possibility of their generating strong experiences. One of the types of semi-propositional metarepresentation incorporates a thought whose meaning we do not fully understand, but which we believe to be true. This allows for extensive interpretative activity, in the pursuit of a difficult meaning. In this way, semi-propositional metarepresentations are like metaphors;

metaphors are often in their coded meaning untrue or incoherent, but they are assumed to be interpretable in ways which produce unspoken truths. Whitehouse (2004: 193) discusses Bloch on religious rituals where the meaning of the rituals is unclear. In our terms rituals are examples of metarepresentations with inadequately specified contents, hence semi-propositional. Amongst the various ways in which the participants might respond to this is to invent possible meanings, for example in response to an outsider asking about them. But instead, 'people might engage in a more prolonged search for "deep" and satisfying ritual exegesis', which 'is deemed to cause "rich and revelatory religious experience"'. This is analogous to the epistemic feeling of poetic effects, discussed earlier.

Catching a Thrill, Metarepresentation and the Transmission of Strong Experience

One of the odd aspects of thrills is that we can 'catch' them by remembering our own previously experienced thrill or hearing someone else talking about having a thrill. We do not necessarily need to be exposed to the original trigger for the thrill, for example we can get a thrill by remembering an experience that gave us a thrill. Gabrielsson (2011: 428) describes having this experience: 'I'm almost in tears now when I think about it', where 'it' is a remembered strong experience. Tangerås (2020: 74) hears his interviewee Veronica describe her life-changing reading experience and as she does she says, 'Hmm, ooh, I feel tingly now'. He responds: 'What happened there? Did the tingling come as you were talking about this now?' She answers: 'Yeah, I could feel a nervous energy, like a flutter in my stomach'.

These can all be thought of as ways of catching a thrill, and specifically involve having an arousal-based thrill reaction when thinking about another arousal-based thrill reaction. Catching a thrill must be something other than emotional contagion, which arises for example when a person cries because they see another person crying. Emotional contagion as defined by Hatfield et al. (2009) or Hatfield et al. (2014) results from witnessing someone else's emotion, in a sequence which starts with 'mimicry of facial expressions, vocal expressions, postures and instrumental behaviours of those around them' and from mimicry comes a sense of the emotion itself, to which we can attend, so allowing the emotion to emerge. This is not obviously what is happening when we catch a strong experience. We cannot usually see someone else getting goosebumps for example because the visual evidence is so small, and the evidence for the other person's thrill is sparse and indirect, usually just a mention of getting a thrill. I now explore the possibility that catching a thrill depends not on directly catching the arousal itself, but depends on how the original arousal and its trigger are metarepresented. This would explain why all the types of strong experiences, including those which have no arousal, can be caught in the same way. Though this does not appear to be emotional contagion, it is nevertheless possible that empathy also plays a role. Coplan (2004: 143–144) differentiates empathy from emotional contagion. In empathy we can imaginatively experience the emotional state of another by taking their perspective while being aware of a self-other differentiation. In emotional contagion we experience the emotions of another as our own emotions, without being aware of a self-other differentiation. Coplan uses 'catch' (an emotion) specifically for emotional contagion. But when I talk about catching a thrill, I use 'catch' for something which is neither empathy nor emotional contagion in her terms. We can catch the thrill while being entirely aware of the difference between us and the other whose thrill we catch.

Can the experience of the sublime or epiphany similarly be transmitted from writer to reader? This is Beja's claim, that Joyce's books 'include many epiphanies which he certainly felt – and often meant the reader to feel' (Beja 1971: 81). Similarly Wordsworth in his poem 'Daffodils' (1807) describes the catching of a strong experience by remembering it, where he catches it from his past self. His original experience occurs directly through sense perception of the world and is a sudden and surprising perceptional experience, where the trigger has the common motifs and elements of liminality, the crowd, and the multiple.

> I wandered lonely as a Cloud
> That floats on high o'er Vales and Hills,
> When all at once I saw a crowd
> A host of dancing Daffodils;
> Along the Lake, beneath the trees,
> Ten thousand dancing in the breeze.
>
> The waves beside them danced, but they
> Outdid the sparkling waves in glee: –
> A poet could not but be gay
> In such a laughing company:
> I gaz'd – and gaz'd – but little thought
> What wealth the show to me had brought:

Then in the next and final stanza, he recalls the first strong experience and has another strong experience as a consequence.

> For oft when on my couch I lie
> In vacant or in pensive mood,

> They flash upon that inward eye
> Which is the bliss of solitude,
> And then my heart with pleasure fills,
> And dances with the Daffodils.
>
> Wordsworth (1807, vol 2, pp.49–50)

This is the kind of evidence that suggests that representations of strong experience might themselves cause strong experiences. I now explore why this might be.

One possibility is that a represented strong experience is perceived as discrepant because there is something inexplicable or irrational about how it is triggered. In epiphany, the feeling of significance is triggered by a perception of something which is not in itself significant. Similarly, the thrill is what we might get in response to some frightening or sad event, but in strong experiences the thrill is often in response to some fiction, some formal change, or something else which is not inherently frightening or sad. Thus the relation between the trigger and the response is mismatched, relative to deeply embedded schemata for experience itself and in particular the schematic expectation of a rational relation between a trigger and an experience. The irrationality of the triggering in strong experience can thus be perceived as a discrepancy between an experience and a schema for experience. This is a type of metacognitive surprise and means that thinking about a strong experience can produce a strong experience.

In this light it is useful to consider Foster and Keane's (2015) account of secondary surprise. In their theory, surprise can arise from a post hoc appraisal of the discrepancy between a perception and what is already known. They quote Adler (2008) who suggests that a person can be secondarily surprised by a remembered event, even if it did not originally surprise them, if they later learn that the event is discrepant with what is generally known. This allows for surprise in the absence of the original trigger, which is happening when strong experiences are infectious.

There is another possible approach to this problem. We might attempt to metarepresent the experience, but find that it can only be represented with a semi-propositional representation, which we can embed inside our belief that whatever is represented actually occurred. This constitutes an attitude of belief towards strong experiences which is like our attitude of belief towards thoughts which we do not understand. In turn, this encourages inference and interpretation and can generate feelings of significance. Consider Wordsworth's strong experience that is triggered by his memory of the daffodils. The experience of remembering is described metaphorically as a 'flash upon that inward eye', and the metaphor suggests that the content of the memory itself cannot be directly stated. Perhaps this is how the memory of the strong experience works as a trigger: the memory produces a metarepresentation whose subordinated representation has characteristics that cannot be fully understood. Perhaps also the empathy involved in remembering our own self as we were in the past plays a role in the experience. As a footnote to this discussion, consider Seamus Heaney's poem 'Postscript' (1996) about an analogous experience, of seeing swans by a lake, which 'catch the heart off guard and blow it open'. This poem is intertextual with Wordsworth's poem. Discussing Heaney's poem, Nichols says 'while reading these words, our minds have an experience not unlike the one described in the poem: powerful, memorable, concrete in terms of sensation, yet semantically open-ended' (Nichols 1999: 470).

Feelings of Knowing

In this book I use the term 'epistemic feeling' to describe the feeling that we know something significant. Other alternative terms which have similar meanings to 'epistemic feelings' include 'noetic feelings' (Koriat and Levy-Sadot 1999: 486) and 'cognitive feelings' (Clore and Parrott 1994: 101).

The term 'epistemic feeling' generalizes a term introduced by Hart (1965), who identified our ability to have a 'feeling of knowing', the feeling that we are able to retrieve information from memory but temporarily cannot do so. For example, we are able to correctly predict that we will be able in the future to remember someone's name which is momentarily forgotten or the answer to a question which we momentarily do not know. The feeling of knowing can exist in advance of actually knowing these things, and so the feeling of knowing is thus separate from the content of knowing. The feeling of knowing can be felt more or less strongly (Hart 1965: 208). Hart took from William James the fact that the tip of the tongue feeling is an example of feeling of knowing, in which we know that we know a word but cannot yet produce that word. One of the interesting characteristics of the feeling of knowing is that it is fairly accurate; when tested experimentally, people who felt that they knew the answer to a question but could not state it were later able to state the answer. There is also a 'feeling of not knowing' though this is less reliable (Hart 1965: 209), and O'Connor et al. (2010) list other similar epistemic feelings. Feeling of knowing involves a temporary ineffability, but usually an ineffability that can be resolved by later being able to state what is known; hence, it is not like the ineffability found in strong experiences, which is generally unresolvable.

The tip of the tongue experience is responsible for two kinds of epistemic feeling, first the feeling of knowing which comes in advance of being able to retrieve the word, and then what Mangan (1993: 96) calls the 'feeling of rightness' at the moment we actually retrieve the word. Though this is part of our voluntary conscious activity, it also plays a specific role when we resolve a tip of the tongue feeling, and also when we have a eureka moment, which as Mangan notes involves our knowing something new, and recognizing that it is right. Mangan also says that aesthetic appreciation in general depends on the feeling of rightness: 'Aesthetic phenomenology has at its core an especially intense experience of rightness. It is this feeling that gives aesthetic experience its phenomenological profile: the sense of immediate correctness, of an especially well-integrated or "right" relation of parts, of a primary and metaphysical YES! of cognitive disclosure' (Mangan 1993: 97). I think it is worth considering whether the feeling of rightness exists in some strong experiences, and in particular in the epiphanic type where we appear to see an object as it truly is; perhaps one component of this is a strong feeling of rightness. If this is the case, then it is a feeling of rightness which is generated independently of what it is about, because ineffability means that it is not objectively certain that anything is known in many epiphanies. In a related discussion, Kang et al. (2017: 8) argue that there is a 'feeling of having decided', where decision makers feel there is a moment of having reached a decision during deliberation. Kang et al. asked their experimental subjects to report the moment of decision and looked for measurable evidence that they were in fact making a decision. Often the report was at the moment of deciding, which suggests that there is an accurate ability in people to feel that they have come to a decision, which is an epistemic feeling. Kang et al. suggest that many decisions arise through an accumulation of evidence to a 'termination threshold', which when reached produces the 'aha moment', which is the feeling of having decided. The aha moment is related to strong experiences, but with a feeling of effable significance.

Is specifically the feeling of knowing involved in the strong experience? The strong experiences include epistemic feelings, and notably a feeling of coming to know something significant, but which can often not be put into words. This is superficially like the feeling of knowing, in that we have the feeling of knowing something without being able to say what it is. But it is not specifically what Hart and others described. Their experimental studies of feeling of knowing involved recall of something already known but temporarily forgotten, rather than coming to know something new. Nevertheless, there are some similarities, and it is worth considering what the feeling of knowing might teach us. In experimental contexts that explore the feeling of knowing, a subject is asked a question and asked to judge whether they know the answer to it. Whittlesea and Williams (1998: 162) note that such a question can be more or less fluently processed and suggest that the feeling of knowing arises when an eliciting question is particularly fluently processed.

Fluent processing produces many side effects, and this seems to be one of them (fluency is discussed further in Chapter 5). Whittlesea and Williams think that the feeling of knowing arises from a discrepancy between the fluent processing of the question and the feeling that the answer is not known; it is worth noting that this is another case where a discrepancy between mental states produces a particular epistemic effect.

Don Kuiken and his colleagues have discussed ways in which feelings of knowing might have a more profound aspect, analogous to the strong experiences discussed here. Kuiken and Douglas (2017) describe a type of absorption which they call 'expressive enactment' and which is an intense epistemic experience of coming to understand a text beyond what it directly says and which can enable a feeling of the sublime. Kuiken, Campbell and Sopčák (2012: 12, 17) discuss what they call a 'felt sense' (following Gendlin 1997), 'an inexpressible meaning that seems tangibly "there" at the moment of its emergence. This moment is brief', and they suggest that it is analogous to the feeling of knowing. They compare feeling of knowing with 'the felt sense of something inexpressible'. Kuiken and Oliver (2013: 304) discuss a 'feeling of familiarity' or 'feeling of knowing' in the experience of aesthetic objects. The feeling of familiarity arises when the subject's previous distress is echoed in the aesthetic object, so that 'a familiar felt sense emerges as an inexpressible meaning that is nevertheless palpably "there"'. They suggest that it is analogous to the thrill responses to music which they call 'moving moments'. This is a different sense of 'feeling of knowing' from that discussed by Hart, because it is about emotional knowledge rather than knowledge of content, but it does share the characteristic that what is known as a memory which is not yet fully accessible.

The Feeling of Significance

The primary epistemic characteristic of strong experiences is that they involve a feeling of significance. The other epistemic characteristic, discussed shortly, is a feeling of ineffability. I assume that there is no single source of the feeling of significance, but that it can arise for various reasons. One possible source of the feeling of significance is that the contents of a thought or set of thoughts are inherently significant and that we just recognize them as such. Thus Barnett Newman (1968: 553), for whom 'the sublime is now', says that '[t]he image we produce is the self-evident one of revelation, real and concrete, that can be understood by anyone who will look at it without the nostalgic glasses of history'. Another possibility is that the feeling of significance of a thought depends on an ability to estimate the number of inferences which can be derived from that thought, without actually formulating them. This would be one of the types of epistemic feeling, and may be what happens when we experience what Sperber and Wilson (1985) call poetic effects, if the large number of implicatures involved are not all actually formulated. Bell and Lyall (2002: 151) discuss under the heading of 'the accelerated sublime' an implicature-rich source of this type: 'the accelerating density of the tourist's experiences. A day may now be so event-rich (so folded) that it is endlessly unpicked (retold – unfolded)'. A third possible source of the feeling of significance depends on our ability to judge the coherence of any new thoughts relative to our existing thoughts. This is one of the cognitive effects in relevance theory, where new thoughts can be rewarding and worth deriving because they interact with existing thoughts. Perhaps we get a feeling of significance that positively correlates with a judgement of coherence between a new thought and the thoughts that are already known. This could be another measure of relevance and future reward. This is what Laski (1961: 341) describes when she says of an ecstasy that 'the sudden discovery of significance in a few words, often in words previously known, must seem to depend on the fact that these words chime and fuse with material already collected'.

However, the contrary situation might also lead to significance, where it is not the coherence with what is already known but the incoherence of the new thought which triggers the judgement of significance. This idea relates to Foster and Keane's (2015) sense-making theory of surprise, where greater surprise arises from greater incoherence. This in turn relates to Charlesworth's (1969) suggestion that insight is a type of surprise where we find a discrepancy between two ideas. Foster and Keane suggest that the subject who is presented with a surprise-causing discrepancy is rapidly able to work out the size of the discrepancy which triggers the surprise, by conceptually linking the surprising outcome to the scenario in which it unexpectedly occurred. They suggest that the amount of work expended in this rapid computation acts as a proxy that determines the degree of surprise experienced, so that 'some surprises are more surprising because they are harder to explain'. More specifically, 'the perception of surprisingness is based on a metacognitive assessment of the effort to explain, the amount of cognitive work carried out to explain the outcome' (Foster and Keane 2015: 80). Surprise is one of the characteristics of some strong experiences, but it is not identical with what is here called a strong experience, because for example surprise does not automatically produce a sense of significance. But perhaps the feeling of significance is produced in an analogous way, where the output of some other rapid computation acts as a proxy for the magnitude of significance. Perhaps we have the capacity to make a rapid metacognitive assessment of cognitive effects. This is what Wilson and Sperber (2004: 626) suggest: 'relevance theory does not provide an absolute measure of mental effort or cognitive effect, and it does not assume that such a measure is available to the spontaneous workings of the mind. What it does assume is that the actual or expected relevance of two inputs can quite often be compared'. Sperber (2005: 65) discusses the assessment of cognitive effects, including physiological proxies for cognitive effects. While such an assessment can only be very brief and preliminary, nevertheless small differences in the assessment might scale up to cause big differences in the feeling of significance.

There are other possible explanations for the feeling of significance. It may be that the experienced event has a particular interest for the subject, for example that the experience may form an important episode in the narrative of the self (Öhman and Wiens 2003: 262). Significance might also be correlated with aversive consequence, where an entity moving towards the observer might be judged as more significant because it might be a threat such as a predator, and the looming effect in the sublime might produce an effect of significance for this reason. It is also possible that the feeling of significance might be influenced by brain chemistry. McNamara (2009: 144) discusses the underlying neurochemistry in producing insight, for example when a mystical experience is stimulated by an entheogen drug such as LSD or psilocybin, both of which were cited by Maslow (1976: 27) as possible sources of peak experiences.

The Feeling of Ineffability in Strong Experience

Ineffability is the impossibility of putting a meaning or knowledge into words and is often a characteristic of strong experiences. William James's mystical experiences involve 'states of insight into depths of truth unplumbed by the discursive intellect. They are illuminations, revelations, full of significance and importance, all inarticulate though they remain' (James 1982: 380). In similar terms, Botterill (1988) says that Dante's *Paradiso* declares that language cannot express the reality of Paradise, and he concludes that 'ineffability is a condition of, not an obstacle to, mystical experience' and that mystical experience 'is indissolubly bound up with the impossibility of remembering it and expressing it fully; in a word, with its ineffability'. Miller and de Baca (2001) say about their strong experience, called a quantum change, that it has 'an elusive, ineffable quality'. Gabrielsson (2011: 374) notes that when people describe their strong experience of music, they sometimes characterize it as unverbalizable. For example, '[i]t was an experience that far exceeded my verbal and intellectual capacity, it includes things that I verbally can only touch upon'.

As an example of ineffability associated with the strong experience, here is Wordsworth's description of an ineffable strong experience, in which the landscape has a 'visionary dreariness' which cannot be expressed in words and is also inexpressable in existing paint colours.

> Then, reascending the bare common, saw
> A naked pool that lay beneath the hills,
> The beacon on the summit, and, more near,
> A girl, who bore a pitcher on her head,
> And seemed with difficult steps to force her way
> Against the blowing wind. It was, in truth,
> An ordinary sight; but I should need
> Colours and words that are unknown to man,
> To paint the visionary dreariness
> Which, while I looked all round for my lost guide,
> Invested moorland waste and naked pool,
> The beacon crowning the lone eminence,
> The female and her garments vexed and tossed
> By the strong wind.
> Wordsworth *Prelude* 1850 book XII, Maxwell 1986: 481

William James in his 1902 book *The Varieties of Religious Experience* says that ineffability is a characteristic of what he calls 'mystical experience', and which I take to be a type of strong experience.

> The handiest of the marks by which I classify a state of mind as mystical is negative. The subject of it immediately says that it defies expression, that no adequate report of its contents can be given in words. It follows from this that its quality must be directly experienced; it cannot be imparted or transferred to others. In this peculiarity mystical states are more like states of feeling than like states of intellect. No one can make clear to another who has never had a certain feeling, in what the quality or worth of it consists. (James 1982: 380)

Again, there is the sense that the meaning can be 'felt' but cannot be directly expressed.

Marghanita Laski found that people sometimes thought of 'ecstasy' as involving ineffability. She asked people to tell her: 'how would you describe the sensation of transcendent ecstasy?' (Laski 1961: 448, 461). Ecstasy is one of the types of strong experience. Here are four answers to this question (the letter-number identifies an individual who responded).

> Q25 Indescribable – I know but I can't describe it – a shock of joy – something perfectly apprehended, not formulated, a recognition.

Q62 I can't [describe it] – it's a most marvellous feeling – whatever words I used would be inadequate.

Q39 You can't describe it, because the more you describe, the further you get from it.

Q24 [...] it's a mental sensation – it is to me perfectly described in Cassian, where the heart without words leaps like a fountain – a wordless feeling of sudden tremendous expansion, sudden glory [...]
(Laski 1961: 384, 398, 389, 383)

These examples suggest that the ineffability of certain kinds of knowledge is conventional; there is a 'trope of ineffability'. As Laski (1961: 31) notes: 'Demonstrably these experiences are *not* ineffable; few kinds of experience can have been so fully and so consistently described. But such experiences obviously *feel* ineffable, and to say that they are ineffable (or indescribable, etc.) is a typical part of their description'. Similarly Botterill (1988: 333) talks about '[t]he first of many declarations of language's inadequacy to convey the reality of the experience of Paradise – declarations which have collectively become known, through the elaboration of an insight of E. R. Curtius, as the "ineffability topos"'. We know about the ineffabilities in strong experiences because they are explicitly reported to us, sometimes using the term 'ineffability'. The conventionality of the ineffability means that is not always clear that there really is a felt experience of ineffability, as opposed to a convention of saying that it exists.

As another example of ineffability and its association with strong experience, consider Proust's experience triggered by the taste of the Madeleine cake he eats.

And soon, mechanically, oppressed by the gloomy day and the prospect of a sad future, I carried to my lips a spoonful of the tea in which I had let soften a piece of madeleine. But at the very instant when the mouthful of tea mixed with cake-crumbs touched my palate, I quivered, attentive to the extraordinary thing that was happening in me. (Proust 2002: 47)

Proust's strong experience begins with a quiver (*je tressaillis*); he experiences a strong emotion of powerful joy (*puissante joie*), but cannot identify its cause. He finds a truth within himself (*la vérité que je cherche*), but does not know how to interpret it; he realizes that he has to create the truth, by 'entering into its light'.

In sum, ineffability is often claimed as a characteristic of various kinds of experience, in which what is known is felt but cannot be put into words. In the next section I consider why ineffability is possible, and why we feel that certain meanings are ineffable.

What Makes Ineffability Possible

Diana Raffman (1993) explores ineffability relative to music and offers an account that is compatible with the representational theory of mind which is used in the present book (from Fodor 1975). She classifies ineffability into three broad kinds, each of which can arise in the experience of music: structural ineffability, feeling ineffability, and nuance ineffability. Our experience of structural ineffability is our consciousness of having knowledge of a musical form without being able to describe how exactly it is known, which may be an abstract mental representation of musical form below the level of consciousness. An example would be the ability to tell when a piece has reached a tonic chord, and so might be ending, as in a Romantic symphony. Raffman notes that our ability to make the judgement is based on cognitive processes and structures which are not available for introspection (Lerdahl and Jackendoff 1983). She calls this inability to verbalize our mental structures for music a 'structural ineffability'. Raffman's second kind of ineffability is 'feeling ineffability', which she explains by referring to our experience of feelings communicated by the music that cannot be directly verbalized. As part of this discussion, Raffman (1993: 44) suggests that the experience of having feelings which cannot be verbalized is inherently surprising, in part because the structural regularities of music trick us into thinking that music should encode meaning as language does. Because we are repeatedly surprised in this way by the same piece of music, we are encouraged to learn from the music, repeatedly, just as surprise always encourages us to learn something new. Raffman's third kind of ineffability is 'nuance ineffability', which as it applies to music involves our awareness of the nuances of music which are not categorizable in a way which allows for verbalization. Raffman assumes that each experienced listener has a musical knowledge in the form of underlying structural representations, but that these representations do not fully determine the range of actual musical differences which can be discriminated in performance. Thus for example a person who is able to form in their mind structural representations of the tonal hierarchy in music, allowing for sounds to be divided into tones and semitones, can nevertheless discriminate much smaller intervals such as a twentieth of a tone. For example, Indian classical musicians can discriminate more nuances than they can categorize. Each such discrimination cannot be categorized (schematized), remembered or verbalized, and so this is a nuance which is ineffable. Nuance ineffability should hold of any perception that is more granular or finely detailed than can be expressed in words, and this ineffable granularity may be one of the features of an epiphany. All the kinds of ineffability arise from ordinary properties of music, and in the remainder of this section I consider how ineffability can also arise from the ordinary properties of language.

The finiteness and generality of language can never match the infinity and specificity of what we can know and so ineffability is inevitable. To illustrate this general point, here is Sullivan (2017: 33) on ineffabilities: 'there may be a disjointedness between public words and inner images, metaphors and feelings; what Murdoch (1992) refers to as "private, insoluble difficulties; mysterious half understood mental configurations"'. Most words stand for schemata, and hence the words express generalities rather than the specificity of our actual perceptions. If we want to describe specific and unique things, language will not usually be adequate. However, there are elements of language that are matched not to schemata but to unique elements in the world. This includes names, which in principle can refer to unique entities which may not be captured by schemata, and names can be conceived of as directly referring to unique parts of reality itself. A different kind of exception to the schema dependency of language is offered by pronouns and other deictic terms, which can be used to point outside language directly at the world and its unique entities, so that the meaning of the deictic lies outside the schematicity of language.

Strong experiences often depend on a specific perception whose specificity is both a source of the profundity of the experience, but also threatens to be ineffable because the specific may not fit with the schematicity of language. In this regard, it is interesting to note that strong experiences are sometimes represented in literature by using the less schematic aspects of language. Thus, Beja (1971) notes that one of Woolf's favourite words for what is revealed in a literary epiphany is the pronoun 'it'. Making a related point about demonstratives such as 'that' and 'there' as deictics, Zhang (2014: 56) discusses Woolf's use of demonstratives at moments of strong experience. An example comes at the end of *To the Lighthouse*, where the deictic 'there' is used to stand for the distinctive thing which is created and perceived.

> With a sudden intensity, as if she saw it clear for a second, she drew a line there, in the centre. It was done; it was finished. Yes, she thought, laying down her brush in extreme fatigue, I have had my vision. (Woolf 2006: 170)

We might similarly note the end of *Mrs Dalloway*, where the strong experience triggered in Peter by Clarissa Dalloway involves three escapes from the schematicity of language, a name 'Clarissa' and two deictics, a demonstrative 'there' and a pronoun 'she'.

> 'I will come,' said Peter, but he sat on for a moment. What is this terror? What is this ecstasy? He thought to himself. What is it that fills me with extraordinary excitement?
> It is Clarissa, he said.
> For there she was.
>
> (Woolf 1969: 215)

The limitations of language can produce ineffability because we have an ability to perceptually discriminate at a much finer grain than we have words for the distinctions. For example we can perceptually discriminate between very similar colours or microtonally close sounds, but not have words for these distinctions. De Clerq (2000) discusses various accounts of this kind of ineffability of microperception in music including Davies (1994) and what Raffman (1993) calls nuance ineffability. Scherer (2009a: 3467) discusses how the qualia of feelings are only partially captured in language, making them ineffable (also Scherer 2009b: 1321, citing Dennett). Scruton (1997) suggests that our ordinary ability for empathy involves ineffabilities, ways of taking another perspective in a way which cannot be put into words, and this again links empathy with strong experience.

In communication, thoughts can be communicated which cannot directly be put into words. The words are evidence for the thoughts but need not directly express them. The meaning is derived by considering the utterance in its context. Ineffability might thus ordinarily arise in communication in at least two ways. The first is that we are able to communicate a thought which can in fact not be expressed directly in words. Metaphors might be like this. Similarly, Nelson (1956: 336) describes allegory as an attempt 'to deal with the ineffable', by its indirectness. Or the communicated thought might be a metarepresentation whose subordinate representation is semi-propositional. The second kind of ineffability involves Sperber and Wilson's 'poetic effects', which arise when the hearer is aware of a large number of possible meanings as potentially communicated, without being able to attribute these to the speaker with any certainty. Communication depends on context for the full meaning of utterances to be communicated, and a contextually dependent type of ordinary ineffability is cited by Scharfstein (1993: 26) who, drawing on a theoretical claim made by Penfield, says that 'a memory we can recover and put into words in one mood may in another be irrecoverable and, in this sense, ineffable'.

An ineffability is ordinary if it can be found throughout our everyday experience. There is a more specialized but also widespread type of ineffability which is found in our experience of aesthetic objects. Because it is spread out across a literary text, and rather common, this is not the ineffability which is particularly associated with strong experience, but it may be related to it. The idea that there is a residue of unclarity in the appreciation of an aesthetic object is central to the New Critical heresy of paraphrase: 'Whatever statement we may seize upon as incorporating the "meaning" of the poem, immediately the imagery and rhythm seem to set up tensions with it, warping and twisting it, qualifying and revising it' (Brooks 1947: 197). A similar view about literature can be found in other cultures. Thus, Owen (1992: 149) summarizes the Chinese theorist Lu Chi: 'Meaning is an event that occurs beyond words and "after the words have ended". Without that sense of some significance, flavor, or whatever beyond the surface of the text, the literary work seems flat'. McGregor (1984: 22) describes the practice associated with the Nath religion of Northern India, of composing vernacular poetry in an upside down language, an 'obscure allusive style in which suggestive dualities and incongruities (*ulatbamsi*) asserted as paradoxical truths bear much of the meaning'. Many of these descriptions of aesthetic practices work on the basis that the text cannot directly express a meaning, but that the meaning can perhaps be inferred on the basis of the evidence offered by the text. This recognizes that many aesthetic practices are very indirect in their modes of communication, but also recognizes that they are modes of communication and so they draw on the general way in which 'ineffability' is a convention about knowledge and the limitations of language.

Summary of Chapter

This chapter assumes a representational theory of mind, as proposed for example by Fodor (1975), and used in relevance theory (Sperber and Wilson 1995), and in the anthropological and cultural theories of Dan Sperber. Representations include schemata, which are generalized knowledge of things and events. Schemata are matched with new perceptions, and surprise is triggered when the perceptions are strongly discrepant relative to the schemata. It is possible also to be surprised by experience itself, when an actual experience is strongly discrepant with deeply embedded schemata for experience; this is 'metacognitive surprise'. Surprise is the starting point for a strong experience. One of the types of representation is a metarepresentation, that is, a representation of another representation. This chapter explores some of the characteristics of mental metarepresentations, which are thoughts about thoughts, and whose characteristics make strong experiences possible. One of the characteristics is that the mental metarepresentation can contain a semi-propositional representation, allowing us to have thoughts which we do not understand. The chapter concludes by looking at ineffability as a characteristic of strong experiences, and then considering why ineffability might arise from the ordinary characteristics of language and communication.

Chapter 4
AROUSAL, EMOTION AND STRONG EXPERIENCES

In this chapter I look at the bodily feelings, kinds of phasic arousal, which are associated with strong experiences, and which constitute the 'thrill' response. This is part of a broader consideration of emotion and its relation to strong experiences.

Phasic Arousal

The poet A. E. Housman in his 1933 lecture 'The name and nature of poetry' argues that poetry should convey strong arousal rather than ideas: poetry stabs the heart, shakes the soul, takes the breath away and brings tears (Housman 1933: 23, 35, 46).

> Poetry indeed seems to me more physical than intellectual. A year or two ago, in common with others, I received from America a request that I would define poetry. I replied that I could no more define poetry than a terrier can define a rat, but that I thought we both recognized the object by the symptoms which it provoked in us. One of these symptoms was described in connexion with another object by Eliphaz the Temanite: 'A spirit passed before my face: the hair of my flesh stood up.' Experience has taught me, when I am shaving of a morning, to keep watch over my thoughts, because, if a line of poetry strays into my memory, my skin bristles so that the razor ceases to act. This particular symptom is accompanied by a shiver down the spine; there is another which consists in a constriction of the throat and a precipitation of water to the eyes; and there is a third which I can only describe by borrowing a phrase from one of Keats's last letters, where he says, speaking of Fanny Brawne, 'everything that reminds me of her goes through me like a spear'. The seat of this sensation is in the pit of the stomach.
>
> (Housman 1933: 46)

In these strong experiences, arousal is manifested as piloerection in which the hairs rise, and also manifested as tears, and as an enteric reaction in the stomach. Housman is not claiming that these experiences are responses to conventional emotional triggers: the hair does not stand up because the poem frightens him, for example, and he does not shed a tear at a poem which is sad. Instead, he implies that these arousal responses are part of an epistemic feeling that 'something is a poem'. This is a knowledge which is ineffable because he says it cannot be put into words. In this chapter I look at these arousal responses as components of strong experiences.

The strong experiences sometimes involve chills, tears, shuddering, freezing or some other sudden and transitory response. The thrill type of strong experience by definition involves this kind of response, the sublime often involves arousal and perhaps sometimes also epiphany. These responses are kinds of arousal in response to a trigger, and when I use the term 'arousal' this is shorthand for specifically 'phasic arousal', in which the arousal lasts a short time. Phasic arousal is different from 'tonic arousal' which is the general or background bodily state, manifested for example in a level of general alertness. Arousal can manage homeostasis, as when our hair raises in a cold environment in order to trap warm air over the skin; though generally not our concern here, this homeostatic function may be loosely related to the strong experience, as Panksepp has argued. For our purposes arousal is interesting as an essential component of an emotion, so for example the emotion of fear can involve the raising of hair, and in the next section I consider emotion.

Emotion

Given that arousal can be part of a strong experience, and is part of an emotion, we might ask whether strong experiences just are emotions, since they both can include arousals. But there are several reasons for thinking that strong experiences are not emotions. First, many theories of emotion define emotion as having arousal as a necessary component, but there may be kinds of strong experience which appear not to include arousal, though it is possible that there is always some arousal even if it is below the threshold of conscious awareness. Second, strong experiences often have an epistemic component, and yet this is not part of the definition of an emotion. Third, strong experiences are rare, sometimes extremely rare, while emotions are very common. One way of thinking about the relationship between emotion and strong experience is that if arousal can be a component of an emotion, and can also be a component of a strong experience, then when strong experiences include arousals there is also an emotion present. The arousal would be part of the emotion, and the emotion is part of the strong experience.

An emotion is a psychological episode which feels unified and with a beginning and ending, involves some kind of arousal, and is valenced, which means that it is experienced as positive or negative. The person experiencing the emotion may give it a name such as 'sadness', 'happiness' and 'fear'. An emotion is triggered, in which it differs from a mood. There are various theories of emotion, which I summarize now, the summary based on Scherer (2009c).

Basic emotion theories argue for a fairly fixed relation between the parts that make up an emotion, so that there are universally definable and distinct basic emotions with well-defined characteristics. In this sense, emotions are natural kinds. Basic emotion theories are proposed in Charles Darwin's 1872 book *The Expression of the Emotions in Man and Animals* and are endorsed by Silvan Tomkins and more recently by Paul Ekman and Carroll E. Izard (Frevert 2014: 23). Among emotion theories, basic emotions theories probably have the greatest influence on literary and cultural theory, and the basic emotions were even personified in the Pixar cartoon *Inside Out* (2015, with Ekman's group advising).

A second group of theories of emotion are constructivist theories. Constructivist theories of emotion model an emotion as an arousal, having positive or negative valence, where this combination is interpreted by the experiencer as being a particular kind of emotion. The 'constructivist' part of this is the view that our interpretation and hence our experience can be influenced by our cultural context. William James is an predecessor of constructivism in his 1884 account of emotion in 'What Is an Emotion?', an article which also mentions thrill experiences. James thought that emotions are a particular kind of sensation, and to this, Schachter and Singer (1962) added an interpretive component. In these constructivist approaches, emotions are composite entities. A variant of constructivist theories is the circumplex model of Russell (1980), which treats emotions as located in a two-dimensional space whose axes are defined by how high or low the arousal is and how positive or negative the valence is. Barrett (2011: 362) also includes people's idiosyncratic language-based and culture-based conceptualizations of emotion. In this approach, the same arousal state can be experienced as different emotions (Barrett 2011: 365). Constructivist theories allow for a wide range of variation between individuals and cultures in what emotions arise.

Another set of approaches are the componential theories of emotion, in which the experiencing subject appraises the components, the event causing the emotion, and their own relation to event and emotion. As a consequence of the appraisal, the emotion is externalized. The importance of appraisal in constituting the experience of an emotion was pioneered by Magda B. Arnold (1960) and by Richard Lazarus (1991), and major componential theorists include Nico Frijda (1986) and Klaus Scherer. The appraisal can be conscious or unconscious. In this approach, the triggering event does not determine the type of emotion; instead, different people will derive different emotions from the same event if they appraise it differently. For example, in Scherer's (2009b) component process model, emotional reactions to an event depend on four factors: the relevance of the event, the implications of the event, the experiencer's coping potential and its significance for the experiencer's self-concept and for social norms and values. This multi-component approach is useful for the study of strong experiences, because it focuses on the role of the experiencing subject in appraising the situation and producing a response accordingly. This fits with the metacognitive aspects of strong experiences.

It is possible that when strong experiences include arousal, then they also include an emotion built around the arousal; for example, in a circumplex theory, arousal plus valence produces an emotion. However, strong experiences present a problem relating to valence. Thrills as types of strong experience are typically pleasurable when they are accompanied with arousals such as chills or tears, but these same arousals are otherwise associated with negative emotions such as fear and sadness. Exactly what is happening here has been studied experimentally, particularly for the experience of the sublime, but with different experiments producing different results. For example, focusing on the sublime, Eskine et al. (2012) undertook an experiment in which they presented subjects with abstract paintings by El Lissitsky, these paintings rated for sublimity by participants on a five-point scale containing elements of sublimity drawn from Burke (1987). Arousal levels were tested, showing that physiological arousal generally correlated positively with sublime rating. The brain area of the right anterior insula showed greatest activity during positively valenced aesthetic judgements, which was unexpected given that this region is normally associated with negative emotions such as disgust and fear (Eskine et al. 2012: 1073). These findings are however different from those found in an fMRI experiment by Ishizu and Zeki (2014), which studied brain activation when viewing pictures rated as sublime, where there was no activity in the insula or other brain areas such as the amygdala associated with negative emotion; they found deactivation of those parts of the cerebellum which mediates fear and deactivation of the anterior cingulate and medial prefrontal cortex which are associated with the experience of negative emotions.

If we step back from the experiments, to consider the more general problem, we can see that there is an oddity which is that what ought to be a negatively valenced arousal is found in a positively valenced experience. But this is characteristic of our response more generally to aesthetic objects, and so we could consider our problem of valence in strong experience as a version of the familiar problem of emotion in response to aesthetic objects (Nadal and Skov 2013: 6–7). Two problems present themselves when we consider emotional responses to artworks, with their often fictional subject matter. First, it is not clear why we respond emotionally at all to events and objects which are fictions. Second, we can respond with tears that are normally responses to negative events but here are positively valenced as pleasurable. One solution to these problems is to say that an emotion can have an ordinary form and an aesthetic form, so that there would be an ordinary sadness and an aesthetic sadness. Taruffi and Koelsch (2014: 14) suggest that this is ordinary sadness but '[b]ecause music-evoked sadness is not linked to an extramusical event, the listener can take pleasure in so-called negative emotions'. Levinson (2006) accounts for the gap by suggesting that aesthetic emotions are separated from real-life implications and that this allows the valence to switch from negative to positive. Scherer (2004) suggests a distinction between kinds of emotion, between utilitarian emotions and aesthetic emotions based on the appraisal criteria, such that aesthetic emotions involve appraisal not so much in terms of goal relevance or coping potential, but instead via cultural values, norms and personal values. Rickard (2004: 384) suggests that the study of arousal responses to music shows that both in emotional responses to real-world stimuli and in emotional responses to music, the same increase in physiological arousal is found, suggesting a common mechanism.

The issue of whether we respond with distinctive emotions to aesthetic objects is related to the issue of how we respond to fictional situations and characters. Again, it is unclear why we have any kind of strong response to something which we know to be fictional. Gerrig says that we do not engage in fiction-specific kinds of cognition: 'there is no psychologically privileged category "fiction"' (Gerrig 1993: 197, also 102, 180). Similarly Konijn et al. (2009: 314) argue that 'neural responses to mediated events and actual events are similar' and hence that humans do not have separate psychological systems which judge real vs. fictional events. If there are no fiction-specific kinds of cognition, then there may be no fiction-specific kinds of emotion; and this means that 'the experience of narratives is largely unaffected by their announced correspondence with reality'. However, even if there is no inherent difference between fictional and factual representations, they still might be processed differently for other reasons which relate to their being fictional or factual. For example, one of the characteristics of representations of fictional things is that they tend to be thinner or sparser than representations of real things in having less inherent detail, and having fewer connections to other representations. Fictional representations are connected mainly to other fictional representations, in a relatively small network such as the network of representations forming the world presented by a novel, and they do not interact very extensively with factual representations. Our ability to separate them comes early. Skolnick and Bloom (2006) show that five-year olds are capable of understanding that two fictional characters, Batman and Spongebob Squarepants, exist in different fictional worlds, and so cannot interact with each other. This is analogous to what Cosmides and Tooby (2000) call the decoupling of a set of representations to produce a self-contained fictional world. Abraham and von Cramon (2009) propose another difference between our knowledge of the real and the fictional. Fictional events and characters have fewer associations with other memories. In contrast, real people are associable with many other memories, and this is even more true for real people who we personally know, so that all of our personal memories can also be invoked. They show that thinking about real people involves different brain areas from thinking about fictional people, specifically stronger activation in the anterior medial prefrontal cortex and the posterior cingulate cortex, in the default mode network; but this is also where we process information which has greater personal relevance. So we do think differently about real and fictional events/people, but this is not because of their inherent reality, but because of the greater personal relevance of the real and because real people are much more easy to associate with our other knowledge, including knowledge of personal relevance, and real people are therefore cognized in these areas.

If we now turn from this to the question of emotion, we might speculate that our emotional responses to fictional people and events are only weakly connected to other emotional responses and this is why they are different. It also explains why there is no behavioural response – we do not act on the basis of our emotional engagement with fictions – because we are responding to events and characters that are so weakly connected with the real world in which our bodies exist that we do not initiate bodily actions which might be appropriate to those emotions. Perhaps this gives us another angle on the lack of negative valence in our emotional responses to fictions and art in general. We respond with arousals which should be associated with a negative valence because, for example, this is how we respond to discrepancy. But our appraisal of the triggers as relatively thin, decoupled or lacking personal relevance means that we discount the negative valence in forming our experience. Metacognition, which can take into account the context, allows the experience to be positive. The upshot of this discussion is that strong experiences might contain an ordinary emotion, which contains an arousal. But as a result of metacognitive appraisal, the emotions take on the typically inappropriate relation to the triggers of strong experience. In this way, the emotional components of a strong experience are similar to the aesthetic emotions.

Surprise can trigger the fight, flight or freeze responses, which involve phasic arousal. These are evolved responses that are triggered in a prey animal when they perceive a possible predator and are associated with surprise, because surprise can always hint at a threat. Noordewier and Breugelmans (2013: 1328) say that 'at a neural and psychophysiological level, responses to surprise are similar for positive and negative events'. However, the arousals in surprise might be shared with emotions; for example, the rising of the hair as part of a surprise-driven fight response might also be part of a fear response. Surprise is of course relevant to strong experiences, because strong experiences begin with a moment of surprise, when there is a problem in matching perception to schematic expectation. Huron (2006: 26) says that the fight–flight–freeze responses are emotions that are 'specialized varieties of surprise'. He argues that the fight–flight–freeze reactions evolved to deal with threats, but are also produced in humans when there is no actual threat, for example in aesthetic experience. In this case, the three reactions manifest as chills (fight), laughter (flight) or awe (freeze). Huron's proposal depends on the view that animals, including humans, have fast but poorly discriminating reactions to any surprise, as though it is a threat; but if there is no actual threat then a slower reaction corrects the first response, so that instead of running away we laugh.

Huron suggests that the freeze stage is manifested as awe in an aesthetic context, where the body goes still. He suggests that the fight-or-flight stage is manifested as responses including chills and laughter. Where chills reflect piloerection, this is analogous to piloerection in animal fight behaviour where hair stands up as a signal, or the pale skin of vasoconstriction which reduces the risk of haemorrhage in case of injury because there is less blood in the skin; in these ways, these chill responses are like fight responses. Huron further argues that laughter is a kind of panting, analogous to behaviour which prepares the animal to run away. Sweating on the palms or soles, which is a measurable response in some aesthetic thrills, also enables animals to run or climb more easily away from danger by increasing grip, and may be manifested in skin conductance response changes. Most of the main kinds of thrill arousal are included in Huron's surprise emotions, but tears are not. Tears or other responses characteristically associated with sadness might however be also forms of surprise, if they are interpreted as responses to a discrepancy between perception and schema. Tears can also be more directly responses to surprise which produces a sudden stress; by producing prolactin, tears may calm the organism.

Empathy, and other prosocial emotions, are also sometimes involved in strong experiences. Sometimes the term 'being moved' is used to characterize these arousals and emotions when they have prosocial elements

(Schubert et al. 2016). In broadly the same area, Zickfeld et al. (2020) explore an emotional response of 'being moved' which they call *kama muta* (Sanskrit for 'moved by love') and which 'is evoked by observing or experiencing *sudden intensifications of communal sharing*' and which can involve mild or moderate arousals such as tears or goosebumps. It may be that some of these prosocial experiences also involve surprise, perhaps a surprise at the fact of empathy itself, as I argue in Chapter 5.

Arousal

Various kinds of phasic arousal are found in strong experiences. In his study of responses to music, John (Sloboda 1991: 112) asked people to report on whether and how frequently they responded in specific ways to music, calling these responses 'thrills', a general use of the term which I borrow to use in this book. He found that what he generically called the 'thrill' responses to music included (starting with the most frequent) laughter, a lump in the throat, a racing heart, yawning, pit-of-stomach sensations, sexual arousal, trembling, flushing and sweating. Sloboda says that thrills 'have the benefit of being stereotypical, memorable, clearly differentiated from one another, and easily identifiable. It is hard to be mistaken about whether one is or is not having one of these experiences, and it seems that they are experienced at one time or another by most people'.

Before proceeding, I briefly note the relevant bodily systems. The brain and spinal cord form the central nervous system; the remaining nervous system is peripheral. A part of the peripheral nervous system is the autonomic nervous system which is further distinguished into two parts: the parasympathetic nervous system and the sympathetic nervous system. Many of the phasic arousals involve one or both of the two parts of the autonomic nervous system. Other arousals involve the enteric nervous system that controls the gut and the musculoskeletal system as in shivering. Further, bodily arousals can be produced and also perceived by the somatic nervous system that sends information from the peripheral body into the central nervous system including the brain. The potential gap between what happens in the body and what the brain thinks is happening is sometimes relevant. In the three sections which follow, I have put phasic arousals into three groups: the cold-temperature-related ones such as chills, the tears-related ones and the others. However, the moment of strong experience can sometimes combine several kinds of arousal at the same time. And, though there are some possible correlations between kinds of trigger and kinds of arousal, there is no consistent causal sequence whereby a particular trigger leads to a particular arousal. What seems to be the same trigger might lead to a particular arousal in one person and a different arousal in another, though it is possible that the trigger is in this case appraised differently by the different people.

This chapter focuses primarily on observable arousal responses, rather than the responses people report, but Rickard (2004: 383) notes that what is observed is not always the same as what is reported. Maruskin et al. (2012) take the relatively radical approach of defining thrills not in terms of objectively observed arousal but in terms of subjective judgements of arousal that need not match what is objectively observed. Self-report always plays a role in shaping our understanding of strong experience, including in experimental studies of this kind; most of what we know about strong experiences including thrills is based on self-report. Self-reports can be elicited in a structured way, for example, by asking the subject questions or can be reported in an unprompted manner by the subject. Most of the self-reports are unstructured, with the subject deciding how to describe a strong experience, including what to call it. The reported experiences are usually remembered rather than described while they are happening, and they may be partially or fully fictional. Strong experiences are usually reported as small stories, often relative to some larger story of the self. All of these factors mean that what we can know retrospectively about a strong experience might be a long way from what happened in the physiological event itself.

Many strong experiences involve phasic arousal, which is sudden and brief. But there is also background or tonic arousal, which is the general arousal state of the body, both continuous and changing; for example, being sleepy and being very alert are different tonic arousal states. This is relevant for strong experiences, because sometimes the experiencer appears to be in a high tonic arousal or hyperaroused state, or a low tonic arousal or hypoaroused state. Wordsworth experiences most of his strong experiences or 'spots of time' in *The Prelude*, when he is highly active, such as running, rowing, climbing and so on and so perhaps in a hyperaroused state. The hyperaroused state might also be a factor in the sublime experience of speed, as in the accelerated sublime of Bell and Lyall (2002), in touristic journeys such as boating through rapids. Similarly, Ferri (2012: 559) notes:

> the experience of speed becomes for Alfieri a source of the sublime, from sleigh racing, which he practices with 'furious' impetus in Scandinavia, to horseback riding, which causes in him a similar excitement of the senses and the mind. In an earlier passage of the *Vita* he describes the bodily and spiritual exaltation that he experiences in the reckless speed of horse racing [...] the physical stimulus of speed mimics the feeling of

terror by producing an absolute subjugation of the senses that affects the mind.

Laski (1961: 197) thinks that speed and regular rhythm can help trigger ecstasy; in fact, she cites Wordsworth skating as an example (though this particular example has another characteristic involving the dizzy feeling when the skating stops). We might also recall Burke's claim about the rhetorical sublime that '[t]he mind is hurried out of itself'. It is also the case that people sometimes get strong experiences when they are lying down and perhaps hypoaroused; Proust presents a good example of his fictional persona as a generally hypoaroused experiencer, and Wordsworth experiences the enhanced strong experience while resting at the end of 'Daffodils'.

Chills and Other Cold-Related Arousals

I begin with a group of phasic arousals that can all arise as a response to environmental cold, and which are also found in strong experiences. They include piloerection that produces goosebumps, vasoconstriction leading to pale skin, and shuddering. The chill response is felt as a spreading tingling in the skin, but with an unclear physiological basis. Some but not all experimental evidence suggests that though chill arousals in response to music may involve a sensation of coldness they involve no change in measured skin temperature (Rickard 2004 and Craig 2005: 279, but not Salimpoor et al. 2009).

Goosebumps is the pimpling of the skin produced by piloerection, the raising of the hairs by the arrector pili muscles. The sympathetic nervous system is involved. Piloerection preserves body heat by trapping a layer of still air and so is a functional response to environmental cold (Chaplin et al. 2014). Piloerection is also a fight response; in its function as a response to a real threat, it is a sign of aggression, and also fear. Piloerection can also be triggered as part of strong experiences of the kind self-reported as chill, but it is possible to feel a chill without observed piloerection, and vice versa (see Craig 2005; Benedek and Kaernbach 2011; Sumpf et al. 2015; Grewe et al. 2007). Piloerection correlates with other arousals, such as increased heart rate (Huron and Margulis 2010: 595–596, Sumpf et al. 2015), and in some but not all experiments deeper breathing (Benedek and Kaernbach 2011: 326, but Sumpf et al. 2015: 8). Piloerection-produced goosebumps can also occur along with tears as a response to the same trigger, and overlap at the peak moment, as Wassiliwizky et al. (2017b) show, using the term 'goosetears'. In their experiment they found that the highest intensity of psychophysiological arousal involved a combination of tears and goosebumps, with tears alone at a lower intensity, and goosebumps alone also at a lower intensity

(Wassiliwizky et al. 2017b: 7). They note that goosebumps and tears involve different systems, sympathetic vs. parasympathetic, and suggest that this is a 'complex antagonistic interplay of the two subdivisions of the Autonomic Nervous System resulting in an intense physiological activation and a unique subjective bodily feeling'.

Another cold-related arousal which may play a role in strong experiences is vasoconstriction, where blood vessels are constricted by action of the sympathetic nervous system. Vasoconstriction is a response to cold because by keeping blood away from the surface, it limits heat loss. It is also an emotional response. Pale skin is not widely reported in strong experiences, though Panksepp (1998: 278) suggests that chill experiences in the skin might include vasoconstriction. The presence of vasoconstriction in the chill experience is supported by Maxwell (1902). Additional evidence for vasoconstriction comes from studies showing reduced blood volume pulse in chill moments (Benedek and Kaernbach, 2011; Salimpoor et al. 2011; Salimpoor et al. 2009).

A further cold-related arousal is trembling or shivering, which involves the skeletal muscles and the somatic nervous system. This works as a response to cold because the vibration increases body heat. Trembling also manifests emotion and is reported in strong experiences. Burke (1987: 63) cites a passage in the Book of Job which is 'amazingly sublime' in which it is said of Job that 'fear came upon me and trembling, which made all my bones to shake. Then a spirit passed before my face. The hair of my flesh stood up'. Here, note the combination of trembling and piloerection, both of which are also responses to cold. Moses Mendelssohn (1997) frequently refers to shuddering (*Schauern*) in his descriptions of how the sublime makes us feel: *das schaudernde Gefühl des Erhabenen* (the shuddering feeling of the sublime), *ein Schauern, das uns überläuft* (a shudder that runs over us), *einen süssen Schauer, der uns ganz durchströmt* (a sweet shudder which flows right through us), *eine schauervolle Empfindung* (a shudder-full feeling), *das Schauer auf Schauer erregt* (that shudder after shudder arouses).

Most of the work on thrills is on thrills caused by music, but there is some research on other kinds of trigger. Grewe et al. (2011: 233) made participants get chills by recalling emotional events, with a significant difference in heart rate preceding the chill, unlike the externally triggered examples. Inbody (2015) discusses a Pentecostal congregation where emotion is manifested as chills, sometimes interpreted as communication from God, and there are some of the same causal factors in the heard music. Schurtz et al. (2012) relate chills to awe as part of an approval response to powerful others. Wassiliwizky et al. (2015: 407) say that chills elicited by sadly and joyfully moving film clips should correlate positively with the intensity of being moved, which they treat as a distinct type of emotion and also suggest that the 'sadness' in being moved is balanced out by the positive components of the response. Konečni et al. (2007) also discuss literary stories and chills. Benedek and Kaernbach (2011: 325) claim that films are better able to cause piloerection than music and suggest that this is because films carry more information.

Panksepp (1995: 185) connects the experience of chills, which he also calls 'skin orgasms', to sadness. He claims a correlation between judging a piece to be sad and that piece generating chills and suggests that the correlation of sad triggers and chills is particularly strong in females (Panksepp 1995: 176). He claims that emotional chills have an evolutionary origin, triggered in females by the cry of a baby separated from its mother, with the mother's feeling of coldness making her want to cuddle the baby. He suggests that sounds that trigger chills have something acoustically in common with a baby's cry. The responses such as piloerection (goosebumps) are experienced as ways of managing or eliminating feelings of separation, because as ways of defending the body from cold, they feel as though they are making the coldness go away. Panksepp (1995: 200) suggests that the chemical predictors include oxytocin, opioid systems and prolactin. These chemicals are particularly important in controlling distress in mothers separated from their children. (For further discussion of Panksepp's theory see Taruffi and Koelsch 2014: 2; Huron and Margulis 2010: 596 and Maruskin et al. 2012: 137.)

The chill response is a spreading tingling sensation, which feels as though it is a response to cold, but which also arises in strong experiences. It has been extensively studied by psychologists particularly in response to music. The chill response is sometimes called chills, tingles, shivers or the shiver down the spine. It is not entirely clear what physiological events correspond to chills, but one possibility is that it is a combination of two kinds of response already noted, piloerection and vasoconstriction; thus Panksepp (1998: 278) says that '[t]o the best of our knowledge, this response reflects a mixture of vasoconstriction, local skin contractions caused by piloerection, and perhaps changes in evaporative cooling in the skin surface'. Grewe et al. (2011) define chills as goosebumps and shivers down the spine. A different view is taken by Goldstein (1980: 128) in one of the first articles to study thrills scientifically. He thought that the apparent skin sensation did not involve actual activity in the skin and instead involved activity in the sensory areas of the brain's cortex which map out the body's surface. Maruskin et al. (2012: 136) note that '[m]uch of the chills literature is based on the unstated assumption that the various chills sensations cohere as a unitary construct'. However not everyone agrees that the chills form a single type of arousal. Panksepp (1995: 199), for example, thinks that cold-related arousals have a special status, and Maruskin et al. (2012) suggest that there are two kinds of chill, differentiated by valence, goose-tingles for the positive and goose-shivers for the negative.

Chills are felt in particular parts of the body and can spread around the body. Different people experience them in different places (Laski 1961; Goldstein 1980; Craig 2005; Konečni et al. 2007: 619). Some people seem to get them laterally, more on one side of the body than the other; I am one of these, and get chills predominantly on my right side. This lateralization is an interesting and rarely studied characteristic of chills and also piloerection, and perhaps tells us something important. Lateralized piloerection is a characteristic of some ictal piloerections (Loddenkemper et al. 2004: 879). As a physiological response, lateralization of piloerection has been explored in some animal research, but there is no currently published research that I know of on lateralized piloerection as a strong experience response in humans.

In a much-cited paper on chills and other arousals, Blood and Zatorre (2001) demonstrate experimentally that there is increased cerebral blood flow in some brain areas associated with reward and motivation, emotion and arousal and reduced cerebral blood flow in other areas, correlating with the self-reported intensity of 'intensely pleasant emotional responses, including chills' in response to self-selected piece of music. They suggest that the brain structures relating to musical chills are not the same as those involved in response to musical dissonances or consonances. (For further discussion, see Konečni et al. 2007 and Salimpoor et al. 2011: 260.)

Goldstein (1980) suggested that the chills might involve endogenous opioid peptides (endorphins). These are brain chemicals (neurotransmitters) that are released into the bloodstream in response to stress and have a role in modulating pain (Longstaff 2011: 89). Goldstein offers experimental evidence, based on the fact that naloxone attenuates thrills, and since naloxone blocks opiate receptors and so reduces opioid presence, this suggests that reduced thrills correlate with reduced opioid peptides. Biederman and Vessel (2006: 252, 354) suggest something similar, specifically that novel triggers stimulate more neurons than familiar triggers and so release more opioids: 'as one struggles to comprehend a new idea, there is increased pleasure with repeated exposure, which peaks at what has been called the "click" of comprehension'. Panksepp (1995: 200) suggests that the chemical predictors of chills should be opioids, oxytocin and prolactin. They are all pleasurable, and probably contribute to the positive valence. The chemical effect of strong experiences should thus be similar in some ways to drugs which increase opioid presence in the body: morphine, methadone, heroin, oxycodone and nitrous oxide (laughing gas), for example. Humphry Davy, who isolated nitrous oxide, described one experience as beginning with 'a thrilling, extending from the chest to the extremities', along with an apparent sharpening of perception, he experienced the effect of insight into the reality of the universe, and immediately after being aroused, his 'emotions were enthusiastic and sublime' (Ruston 2013: 169).

Tears and Other Sadness-Related Arousals

Bindra (1972: 283, cited by Williams and Morris 1996: 480) found in his experimental subjects that tears were sometimes associated with elation and could be associated with 'an aesthetic feeling arising from reading or writing poetry or prose or from listening to music'. Tears can arise for various reasons, including as a way of ridding the eyes of irritants, but the tears which arise in strong experiences are triggered in ways which suggest that they are variants of emotional tears, or crying, which is defined as 'the secretion of tears in an emotional context' (Vingerhoets et al 2000: 354). Crying, including watery eyes and welling up, can be produced in response to many kinds of stimuli, some of which can be called 'sad' and some not (Provine 2017: 242). There may be an important role for prosocial emotions associated with tears (Wassiliwizky et al 2017b, Zickeld et al. 2020), and this connects this type of thrill to empathy, also an important component of strong experiences. Williams and Morris (1996: 480) say that Charles Darwin noted that tears can be stimulated 'for sympathy with the sorrows or with the happiness of others (including fictional characters) and in response to music' and tears might be a response to music 'especially when we are already softened by any of the tenderer feeling' (Darwin 1965: 217). James describes tears in a response to literature or to music, Housman describes tears and a lump in the throat in a response to poetry, and most of Sloboda's (1991) respondents said that they experienced tears in chill responses to music. Elkins (2001: 186), in an extended study of crying in front of paintings, sees tears as a potential manifestation of ecstasy and epiphany, both of which are kinds of strong experience. Pelowski (2015) discusses examples of tears in front of artworks, arising from schematic discrepancy and its resolution and the feeling of insight it brings. It is not obvious whether all kinds of emotional tears can be understood as the same kind of psychological event; for example Vingerhoets et al. (2000: 358) ask '[i]s sobbing fundamentally different from simply getting silent watery eyes, as when one is moved?' – and say that the answer is not yet clear. A related type of response is the lump in the throat, which was the third most common thrill response to music reported in Sloboda (1991), and also one of the chill responses described by Strick et al. (2015: 58). The globus sensation of a lump in the throat arises from a conflict between the fight-or-flight need to keep the throat open in order to breathe deeply and the sadness-driven need to swallow which closes the throat.

The basic claim I make about strong experiences is that they are kinds of surprise, as responses to some surprising match between perceptions and schemata. The chill responses discussed in the previous section are classified by Huron as among the surprise emotions, but the crying responses are not. Mori and Iwanaga (2017) also differentiate the chill response from the tears response. So, can crying be understood as a response to schematic discrepancy? Efran and Spangler (1979) offer a theory of crying which suggests that it can, as does the different theory of Gross et al. (1994). Both accounts acknowledge that the parasympathetic nervous system is responsible for causing emotional tears (Vingerhoets et al. 2000: 361). Efran and Spangler (1979) offer a two-factor theory in which crying is a post-arousal phenomenon; in their approach, arousal is a response to a schema discrepancy, and when the schema is changed and the discrepancy removed, crying is a way of restoring homeostasis. On the assumption that the arousal involves the sympathetic nervous system and because crying involves the parasympathetic nervous system, crying works to reduce sympathetic arousal. This approach is however not well suited to the claims made in the present book, as it is not at all clear that the discrepancies are resolved in many of these experiences, especially the experiences that combine ineffability and tears, and so tears cannot obviously be associated with the resolution of discrepancy. Gross et al. (1994) argue against the Efran–Spangler approach, and instead propose that crying produces a state of high physiological arousal; in their approach it is not an arousal-reduction mechanism. This fits better with the idea that crying is a response to the first stage of arousal in schematic discrepancy and that this need not be resolved in order to produce crying. In their experiments, subjects viewing a sad film produced tears along with a range of other reactions, most importantly including increased sympathetic nervous system activity such as decreases in finger temperature and increases in skin conductance, along with increased somatic activity. This sympathetic arousal coexists with the parasympathetic arousal involving the tears themselves. This all suggests, then, that tears can be a response to the same kinds of stimuli as cause other types of arousal such as chills, and thus in principle to the schematically discrepant perception, so that we might sometimes cry as a surprise response.

The brain chemical prolactin may also play an important role in crying. This is a hormone associated with the production of milk in females, and it is also released into the bloodstream in both genders in response to exercise, stress and sex, where it produces a positive effect (Brody & Krüger, 2006). It is also increased during sadness, where it has a homeostatic function of mitigating the negativity of the sadness (Huron 2011: 146). Specifically the emotional tears and the tear glands have high concentrations of prolactin (Vingerhoets 2000: 362). The causal sequence has been discussed: Frey (1985) argued that prolactin causes crying, for example, by lowering the threshold for tears, but Vingerhoets and others have shown that prolactin is primarily a consequence of crying rather than its cause (cited Huron 2011: 152). In aesthetic tears, prolactin should produce an overall positive effect, because the tears which are produced are not associated with negative emotion, and so the positive effects of prolactin are not countered by the negative feeling which is otherwise associated with tears.

Other Types of Phasic Arousal

Emotion can cause body temperature to rise in humans, called 'nonshivering thermogenesis', and this is produced by the sympathetic autonomic nervous system (Longstaff 2011: 279, Renbourn 1960). It can be a response to a threat, at least in rats and so possibly humans (Mohammed et al. 2014). A possible example of raised temperature in a strong experience comes from the Methodist John Wesley, describing his moment of conversion (cited Nichols 1987: 19):

> In the evening I went very unwillingly to a society in Aldersgate Street, where one was reading Luther's preface to the Epistle to the Romans. About a quarter before nine, while he was describing the change which God works in the heart through faith in Christ, I felt my heart strangely warmed. I felt I did trust in Christ, Christ alone, for salvation; and an assurance was given me that He had taken away my sins, even mine, and saved me from the law of sin and death.

In part the warmth in the heart should be read as symbolic, and perhaps is also informed by a range of theoretical assumptions about heat and emotion including Methodist physicians' belief that 'violent emotions could produce fevers, by blocking the skin pores thus preventing the escape of insensible perspiration' (Renbourn 1960: 149). However, we might also interpret this as a description of actual raised temperature at a moment of strong experience which has both arousal and epistemic characteristics.

Sweating is an arousal that can be part of a strong experience. Humans have two kinds of sweat glands, both involving the sympathetic autonomic nervous system. One is an emotional response that produces eccrine sweating on the palms and soles or paws, which improves grip and so may be a functional response to a threat because it enhances the ability to run or climb away from a threat (Adelman, et al. 1975). The other kind produces apocrine sweating in hairy skin such as armpits and is both a response to heat and an emotional response. Both kinds of sweating might thus arise in strong experiences, to the extent that strong experiences have triggers that can be perceived as threats. As an arousal, sweating is frequently observed and reported in psychological experiments because it affects the electrical conductance of the skin and so can be easily measured (Rooney et al. 2012). The skin conductance level can depend on the individual or a type of situation and may correlate with personality type (Rickard 2004). Grewe et al. (2011: 233) and Salimpoor et al. (2011) found that a higher skin conductance level correlated with greater subjective feeling of chill. The skin conductance response can be a response to surprise, and skin conductance responses to musical stimuli have been extensively studied (e.g. summarized in Benedek and Kaernbach 2011: 326; see also Guhn et al. 2007). The chill feeling is strongly correlated with increases in skin conductance response (Huron and Margulis 2010: 595, citing Craig 2005, Guhn et al. 2007, Rickard 2004, Hodges 2010). Grewe et al. (2011: 223) say that a reported chill is followed, a second later, by an increase in skin conductance response. Barraza et al. (2015: 142) suggest that raised skin conductance response may be a manifestation of highly arousing negatively tuned cognitive activity. This reminds us again of the paradox in these experiences that what ought to be negatively valenced emotional arousal is associated with something which is not really threatening or unpleasant and is experienced pleasurably. It is worth noting, incidentally, that as another response to heat, flushing or blushing, does not seem to be reported as part of strong experiences. Flushing and blushing are produced by vasodilation, controlled by the sympathetic nervous system. Feldman (1941) provides a description of many situations in which blushing arises, from a psychoanalytic perspective and emphasising the sexual aspects of blushing, but none of the situations resemble the strong experiences under examination here.

Laski (1961: 79) suggests that deep breathing accompanies or follows ecstasy. It is worth noting that several of Wordsworth's epistemic experiences involve situations in which the natural world is itself breathing, or breathing and speaking: 'low breathings coming after me' in the 'snares' experience, and 'a deep and gloomy breathing-place' in the 'Snowdon' experience. Lord Kames (cited Morley 2010: 114) says that in response to a sublime object, the spectator's breast dilates, involving a deep inspiration of breath, as a kind of mimicry of the great object which is viewed. Deep breathing might be one factor in producing a lump in the throat, which arises from a conflict between the glottis being opened for deep breathing and closed for swallowing. The specific respiratory act of gasping is the focus of a discussion by Elkins (2001: 232) who describes gasping in front of a painting. Huron (2006: 31) suggests that gasping, because it involves a freezing stage, is associated with the freeze response, which Öhman treats as the second stage of a response to threat. Huron associates it with awe, as type of aesthetic response.

Emotion-driven or Duchenne laughter is the second most common of the thrill responses to music reported in Sloboda (1991). Mendelssohn (1997: 230) suggests that laughter is close to the experience of the sublime; Collingwood (cited Kirwan 2005) also implies that the sublime is associated with laughter. Huron (2006: 38) notes that an aha experience can produce laughter. He offers a very tentative evolutionary account of laughter, that it originates in unvocalized panting, which occurs in response to threat and arises in surprise. The panting is then vocalized in order to communicate deference, when panting is induced by threat from another member of the social hierarchy. '[V]ocalized panting generalizes to most surprising circumstances' which include laughter in response to surprise (Huron 2006: 30). In a different but related account, Efran and Spangler (1979: 67) suggest that both laughter and crying are responses to schematic discrepancy. They suggest that while crying arises when the discrepancy cannot be accommodated, laughter is a response to accommodation and resolution of the schematic discrepancy.

A rare and complex psychophysiological event which involves arousal in response to artworks is Stendhal's syndrome. This can be considered a type of strong experience and was identified in 1979 by an Italian psychiatrist Graziella Magherini (1995), who noticed a pattern over several years of visitors to Florence who were so overwhelmed by art that they fell ill and ended up in her hospital. She named the syndrome after the French novelist Stendhal, who describes an experience of visiting the Basilica of Santa Croce in Florence in 1817 (Stendhal 1826: 102). He begins in a sort of ecstasy as a result of being among the tombs of famous men, and then becomes so overwhelmed by the combination of his own feelings and the experience of the artworks, and leaves the basilica with a beating heart, life drained from him and in fear of falling. Innocenti et al. (2014) and Nicholson et al. (2009) discuss how Stendhal's syndrome relates to autonomic arousal and emotional response.

There are other kinds of arousal in strong experiences, and I conclude this discussion with a brief note on them. Some experimental studies have found that people breathe more quickly when they subjectively report chills (Salimpoor et al. 2009, Blood and Zatorre 2001). Changes in heart rate are sometimes reported in strong experiences, sometimes involving increased and sometimes decreased heart rate (Lang et al. 1997, Öhman and Wiens 2003, Guhn et al. 2007: 481, Grewe et al. 2011, Rooney et al. 2012: 408, Sumpf et al. 2015: 3–4, Barraza et al. 2015: 142.) Housman describes a response to poetry as 'in the pit of the stomach', and over half of Sloboda's respondents described a pit-of-stomach sensation as one of their thrill responses to music. One of Laski's informants (Q51) said that ecstasy was accompanied by 'butterflies in the tummy and a floating sensation – it can make me feel sick'. Huron (2006: 19) discusses how fear might produce feelings in the pit of the stomach via the paragigantocellularis lateralis. A small proportion of Sloboda's respondents reported sexual arousal as a thrill response to music. It may be that brain chemicals such as oxytocin, prolactin and vasopressin are involved and that this might be related to prosocial emotional responses. Sexual arousal might also be related to flushing or blushing (noted earlier), which are also rarely reported in these experiences. Terms relating to sexuality are sometimes used; Panksepp (1995: 203) uses the term 'skin orgasm' to describe the chill sensation. A final comment on arousal responses is that sometimes the subject reacts with an action, such as clapping or wanting to clap (Elkins 2001: 226). Freedberg (1989) describes actions which involve touching the object, including kissing a statue, or stabbing a painting.

Summary of Chapter

This chapter has explored the various kinds of arousal which can be part of a strong experience. One of the most frequently reported kinds of arousal involves sensations associated with cold, such as the range of feelings described as chills, frissons, goosebumps, shivers down the spine and so on. These have been intensively examined by psychologists, looking specifically at responses to music to understand what the sensations are and what they correlate with. Another frequently reported and widely explored range of arousals are the responses which are normally associated with sadness, such as tears, and a lump in the throat. Then there are a range of other arousals, including increased temperature, sweating, changes in heart rate, changes in respiration and laughter. Most of the arousals, and perhaps all of them, can be understood as manifestations of surprise, and this would fit with the general claim of this book that strong experiences arise as types of surprise. As manifestations of surprise, the arousals have defensive and homeostatic functions, which seem to have been adapted to produce pleasurable results in aesthetic experience. There is evidence that empathy may also play a role in some of the arousals, and empathy in turn may play a role in some strong experiences. The psychological study of arousal is important in showing that surprise and social cognition have an important triggering role, which I have suggested carry over more generally to strong experiences of all kinds. We have seen that in many cases, the arousal may be part of an emotion, which is in turn part of a strong experience. The arousal and the emotion are triggered in the ways which we would normally expect, often as responses to something odd in the relation between a perception and a schema, and with other contributory factors. We have also seen a similarity between strong experience and aesthetic experience. In both cases, the arousal does not quite fit the trigger. I suggest that this discrepancy is itself surprising, so that strong experience can itself trigger strong experience, as when we 'catch a thrill'.

Chapter 5
THE PSYCHOLOGICAL BACKGROUND

In the previous chapters I have explored the epistemic feelings and the arousals which are the main features of strong experiences. In this chapter I begin by returning to surprise, which is the foundation of strong experience, and then consider various other aspects of our psychology, including processing effort and attention and empathy, in order to gain a fuller understanding of strong experience. In particular, I address the problem of why ordinary objects can sometimes surprise us, as in many modernist epiphanies. I conclude this chapter by exploring some of the variability in how people have strong experiences, and how reliable their reports of a strong experience are.

Surprise

I have argued that strong experiences are a type of surprise, and one reason for saying this is that like surprise, strong experiences are often sudden. Here, for example is the diarist Hester Thrale's 1777 account of a sudden sublime experience.

> Burke would have liked it – so well does it tally with his Notions of the Sublime.
> A little Girl of ten Years old – a Shopkeeper's Daughter, was carried to see Wanstead House – the long Suite of Rooms were suddenly thrown open, the whole blaze of Splendour burst upon her Eye – She said nothing, but cried copiously, such was the violence of its Effect upon her Mind. (Thrale 1942: 21, cited in Burke 1987: xxxiii)

There are other examples of the sudden sublime. Writing in 1747, Baillie (1996: 88) says, 'a flood of light bursts in, and the vast heavens are on every side widely extended to the eye, it is then that the soul enlarges, and would stretch herself out to the immense expanse'. The painter Joshua Reynolds said that the greatest paintings elevate the spectator 'at a single blow' (Ashfield and de Bolla 1996: 159). Moses Mendelssohn (1997: 198) says that the soul is momentarily stopped in its tracks by the sublime. Kant (1952: 91) says that the sublime is 'brought about by the feeling of a momentary check to the vital forces followed at once by a discharge all the more powerful'. Santayana (1896, cited Kirwan 2005: 135) describes the sublime as a 'sudden escape from our ordinary interests and the identification of ourselves with something permanent and superhuman, something much more abstract and inalienable than our changing personality, all this carries us away from the blurred objects before us, and raises us into a sort of ecstasy'. The term 'astonishment' is sometimes used in describing strong experiences, which might be considered a stronger version of surprise, and perhaps with the stronger epistemic content which we find in sublime experiences. Joseph Addison (Monk 1960) says that '[w]e are flung into a pleasing astonishment at such unbounded views, and feel a delightful stillness and amazement in the soul at the apprehension of them'. The OED cites Addison to illustrate its meaning of '[m]ental disturbance or excitement due to the sudden presentation of anything unlooked for or unaccountable; wonder temporarily overpowering the mind; amazement'. Burke (1987: 57) describes the emotional response to the sublime as astonishment, which is 'that state of the soul in which all its motions are suspended, with some degree of horror [...] Astonishment, as I have said, is the effect of the sublime in its highest degree; the inferior effects are admiration, reverence, and respect'. Miller (2007) explores surprise and its relation to epiphany, focusing on Wordsworth but looking back to Dante and Petrarch, and forward to theorization of the literary epiphany.

If surprise is the basis of a strong experience, why do only some surprises turn into strong experiences? The answer must partly depend on the quality of the response: if the arousal produced by the surprise is very strong or the epistemic feeling produced by the surprise feels as though it carries high significance. The feeling of ineffability may also be important; if the surprise produces a sense of knowing something which cannot be described, this may set the surprise on the route to becoming a strong experience. But there is also a role for metacognition, and what sense we make of the surprise. The following is what Whittlesea and Williams (1998: 160) say about the various ordinary ways in which we metacognitively make sense of surprise; I suggest that having a strong experience may involve a metacognitive interpretation of surprise.

> This suggests that surprise may be engendered in many ways, and that a feeling state is the inevitable consequence of that surprise. The feeling might be one of fear, as in the case of sudden noise, or of hilarity, in the case of a surprising punch-line to a joke, or unease or bewilderment, in coming home to find the furniture re-arranged, or of familiarity, in the case of unexpectedly fluent processing of a face seen at a bus-stop.

Which of these is felt depends, we suspect, on one's interpretation of the possible meaning of the surprising event, as being dangerous or pleasant: The interpretation depends on the intuitive theories one has about the possible causes of various types of experience.

Meyer et al. (1991: 296) say that 'surprise is elicited by events that deviate from a schema' and 'if a discrepancy between schema and input occurs, surprise is elicited. The main function of surprise is to enable processes that help to remove this discrepancy'. This is the notion of schema as defined by Rumelhart and as used in this book. Though their discussion is in terms of surprising events, I carry it also over to surprising objects and their schemata, because objects are always part of events. Reisenzein (2000: 264) proposes a related theory of surprise in terms of a sequence of three stages (see also Meyer et al. 1997 and Reisenzein and Meyer 2009). In stage 1, the perception is appraised relative to its schema. There is a tolerance of a certain amount of discrepancy which is the normal range of variation between perception and schema discussed earlier in this book, which is expressed by setting a threshold. If the discrepancy exceeds the threshold, the perception counts as unexpected, and this initiates stage 2 which is the feeling of surprise. Stage 3 can involve changing expectations and schemata so that they better match actual perceptions. The intensity of the experience depends on the discrepancy of the event.

Huron (2006) is one of the major influences on the present book. He discusses surprise in response to music and suggests that there are four kinds of surprise. The four routes to surprise start with four kinds of memory that produce four kinds of expectation, which when violated lead to four kinds of surprise (Huron 2006: 224, 239, 269), as follows. First, semantic memory is where we hold our schemata (Chapter 3). This type of memory allows for schematic expectations, which when violated produce 'schematic surprise'. This is the 'surprise' of Meyer et al. (1991), as already noted. Huron illustrates it by citing a situation where the music violates a schema which the listener has 'brought to the listening experience'; that is, the schema is not just a part of the listener's memory but is sufficiently salient in memory to be available for matching to the perceptions of the music, such that the perception can mismatch the schema. Second, episodic memory is our memory of specific episodes, often with an autonoetic component (but with a complication as discussed in Chapter 3). Episodic memory makes it possible to form veridical expectations, these being expectations based on our knowledge of facts, and which we expect to remain facts. This in turn can produce 'veridical surprise' if there is a discrepancy. This occurs when we believe that we already know the characteristics of a particular musical piece (or text), but the text turns out to have some new and unexpected characteristic. Huron suggests that performance error, misquotation or intentional parody might all achieve this. Third, our short-term memory of what has just happened is the basis for dynamic expectations which allow expectations to be manipulated during an artwork, and this produces 'dynamic surprise'. Here the musical piece creates specific expectations, which when violated produce surprise. Given the schematic nature of musical form, it is possible that these specific expectations still depend to some extent on schematic knowledge. An equivalent in literature is the way that a literary text will lead us to expect that it will develop in a certain way, for example, in its narrative, and then this expectation is disappointed, producing surprise. Fourth, Huron refers to working memory, which is where we formulate conscious and explicit expectations. Violation of these expectations leads to 'conscious surprise'. This arises when a work draws on what a skilled listener might expect, and then subverts those expectations. It is worth noting that thrill experiences may be enhanced by skill and knowledge and also that conscious surprise must depend to some extent again on schematic knowledge, which is how that skill and knowledge is laid down in memory. In all these kinds of surprise, there is a discrepancy produced by a new perception. This can be discrepant relative to something we have known for a while and is the schematic surprise which is the primary concern of the book. But it can also be discrepant relative to expectations that we are formulating in the moment. One of the reasons I focus primarily on schematic surprise is that I suggest that the feeling of significance is more likely to attach to surprises relating to deeply embedded schematic knowledge, rather than the more transient expectations associated with specific events and objects and which constitute the other three kinds of surprise.

Öhman and Wiens (2003) offer another sequential account of surprise, based around the sudden attentional shift of the orienting response; their approach is similar to the Meyer and Reisenzein approach and to Huron's (2006) approach. They focus on the responses that an animal makes when encountering a predator, and on how imminent the threat is. Humans have an evolutionary past as prey animals, and though our response to a literary text is not actually a response to a predator, it may exploit this response; that is, we may respond to art in ways that reflect our evolutionary past. There is an implication of threat whenever a stimulus is novel because it 'fails to find a matching memory model', by being a schematically discrepant perception (Öhman and Wiens 2003: 262). This triggers the orienting response by demanding attention and controlled rather than automatic processing. The orienting response involves attention drawn to the potential threat. In the first stage, the parasympathetic nervous system dominates and heart rate decreases. In the second stage, the animal keeps very still in the freeze response, preferably in a position of shelter; the associated heart rate deceleration associated with fear also makes the animal more open to environmental stimuli, while it scans the environment. In the third stage, there is a switch to sympathetic nervous system activity and a rise in the heart rate; this enables the animal either to fight or to run away in the fight-or-flight response. The whole sequence is associated with fear as an emotion, and with arousals associated with fear, as discussed in the previous chapter.

Foster and Keane (2015) offer an account of surprise which is different from the schema-based approach used in this book, but which I have found useful to refer to. Foster and Keane's approach is associated with sense making and involves the perceiver testing the coherence between a perception and anything that is already known. It does not depend on matching new perceptions to a pre-existing expectation, and the surprise can be generated after the perception. The magnitude of surprise depends on the degree of incoherence, the amount of processing effort required to establish the coherence and the emotional intensity. Some surprises are more surprising because it is more difficult to make them coherent with existing knowledge. Foster and Keane suggest that this type of approach works better than the schema–discrepancy approach when explaining surprise in everyday scenarios with a large number of possible outcomes, where mental capacity prevents all these outcomes being assigned probabilities. A way of addressing these concerns is found in Chumbley et al. (2014), and Clark (2013) who describes how it is possible to be very surprised in situations in which the subject has very little expectation as to what will happen.

Surprise and Fear

Strong experiences begin with a schematically discrepant perception. This always raises the possibility of a new risk, of a predator or other danger, and so the immediate responses to discrepancy can often be related to fear, these being the responses of freeze, fight or flight. Huron (2006) suggests that fear is the first response in surprise, even if it is then overtaken by some other emotion. This means that if strong experiences arise as a kind of surprise, then they have a relation to the fear emotions. Such a relation is conventional in descriptions of the sublime, which is often associated with fear or terror, and with arousal responses that are appropriate to fear, such as trembling or chills. Kant says that fear, modulated and checked, plays a role in the experience of sublime things where 'provided our own position is secure, their aspect is all the more attractive for its fearfulness; and we readily call these objects sublime, because they raise the forces of the soul above the height of vulgar commonplace, and discover within us a power of resistance of quite another kind, which gives us courage to be able to measure ourselves against the seeming omnipotence of nature' (Kant 1952: 110).

Fear involves the brain component called the amygdala, described by Aggleton and Mishkin (1986) as the 'sensory gateway to the emotions'. Sander et al. (2003) suggest that the amygdala is particularly designed to detect events that are 'subjectively appraised as relevant given the individual's current goals, needs, values, and concerns'. The amygdala for example controls the freezing response. LeDoux (1996: 164) showed that fear-inducing sounds reach the amygdala by two distinct auditory processing pathways, one faster and one slightly slower, though both objectively very fast. The information carried by an auditory signal travels from the ears via the auditory brainstem and midbrain to the thalamus and from the thalamus to the amygdala: this is the fast route. But the information also travels by a more indirect and hence slightly slower route from the thalamus to the auditory part of the brain's cortex where it can be interpreted relative to other knowledge, and then back from the auditory cortex to the amygdala. The slow route, because it goes via the complex information processing possibilities of the cortex, is able to produce a much more discriminating response to the signal. Where a potentially threatening sound is perceived, the amygdala is immediately alerted by the fast route. But the slower route allows the possibility of a threat to be appraised, and possibly discounted, so that this information reaches the amygdala at a slightly later stage. The outcome of this dual route is that a threat can thus lead to an immediate response which is then cancelled. LeDoux suggests that something similar might happen with visual threat information. Scherer and Zentner (2001: 365) describe an autonomic low-appraisal route by which emotion is produced, which is similar to LeDoux's fast route to the amygdala. This route may be taken by musical stimuli that sound acoustically similar to cries of fear involving sudden onset and high pitch, and these 'may be appraised by evolutionarily primitive but extremely powerful detection systems and may provoke, like pictures of spiders or facial expressions of fear, physiological defence responses'. Schultz (2002: 255) notes a similarity between LeDoux's approach and the prediction error approach (Clark 2013) in which there is a bottom-up dopamine reward alert signal by the fast route and a top-down, more cortically controlled, slow route for reward discrimination and representation systems.

Huron (2006) offers a theory of how the brain responds to surprises in listening to music. This is directly relevant to the present project, because one of the surprise responses is the thrill response. Huron adapts LeDoux's dual route theory, in which the musical surprise alerts the amygdala to a threat by the fast route, but this alert is subsequently cancelled by the slow route to the amygdala via the cortex, where the aesthetic context is taken into account.

Huron's theory is a development of Meyer's (1956) account of musical emotion, where our expectations of what will happen in the music creates tension, and this tension is released when the expectations are met. Meyer's account was based on Gestalt theoretic notions and was later formalized by Narmour (1990) amongst others; and Patel (2008) offers extensive discussion of the role of expectation both in music and language. Huron proposes that we learn from experience, by statistical learning, what to expect from musical form. These expectations then involve anticipatory arousal and attention, which are tested against stimuli. We get a reward when our expectations are met, but repeated meeting of expectations diminishes rewards, leading to boredom. Where our expectations are not met, we are surprised, leading both to a fast reaction response and to a slower appraisal response, which are the two routes to the amygdala. The fast reaction response is short-lived, rarely reaches consciousness and is immune to habituation, which means that it is difficult or impossible to turn off. Hence in aesthetic experiences the fast response is not turned off and so though this response may not be functionally appropriate, it is nevertheless immune to change. This is why we can thrill repeatedly to the same moment in a piece of music, even if we know that the moment is coming: we do not have the ability to turn off the fast route to the amygdala, and so are repeatedly surprised by the same thing (Huron and Margulis 2010: 596). In contrast the slow appraisal response can take situational and social factors into account and its operations are open to manipulation and change. The looming effect of a crescendo in a piece of music may send a danger signal to the amygdala, but the slow route via the cortex recognizes that this crescendo is part of a piece of music, not a predator, and so will subsequently modulate the amygdala's response. The consequence is that we begin to respond to the music with an arousal appropriate to fear of a predator but because this is then cancelled we do not run away from the music. Huron presents a model for the matching of perceptions to schemata that involves a sequence of five responses, all potentially below conscious awareness, for which he uses the acronym ITPRA, the R and A of which manifest the fast and slow routes. The subject predicts a future event (the I of ITPRA, for 'imagination response') and acts to favour a positive outcome, by for example focusing attention and increasing arousal (T for 'tension response'). Then the event occurs. The subject assesses whether predictions were correct (P for 'prediction response'). Two responses now begin at the same time, a fast and crude defensive response (R for 'reaction response'), and a slower and more precise response that takes context into account (A for 'appraisal response'). The fast reaction response is irrespective of context, and hence not sensitive to the difference between real threats and 'aesthetic' threats such as a narrative surprise. The distinction comes in the slower appraisal response;

the reason we laugh at the surprise in a joke, rather than run away from it, is that the appraisal response modulates the fast reaction response by taking context into account. In this fast–slow distinction we see LeDoux's distinction. The subject's emotional experience of the event is a combination of all five responses.

In principle, if our expectations are not met, we experience negative affect. However, this cannot be how things work in practice, when for example we experience aesthetic objects. This is because our experiences of aesthetic objects are not always satisfied and yet this does not undermine the aesthetic experience. Sometimes the expectations are satisfied, sometimes satisfaction is delayed, and sometimes they are not satisfied at all. Huron (2006: 25) proposes a reason for why this potential negativity is experienced as positive in aesthetic experience. He argues that contrast plays a role in valencing our feelings. An experience which is first valenced as negative and later valenced as positive will be more positive because of the contrast with the previous negative valence: this is contrastive valence. He cites Locke's suggestion that the removal of pain can lead to pleasure and also cites Burke's notion of the sublime which depends on an initial sensation of fear that is later judged inconsequential. When it comes to surprises, the two routes to the amygdala are relevant. A surprise can always be initially assessed as negative, by the fast route to the amygdala; the amygdala prepares the body to freeze, fight or flee. This will apply to any surprise, whether its source is fictional or something of no actual danger to the experiencer such as a mountain viewed from a place of safety. The slow route to the amygdala takes contextual information, such as the lack of actual danger, into account, when it passes through the cortex and then to the amygdala. This corrects the initially negative appraisal of the situation, replacing it with a positive appraisal or possibly a neutral appraisal, and this produces a contrastive valence. What might initially have been threatening and a source of fear is now experienced pleasurably. This arises in some strong experiences: 'frisson arises when an initial negative response is superseded by a neutral or positive appraisal […] contrastive valence transforms the negative feelings into something positive' (Huron and Margulis 2010: 596, citing Huron 2006). Menninghaus et al. (2017: 5) also suggest that the thrills involve an interplay of the positive and negative emotions.

Surprise and Discrepancy Relative to a Schema

A cause of surprise is when there is a discrepancy between a new perception (or thought) and an existing schema. We have seen that surprise could be the cause of the arousal responses seen in strong experiences and that there are other reasons to associate surprise with strong experiences, including the suddenness of the experience, and the epistemic characteristics. Apart from the moment of sudden surprise, discrepancy in general can also cause arousal. MacDowell and Mandler (1989) provide evidence for Mandler's discrepancy/ evaluation theory, in which 'the discrepancy between actual and expected events is considered to be a major mechanism by which autonomic arousal is produced'; the arousal will lead to an emotion depending on how the situation is evaluated. The arousal is greater when the discrepancy relates to expectations about better organized material or more familiar material, as in well-known proverbs. In their experiment they showed that the heart rate rose more after unexpected events. They asked the subject to report on the felt intensity of the experience and found as in other experiments that what subjects feel does not always correlate with the actual arousal they undergo (MacDowell and Mandler 1989: 122). Bohrn et al. (2012) note that discrepancy can raise physiological arousal (citing MacDowell and Mandler), trigger appraisal processes (Scherer 2001) and be accompanied by interest or surprise (Silvia 2008). Discrepancy is important in literature. Zwaan et al. (1995: 387) say that 'discrepancies between real-world constraints and narrative structure are regarded as one of the hallmarks of literature' (citing Bruner 1986; Genette 1983; Striedter 1989; Tomashevsky 1965). Oatley (1994: 56) says that 'arousal is first provoked by discrepancies between the reader's schema and that implied by the work of art,' which are resolved (citing Berlyne 1971; Gaver and Mandler 1987; Cupchik and Lazslo 1994). As often in this project, we find that a characteristic – here, discrepancy – is found throughout an aesthetic object, but that it may also play a role in a strong experience of that object. A puzzling and persistent problem is why a characteristic that is present all along can suddenly play a role in triggering strong experience; perhaps the answer is that the trigger works only in the right circumstances, involving text, context and subject.

Music psychologists often find that when their experimental subjects select their own music, they get more frequent chills (Laeng et al. 2016). Assuming that chills arise because of surprise, this suggests that the schematic discrepancies which may be producing the chills cannot be altered by prior experience of the schematic discrepancies; that is, we can be surprised by something we already know. There are several ways of understanding why this might be. First, given that different performances of music are slightly different, a structural element in music might surprise us in how it is slightly differentiated in a performance. For example, I once had a strong thrill while in a concert, hearing an unexpected deceleration in the last few bars of a performance of Mozart's Symphony 40, a piece I am very familiar with, so that the slight change was very clear to me. Second, to the extent that context plays a role in allowing a trigger to generate a surprise response, then a contextual change in listening to the piece of music, even if the piece is exactly the same as for example in a recorded piece, may mean that the triggering factor remains surprising because the context around it slightly changes.

As a third type of explanation, we can adapt Boyer's (1996, 2001) explanation of why certain triggers continue to stimulate a strong response in us even though we should have become habituated to them. Boyer discusses anthropomorphic projections in religious belief, where for example natural objects or statues are conceptualized as though they are people, as walking around or feeding on sacrifices or listening or speaking to people, all of which should be impossible. Another type of anthropomorphic projection is where the property of personhood is attributed to non-corporeal or supernatural beings. Such anthropomorphic projections exist also in literature and art, and particularly in the sublime, where inanimate and natural objects are often attributed animacy. Though Boyer does not say so, it is worth noting how similar this is to inanimate but also animate objects such as the automaton which is a trigger of the uncanny for Jentsch (1906) and Freud (1919), and I have suggested that the experience of the uncanny is a type of strong experience. Boyer argues that these projections are powerful because they violate intuitive ontologies that are genetically determined as part of our evolutionary heritage, such as the intuitive ontological distinction between animate and inanimate things. Boyer can be interpreted as saying that these anthropomorphized objects violate schematic expectations: even if we are habituated to the feeling that a statue can hear us, it is still surprising that it can. He comments that it is the counter-intuitiveness of the violation of schematic expectations which explains 'why they trigger significant cognitive investment on the part of the people concerned'. If we transfer this idea to the theory of surprise, it means that we may be unable to learn and generalize from certain perceptions, including perceptions of apparently impossible things such as religious objects. Since we cannot change schemata which we have acquired from our evolutionary past, for example relating to basic knowledge of the physics of the world in which we live, it is tempting to wonder whether the creation of a work of art is the creation of an apparently impossible thing, presenting us with anomalies which we cannot learn, and so consistently surprising us.

A similar approach to why we are surprised repeatedly by the same thing is taken by Bharucha (1994, cited by Huron 2006: 224) in his explanation of why a piece of music can surprise us twice. It involves a distinction into two kinds of expectation, one called a 'veridical expectation' of the text as a unique token, and the other called a 'schematic expectation' of the text as a type with its generic characteristics. Moving from Bharucha's account of music to our interest in literature, we might say that during our reading of a novel for the first time, we formulate expectations of what will happen next. Some of those expectations are drawn from our knowledge of what happens next in this genre of novel. Any expectation can be violated; what we expected to happen does not happen, and when this is the case in the novel we are reading, we learn that something else happens instead. One would imagine that once the expectation has been violated once, we would no longer form the original expectation again, but would have changed it. This is true for veridical expectations in which we come to know exactly what will happen in the novel and so will not be veridically surprised again after the first reading. But a violation of expectation when we first read a novel can also violate a schematic expectation about narratives in novels. This schematic expectation is hard to change, even if we can formulate a veridical expectation which contradicts it. We brought a schematic expectation to our first reading and that schematic expectation is unchanged when brought to the second reading. So while the veridical expectation is changed or newly formed on the basis of the first reading, the schematic expectation is unchanged, and we can be schematically surprised even by an event which we know is going to occur. This is in part what allows us to return to an aesthetic object which we already know, and to be surprised by it again. Huron argues that it is these hard-to-change schematic expectations that allow us to be surprised by moments in pieces of music which we already know. Gerrig (1993: 172–173) endorses the extension of Bharucha's ideas to literature; he discusses the 'anomalous suspense' experienced by a reader who actually knows what will happen, and refers to the Bharucha model in analysing narratives. He says that we have schematic expectations of narrative that are difficult to overturn, and so our veridical knowledge of what will happen in the narrative does not prevent our surprise: 'If a veridical expectancy is sufficiently weak with respect to overlearned schematic expectancies, it may never achieve a sufficient threshold of activation to affect conscious experience'.

Curiosity

Curiosity plays a role in strong experiences, as it does more generally in our aesthetic and ordinary experiences. Dan Berlyne described epistemic curiosity as a desire for new information that 'motivates exploratory behaviour and knowledge acquisition' and as a characteristic of our aesthetic experience (Berlyne 1954, cited Lipman 2005: 559). Curiosity, which can begin with surprise, is driven by the need to resolve a discrepancy between what is perceived and the schemata that constitute what we know. Loewenstein (1994: 86) describes an information gap between what we know and what we want to know, and this produces a curiosity which peaks when we feel that the knowledge gap is almost closed (Oatley 1994: 57). This peaking might be part of a strong experience. This is particularly true of what

Loewenstein (1994: 88) calls 'insight problems' that are solved suddenly. The particular relevance of curiosity in strong experiences is that at some point in closing the knowledge gap, the curiosity suddenly increases. There is a sudden increase in attention, which then increases more gradually until the gap is closed, and the knowledge is acquired. The closing of the gap is 'sense-making', and Chater and Loewenstein (2016: 152) say that 'the experience of sense-making is itself pleasurable: we may experience a momentary positive "frisson" when we suddenly "find" an elegant interpretation'. In all these ways, curiosity is associated with the moment of strong experience. But it is worth returning to Berlyne's notion that curiosity is a continuous characteristic of our experience of literary texts, which again relates the strong experience to the general experience of literature.

Processing Effort

A surprise, and hence potentially a strong experience, is initiated by some change in what we perceive or think. One possibility is that the change is in the content of our perception or thought, that is, in what the perception or thought is about. But there is another possible kind of change which might trigger strong experience, and which I explore in this section, which is that there is a change in the energetic demands of the perception or thought. To put it another way, there is a change in how much effort is involved in the processing involved in the perception or thought, and the sequences of further processing they entail. This involves us in three existing strands of research. First, there is the research on 'defamiliarization' and related notions, which suggests that literary texts produce particular effects in readers by putting them to additional work involving higher processing effort. Second, and going in the opposite direction, there is the research on fluency of processing, which suggests that a reduction in processing effort (which can be enabled by regular form in a literary text) can also produce aesthetic effects, including both arousal and epistemic effects. The third possibility is that a sudden change in processing effort, whether from low to high or from high to low, might trigger a strong experience, and I explore whether this might be happening in poetic closure, in Smith's (1968) account.

The experimental psychological study of processing effort is often a study also of working memory and of focused attention. In many accounts, working memory is the part of our mental activity in which much of the processing of new perceptions and of thoughts occurs, and this is also the part of our mental activity in which we attend to perceptions and thoughts, though we do not have conscious access to all of working memory. In all kinds of memory, information is stored. Psychologists distinguish a memory store in which information can be kept indefinitely, often called 'long-term memory', which includes semantic memory and episodic memory, and schemata are kept in long-term memory. This is distinguished from a part of memory called 'working memory' in which information is held briefly and where that information is processed. The idea that a single system of working memory is used both for holding information and for processing information is an innovation of Baddeley and Hitch (1974). What in everyday language we mean by memory is 'long term memory'; in contrast, 'working memory' with its very short timespan is closer to what we ordinarily mean by conscious attention or 'what I'm thinking about right now'.

There are different approaches to working memory, and I assume here an approach in which working memory is treated as cognitive system which is divided into distinct component parts (Baddeley 2000). Working memory has three relevant characteristics. First, it is severely limited in storage capacity, unlike long-term memory which has indefinitely large storage capacity. In Baddeley's approach, the phonological loop which stores sound is limited by temporal characteristics of what is being stored or processed, while the central executive is instead limited by the amount and structure of the information which can be stored. The widely repeated notion that about seven items can be stored in working memory expresses this latter type of capacity limit, though it is no longer considered correct; the capacity is more likely to be four chunks of material, where each chunk can be internally complex (Cowan 2000). Limitations on capacity are not directly relevant in the present project, though in Fabb (2015, 2016) I argued that some regular aspects of poetic form in the world's literatures are controlled by information limits on working memory capacity. Second, and of particular relevance to the present project, working memory is where a large amount of the processing of information takes place. This is relevant because differences in the amount of processing effort have known side effects which are relevant to aesthetic experience, and these quantifiable differences may also have a role in triggering strong experience. Third, working memory is where our focused attention is concentrated, and attention is relevant in strong experiences.

Processing is generally measured in terms of 'processing effort'. It is worth noting that the psychological literature sometimes hesitates about what is meant by 'effort', and the extent to which it is conscious or unconscious and involves a feeling of strain or not (cf. Bruya and Tang 2018; van der Henst and Sperber 2004: 142). Similar problems apply to the related term 'tension' which is widely used to describe aesthetic objects and our response to them, but which also has varying and uncertain meanings. Psychologists examine processing effort relative to specific experimental tasks, such as recognizing a letter on a page, judging that two images are the same or recalling one kind of information when another kind of information also demands our attention. In experimental conditions, it is possible to quantify aspects of processing by measuring how long it takes to perform a task or by testing what other tasks can be performed at the same time, on the assumption of shared limits on resource such that greater effort on one focused task can interfere with processing of another task. The eyes also reveal processing effort: pupil dilation is greater with increased processing (Beatty 1982; Chen and Epps 2013), and the eyes blink more quickly with increased processing (Ponder and Kennedy 1927). Brain activity can also be measured, in specific places, in order to assess processing effort. For example, Schmidt and Seger (2009: 376) hypothesize that greater processing effort has a measurable effect in the brain's right hemisphere, and Wilson et al. (2008: 236) point to the downgrading of the brain's default mode network when processing effort is increased, for example when readers are very engrossed in a narrative.

It is a big jump from these relatively simple experiments to measuring processing effort in the many and complex tasks involved in reading literature or having any kind of strong experience. However, I assume that the same cognitive systems are potentially involved in all experience, whether testable in a laboratory or not, and this should allow us to extrapolate from the simplified tasks. Experimentally it can be shown that some tasks are inherently more difficult to process than others and place a greater cognitive load on the person processing them; for example, a simple arithmetic task is easier to process than a difficult arithmetic task, and a simple sentence is harder to process than a complex one (Sanford 2002: 188). Craik and Lockhart (1972) proposed that there are levels of processing, and thus that processing can be at a particular depth. For example, determining how many letters there are in a word requires a shallower level of processing, while determining the meaning of that word requires a deeper level of processing. Craik and Tulving (1975: 271) say that depth of processing often requires longer processing time, while also noting that 'highly familiar stimuli can be rapidly analysed on a complex meaningful level'. Just as tasks vary in what they demand, so individuals vary in the processing effort they put into tasks. As Kahneman (1973) noted, levels of tonic arousal that make us sleepy or alert make a difference in the degree of processing effort expended. Skill in performing a task will also affect processing effort, because a skilled reader for example will put more processing effort into a task; this has the slightly counter-intuitive effect that skilled readers may find a text more difficult than unskilled readers. (I tell my first-year English literature students that if they think a poem is easy to read, it may be because they do not yet really know how to read the poem.)

Difficulty of processing may correlate with the complexity of a text, and the view that complexity plays a role in general aesthetic experience is an old notion in psychology, expressed for example by Wundt (1874) and by Berlyne (1971), both of whom suggest that some middle level of complexity in an aesthetic object is appropriate for optimal aesthetic experience. We might speculate that when a text goes above this middle level of complexity, this might contribute to a strong experience. For example, Longinus (1998: 166) suggests that the sublime can be triggered by hyperbaton, which is an inversion of the normal order of words; an inversion of the normal order of words should require an increase in processing effort from the reader, and this in turn may contribute to the strong experience of the sublime. Hernandez et al. (2013) suggest that increased difficulty of processing can reduce the effect of confirmation bias because disfluency demands more analytic reasoning, and Bullot and Reber (2013: 136) suggest that difficulty and disfluency 'make people think' about the artwork they are perceiving. These two findings suggest that increased processing effort involves more complex cognitive activity, and perhaps metacognitive activity, which I have suggested is an important factor in some strong experiences.

Miall and Kuiken (1994) draw on various notions from Russian Formalism to discuss how the foregrounding of formal properties of a text causes it to be read more slowly, indicating increased difficulty of processing, and they suggest that this in turn leads to strong experience. This is what the Russian Formalists called 'retardation' (Zyngier et al. 2007: 658). They say that 'foregrounding may motivate an attentional pause that allows emergence of related feelings' (Miall and Kuiken 1994: 394). Foregrounding is a way of defamiliarizing the content of the text. Miall (2007: 155, 159) says that 'the sublime represents an extreme mode of defamiliarization', and he says that the poet must use language that 'breaks into and disrupts the reader's standard assumptions', by foregrounding, which thereby conveys a sense of the sublime. Graesser et al. (1998: 249) cite Miall and Kuiken 1994 when they say that '[g]ood literature often creates *defamiliarization* and *epiphany* [...] prototypical concepts and experiences are transformed in an illuminating unfamiliar way by stylistic devices (such as metaphor, irony, hyperbole, understatement), unusual points of view (e.g., viewing the world through the eyes of a dog), and deviations from norms (e.g., a character who never follows social etiquette)'. Oatley (1999: 115) cites Sikora et al. (1998) saying that 'literary expressions that cause defamiliarization and affect make insight more likely', where defamiliarization slows down the reading process. There is supportive experimental research that suggests that texts that offer insight are read more slowly (Cupchik and Laszlo 1994; Cupchik, et al. 1998a, 1998b). Oatley (1999: 112) suggests that defamiliarization is a challenge to a schema, and this challenge requires accommodation. This would make defamiliarization a mechanism for producing surprise, and as we have seen, surprise is the key component of strong experience. The increased processing effort demanded by defamiliarization also relates to Foster and Keane's (2015: 80) theory of surprise. They argue that a subject's perceptions of surprise are raised when the surprising perception must be explained by increased effort. Sperber and Wilson's (1995) relevance theory suggests that hearers are able to unconsciously measure the relative processing effort demanded by a speaker's utterance, such that hearers use increased processing effort as a guarantee that a wider range of meanings are being communicated; increased processing effort leads to a larger range of thoughts, and I have already suggested that this can correlate with feelings of significance and ineffability.

The opposite of the difficulty produced by defamiliarization is fluency or ease of processing. Reber et al. (2004a) define perceptual fluency as 'the subjective experience of ease with which a person can process incoming information'. They show that the feeling of subjective fluency is derived from the actual objectively measurable fluency with which tasks are performed; that is, that subjective fluency is introspectively accurate. The feeling of fluency can be characterized as one of James's fringe experiences. What makes subjective fluency interesting is that it leads to a range of fluency effects, which appear to be the result of a mental heuristic (Reber et al. 2004a, 2004b, Whittlesea and Williams 1998: 160). The more fluently processed text might seem more true, or more familiar, or better liked, and there can be other effects, some involving epistemic feelings. These effects might be connected, via for example the mere exposure effect, which is that people like things if they are familiar (Zajonc 1968, Hogan 2013: 322). This is discussed by Bohrn et al. (2013: 2), Bornstein (1989) and Monin (2003), though familiarity and preference can also be dissociated, as noted by Leder et al. (2004). Bornstein and D'Agostino (1994, cited Huron 2006: 135) suggest that familiarity makes a stimulus easier to process, and it is the ease of processing which leads to liking. Fluency of processing can follow from various characteristics of what is processed. In discourse, repetitive and/or predictable forms in a literary text or in ordinary discourse may enable the language to be more fluently processed (Bohrn et al. 2013: 6).

Consider for example metre and rhyme in poetry of the predictable kind found in a sonnet, where often we know in advance something about the form of a line before we hear the line. For example, we know how many syllables it will have, and what the rhythm is likely to be and where the rhymes are. This means that in principle we are able to process it more easily. It may also be the case that any language-based repetition, even if not predictable, makes processing more fluent because it involves less variation in the course of the text. Parallelism and repetition is another type of form that is widespread in the world's poetic traditions, and even in traditions such as English poetry, unsystematic parallelism and repetition may make the text easier to process, because the variety of what needs to be processed is limited. McGlone and Tofighbakhsh (1999, 2000) describe an experiment that produced the result that aphorisms that rhyme (such as 'an apple a day keeps the doctor away') were considered truer than aphorisms that did not (such as 'rolling stones gather no moss'). Because the rhyme makes the aphorism more fluently processed, a side effect is to make the aphorism seem more true. Another angle on how fluency is produced is suggested by Garry and Wade (2005: 365) on the fluent processing of narratives. They compare narratives and photographs and show that narratives are more likely to elicit false memories than photographs. They suggest that narratives allow the subject to fill in the details of events and that this filled-in information is processed more fluently. This in turn gives the impression that the narrated events are familiar even if they are in fact not, which is one of the standard fluency effects. We might add that other fluency effects might arise as well, including truth and pleasure, just from engaging with narrative.

Some literary strategies increase processing effort, and others decrease processing effort. But a single textual strategy can sometimes engage a reader at the same time both in tasks that increase processing effort and in tasks that decrease processing effort. For, example, a poem which is metrical demands greater processing than a free verse poem, because its literary form is something additional to process. But the metrical poem also produces greater fluency, by making the verbal material more predictable. Similarly, a narrative surprise should present difficulty of processing, since we have to make sense of something which is unexpected; but on the other hand a narrative surprise stimulates faster reading (Cupchik et al. 1998: 378), so in some cases it forces a greater fluency of processing as a result. It is possible that these difficulty-plus-fluency situations are sequenced, such that an initial difficulty is followed by a later fluency, like the contrastive valence which Huron identifies in strong experience.

All of this tells us that both difficulty of processing (and increased processing effort) and fluency of processing (and decreased processing effort) can have potential effects on a reader, which might play a role in producing a strong experience. Furthermore, a change from difficult to easy processing, or vice versa, may also play a role in strong experience, because a change can be a surprise. To explore this further, I begin with an assumption that any change in what is being processed will temporarily increase processing effort, compared with no change. This means that even if the text changes to become more regular, this will increase processing effort. Note the conflict here: a more regular text should be easier to process, but the change to being more regular in itself raises the difficulty of processing, at least momentarily.

In a literary text, changes may happen at formal boundaries, between lines or stanzas or poetic sections, or chapters. It might be a change in event structure, with an event coming to an end and followed by a new event. Zacks et al. (2009: 309) show that readers slow down at event boundaries, which might involve increased processing effort. Schwan and Garsoffky (2004: 52) show that in event sequences where highly relevant breakpoints follow one another in rapid succession, the processing capacity of viewers may break down. And we might speculate that the appearance of a new form such as metricality in a non-metrical poem or the disappearance of a form such as when the rhyme disappears from a previously rhyming poem, are changes which, just because they are changes, should increase processing effort.

Another change might involve the regularity of a poetic form such as iambic pentameter where the relation of meter to rhythm can be more, or less, regular. Either a shift to greater regularity, or a shift to lesser regularity, is a change and therefore involves greater processing effort. In Fabb (2016), I examine Smith's (1968) evidence for the effect of closure at the ends of poems. She says about the endings of some poems that '[t]he sense of stable conclusiveness, finality or "clinch" which we experience at that point is what is referred to here as *closure*' (Smith 1968: 2). The feeling of closure is a psychological effect that can be aligned with James's fringe experiences and perhaps sometimes is a strong experience or leads to a strong experience. In Smith's account, closure is epistemically distinctive, and it comes suddenly, usually in the last few lines of the poem, and so we might see the experience of closure as a strong experience; Wassiliwizky et al. (2017a: 1235) suggest that closure can trigger thrills. The epistemic distinctiveness of closure includes epistemic effects that are ineffable because they involve a knowledge of the unparaphraseable wholeness of the text. Smith argues that closure can be produced by the manipulation of poetic form such as metre or rhyme; the closural part involves a return from relative irregularity to regularity which produces the closure. However, in Fabb (2016) I pick up on Smith's proposal that 'any terminal modification of form will strengthen closure' (Smith 1968: 53), and I argue that Smith's examples show that poems with closure can end with changes which make form less regular, as well as changes which make the form more regular. For this reason, I suggest that closure can arise just because of the change in either direction and that this causes increased processing effort. This increased processing effort may be one of the triggers for strong experience, which is why closure may produce strong experience.

Attention

Attention is a form of processing effort and operates in working memory; it is the allocation of limited resources to specific information. When attention is focused on a specific piece of information, it cannot be allocated elsewhere; we can for example only focus on a limited number of objects within a particular space or during a particular timespan (Chun et al. 2011: 80). Attention can be internal or external. Internal attention focuses on information in 'self-generated thought' (Smallwood 2015: 234, taking the term from Frith). Internal attention operates during mind-wandering, or daydreaming, and during other activities of the default mode network which is operational when the mind is not focused on a specific task. Self-generated thoughts take up about half of our waking experience (Smallwood 2015: 236), and when we recover or reconstruct material from memory, we are focusing internal attention.

Internal attention may be relevant to strong experience. For example, eureka and aha-moments may involve internal attention, as may strong experiences which rely on reconstructing events from memory. Cupchik et al. (2009: 89) say that in aesthetic viewing 'maintaining attention on internally generated cognitions may be an important component of this experience', which again shows that a strong experience may emerge from a background of general aesthetic experience.

In contrast, external attention focuses on information that comes to the subject via the senses from the external environment or from representations presented to the subject, as for example, when reading a novel. Bohrn et al. (2012: 4) suggest that the literary techniques of foregrounding and defamiliarization correlate with increased external attention, as demonstrated by measurements showing increased processing effort in the bilateral frontoparietal attention network.

A balance is generally kept between internal and external attention, managed in working memory, as an interface between external perception and internal long-term memory (Chun et al. 2011: 85). Bruya and Tang (2018) discuss the relation between attention and processing effort, as part of their criticism of Kahneman (1973), who proposed that attention is the same as processing effort. They suggest that in fact there are two kinds of attention. One kind of attention involves focusing on a specific task and involves sympathetic nervous system dominance; it feels effortful and might be identified with processing effort. This is indicated by pupil dilation, which they interpret as a readiness to expend resources. The other kind of attention is the kind of attention involved in meditation, which feels effortless and involves parasympathetic nervous system dominance. Both kinds of attention might be relevant in strong experiences. For example, strong experiences might arise as an end result of curiosity or exploratory behaviour, as when a person seeks out sublime experience and in this case might involve a similar type of parasympathetic and effortless attention found in meditation.

It is possible that objects that trigger epiphany do so by being attended to in a particular way. Panzarella (1980) argues that there is a 'withdrawal ecstasy', where external attention is focused on the aesthetic object, and its surroundings no longer attended to; this decontextualization of the object may be one of the ways in which it becomes discrepant and would be similar to the decontextualization of objects under déjà vu. This suggests that epiphanies might arise from a forced shift in attention. This is exogenous control of attention, when something captures our attention and is involuntary or a reflex. Exogenous attention is transient, and faster to occur than endogenous attention, when we choose to focus on something (Folk 2015: 5–6). Many object epiphanies seem to capture the attention, demonstrating exogenous control. Folk (2015: 15–16) describes some of the external elements which can capture our attention, including when objects come closer or 'loom' up on us, which is one of the causes of surprise and some of its arousal components (Gibson 1958; Chun et al. 2011: 80). Our attention is also captured by rare and unexpected stimuli and rewarding stimuli. It is probable that emotionally charged stimuli capture attention (Chun et al. 2011: 89). On the other hand, it seems that our attention is more likely to be captured by something new if it is also within the range of what we are currently expecting: if we are attending to yellow road signs, then an unexpected yellow object crossing in front of our car will draw our attention better than an unexpected blue object: 'The ability of a stimulus to generate an involuntary shift of attention is contingent on whether the eliciting features match the current top-down control settings' (Folk 2015: 9).

Another relevant topic relating to attention is 'flow'. Flow is a psychological state identified by Csikszentmihalyi (1990), which involves a focus on a challenging task requiring skill, with goals and with immediate feedback from the actions. Flow is usually a state one puts oneself into, and so it is different from the strong experience with its external trigger. Flow is not the same as attention in the general sense of the word, but like focused attention it is a focused activity of the brain in which the default mode network is deactivated. As Silvia (2008) notes in his account of interest as an emotion, there is a relation between Csikszentmihalyi's notion of flow and Berlyne's account of general aesthetic experience which claims that people seek a middle level of novelty and complexity. López-Sintas et al. (2012: 338) distinguish between flow and the 'unforgettable aesthetic experience' before an artwork in a museum. Flow and strong experience are not the same (Privette 1983; Csikszentmihalyi 1990: 251). However, it is possible that strong experiences are potentiated by flow, even if they interrupt the flow. Csikszentmihalyi talks of 'rich epiphanies in response to such simple events as hearing the song of a bird in the forest, completing a hard task, or sharing a crust of bread with a friend'. He quotes a motorcyclist amongst hundreds of motorcycles in Kyoto: 'I understand something, when all of our feelings get tuned up. When running, we are not in complete harmony at the start. But if the Run begins to go well, all of us, all of us feel for the others [...] All of a sudden I realize "Oh we're one"'. This, incidentally, manifests the characteristic individual-in-crowd motif found in some strong experiences.

Attention and Time in Strong Experience

Discussing literary epiphanies, Beja (1971: 231) describes how authors seek to fix 'for all time [...] the throb of one happy moment', preserving 'the adventive Minute', and fixing 'eternally in the patterns of an indestructible form a single moment of man's living'. The epiphany is conceptualized as containing all time within itself (Beja 1971: 217). Bohrer (1994: 217) discusses 'theorists of the moment' such as Robert Musil, Proust with his 'privileged moments', and Browning with his 'good moment'. Arthur Symons in *The Symbolist Movement in Literature* says that '[o]ur real position is made clear to us only in moments of overpowering consciousness which come like blinding light or the thrust of a flaming sword' (Symons 1958: 94). Similarly Walter Pater, in discussion of the school of the Venetian Renaissance painter Giorgione, describes 'exquisite pauses in time, in which, arrested thus, we seem to be spectators of all the fullness of existence, and which are like some consummate extract or quintessence of life' (Pater 1910: 150). This is important to Pater's general philosophy of life, and of art which gives 'nothing but the highest quality to your moments as they pass, and simply for those moments' sake' (Pater 1910: 239). Zemka (2012) argues that reports of time stopping, or indeed of momentariness itself, may depend on social constructions of time, as in an ideology of the significant moment in the nineteenth and twentieth centuries.

Psychology offers another reason why time seems to stop in strong experiences. Attention can alter our perception of time. So the association of attention with strong experiences might have some role in explaining some of their temporal characteristics, at least the slowing of time. Both increased arousal and increased attention to the passing of time produce a perception of time as passing more slowly.

This can be explained by an internal clock model (Gibbon 1977 and Gibbon et al. 1984; the discussion here is based on Gil and Droit-Volet 2012 and Jakubowski et al. 2015, and see Coull et al. 2011 for a revised model). In the internal clock model, a pacemaker in the brain emits pulses at a consistent rate, and we judge a subjective duration in time by counting how many pulses are emitted from the point we start measuring duration to the point we stop measuring duration. When we are aroused, the brain emits pulses more quickly. When we attend to the passing of time we count more of the pulses than if we are distracted. If the matching of objective time and subjective time are compared, the gap between objective time and subjective time is altered when there are more pulses. Relatively speaking, objective time then passes more slowly than subjective time because we seem to be subjectively moving faster through time because more pulses are counted. If we reorient this so that we treat our counting of pulses as always at the same rate, then objective time will seem to have slowed down (Gil and Droit-Volet 2012: 848). Stetson et al. (2007) offer an alternative account, but with the same outcome, that though time might be judged as slower during a frightening event, this temporal slowdown is not experienced while the event is occurring, but is felt retrospectively.

Can these aspects of attention help us understand the focus on the single moment as part of a strong experience? Where the experience involves increased arousal, then it might involve a sense of time slowing, though for very short intervals. If the experience involves attention to duration itself, then duration will be experienced as slowed. By itself this does not explain why time appears to stop or to contain an infinity in a moment. These are best understood as metaphors or ideas about time, rather than a direct experience of time. However, it is possible that the metaphors about time are validated in part by a direct experience of these attention- and arousal-related micro-decelerations in temporal perception.

Delusions and strong experiences

The following narrative of strong experience by an anonymous woman remembering a past experience was used by Laski (1961) as an example of 'ecstasy'.

> In 1916 I was walking along the shore westward out of the Royal Borough of Culross wheeling a pram which contained one child recumbent and one doing everything but lie down. There were three other young children running round me, getting under my feet and asking the silliest questions ... The sun was not shining. I looked across the waters of the Firth of Forth over to the hills hiding the town of Linlithgow, studying the outline against the watery sky, and out of the utter boredom and empty meaninglessness of that afternoon came a stab of knowledge. I *knew* and have known ever since, that there *is* some Reason, some Plan, some Cause, some Soul, call it what you will, which can be relied upon ... For a split second, there upon the shores of the Firth, I *understood*. What I understood I don't know now, but I *know* I understood then and

I have remained firm and calm and unshaken upon that rock – i.e., that once I understood – ever since. I do not say that my whole life was altered from that moment, only say that fear departed and I was left with something firm and secure ... If everything I can think of were taken away this would still remain. Something so infinitely larger, that the rest, though lost, would be of no account. I do not call this a faith. It is not really so active as that, it is *me*. (Laski 1961: 531–532)

This experience may have some aspects in common with the prodromal phase, which can precede what Jaspers (1963) called a primary delusion. This can be characterized in our terms as a strong epistemic feeling in which our experience of the world is transformed (Owen et al. 2004). The delusion can be preceded by a prodromal phase, a phase in which symptoms appear in advance of the full onset of the event:

In prodromal delusional mood, which can last for 'days, months or even years [...] Something is in the air but one is unable to say what.' Jaspers writes: 'Patients feel uncanny[...] that there is something suspicious afoot. Everything gets a *new meaning*. The environment is somehow different.' (Mishara and Fusar-Poli 2013: 281)

Certain reported kinds of strong experience appear to have something like the prodromal phase but without the subsequent psychotic onset, and this may indeed be a way of understanding this narrative on the shore at Culross.

There is a possible explanation of this type of experience in terms of brain chemistry, and specifically the phenomenon of a false prediction error. A prediction error is a neural signal that a perception is discrepant relative to an expectation or prediction. Prediction errors can be 'highly weighted', meaning that they are treated as more significant. This indicates that something relatively unexpected has been perceived, and this prediction error can be propagated up through more complex aspects of cognition, and at some point may be experienced as surprise. A false prediction error has the same meaning, that something discrepant has been perceived, but it is 'false' because it is not a response to a perception but a manifestation of something which has gone wrong, for example a chemical imbalance in the brain, and in particular relating to dopamine which has an important role in coding prediction errors. For example, Fletcher and Frith (2009) note that an excess of the chemical dopamine in the brain can lead to be persistent and highly weighted false prediction errors. The 'learning' that can result from these false prediction errors can however develop into the delusions or hallucinations that appear during psychosis. Schizophrenia, which can involve delusions, can also involve excess dopamine or hyperdopaminergia (Mishara and Fusar-Poli 2013: 283). Mishara and Fusar-Poli say that both reward and salience are signalled by dopaminergic activity. In the early, prodromal phase of a delusion, excessive dopamine activity assigns salience to stimuli which would not normally command it, producing a characteristic prodromal focus on ordinary objects, and perhaps also the overvalued ideas which are characteristic: 'Primary delusions may emerge from the prodromal state as the individual's own explanation of the experience of aberrant salience'. We might wonder whether epiphanies in which ordinary objects are experienced as strange are sometimes produced by false prediction error, and indeed delusions can sometimes begin with a perception of ordinary objects as strange.

Dopamine has been widely implicated both in surprise and in pleasure, and Heilman (2016: 290) suggests that higher levels of dopamine correlate with higher levels of creativity. Drugs can be used to manipulate the activity of dopamine, thereby either reducing or enhancing prediction errors. Some drugs block dopamine receptors and so reduce the effect of dopamine. There are also manipulations in the opposite direction, such as the use of cocaine to make dopamine more available in the brain. William James explored the possibility that what he called mystical experiences could be 'produced by intoxicants and anaesthetics, especially by alcohol', which 'stimulates the mystical faculties of human nature'. James thus allows mystical experiences, which correlate with our strong experiences, to be produced by some internal process which changes our consciousness so that we are able to gain access to a deeper reality. This is what Benjamin Blood had called the 'anaesthetic revelation' (Blood 1874, cited by James), in which on emerging from anaesthetic, the subject knows that 'the genius of being is revealed'. From our perspective, the mystical experiences in this case may arise from false prediction errors generated chemically, which are then misattributed to external triggers. As far as I can tell, there is still no account of how these effects are produced by the anaesthetics which were known to James, such as nitrous oxide, ether or chloroform. However, we do know that a more recently discovered anaesthetic, ketamine, produces the strong epistemic feeling of revelation by raising dopamine levels, which raises the levels of false predictions. It also affects opioid systems, which may also play a role. Ketamine is known to produce aberrant prediction error signals and can also produce empathy, insights, and religious ecstasy (Jansen 2000: 422). Corlett et al. (2006: 617) provide 'behavioral and neurobiological evidence for the existence of a relationship between prediction error-dependent associative learning and the development of delusional beliefs with ketamine'.

The Perception of Objects as Distinctive

In some strong experiences an object takes on a deep significance, as though its inner truth reveals itself. Experiences of this kind are described in Romantic poetry, notably in Wordsworth, as well as in modernist 'epiphanies'. One approach to the experience is to treat it as arising not so much from the object itself, but from some sudden change in how the object is perceived. Stephen sees the clock of the Ballast Office every day, and then something changes in how he perceives it: 'Then all at once I see it and I know at once what it is: epiphany' (Joyce 1944: 188). Here it is not the object itself but his subjective relation to the object which produces the experience. For Bergson (1911: 287) reality is a perpetual becoming, which we are unable to perceive because we perceive reality incorrectly by cutting moments out of time, but we are able by pure perception to place ourselves into the heart of things, transported into the interior of objects. Gerard Manley Hopkins thought that every fact can become an 'epiphany of God' and that it is the mind of the observer which makes this happen, again suggesting that a change in perception might be a source of the schematic discrepancy. Thus he 'inscapes' disparate elements to produce insight into reality.

> before I had always taken the sunset and the sun as quite out of gauge with each other, as indeed physically they are, for the eye after looking at the sun is blunted to everything else and if you look at the rest of the sunset you must cover the sun, but today I inscaped them together and made the sun the true eye and ace of the whole, as it is. It was all active and tossing out light and started as strongly forward from the field as a long stone or boss in the knob of the chalice-stem: it is indeed by stalling it so that it falls into scape with the sky. (Journal March 12 1870, cited Nichols 1987: 84)

The painter de Chirico in 1919 quoted Schopenhauer on moments of insight: 'to have original, extraordinary, and perhaps even immortal ideas, one has but to isolate oneself from the world for a few moments so completely that the most commonplace happenings appear to be new and unfamiliar, and in this way reveal their true essence' (de Chirico 1968: 397). Sometimes, these moments of strangeness are an inspiration to artistic creativity and de Chirico described 'metaphysical moments' in ordinary life when 'I had the strange impression that I was looking at all these things for the first time, and the composition of my picture came to my mind's eye. Now each time I look at this painting I again see that moment. Nevertheless the moment is an enigma to me, for it is inexplicable'.

There are various reasons why an ordinary object should be perceived as distinctive, and so trigger a strong experience. All involve a discrepancy relative to a schema, and thus surprise.

One possible reason is that there is a false prediction error. As explained in the previous section, prediction errors are neural signals that what we perceive is new and different from what we expect. But prediction errors can be triggered incorrectly, for example when there is too much of the neurotransmitter dopamine in the relevant part of the brain; this is what happens in some delusional states, and a delusional state can make ordinary things seem distinctive or weird. Any prediction error, including a false prediction error, can focus attention, making a perceived object more salient, and demanding explanation (Fletcher and Frith 2009: 54). Perhaps by attending to the object more precisely, we change our perceptions of it in a way which makes it radically discrepant relative to its schema, and thus a source of surprise. But all of this may come from a tiny accidental event in the brain, where the prediction error arises incorrectly.

Another possibility is that we perceive the object as the unique manifestation of a schema, so that the token is identical with the type. This is metacognitively surprising for reasons explained earlier, and hence a possible trigger of strong experience. Perhaps this is why unique originals have such an appeal that we seek them out: we want to see the original of the Mona Lisa and not a reproduction, or the original pen with which an important document was signed. What Benjamin (1969) called the 'aura' of unique originals is perhaps their strangeness as tokens which are unique instantiations of their type, and thus identical with them, and so metacognitively surprising. This may all be related to the special attraction which is presented by rare objects, people and events.

An object may be perceived at a high level of granularity, as having details which are not captured by our schematic knowledge of it. These granular properties are unique, aschematic and perhaps if focused on very intensely, they are surprising. Meditative practices such as gazing at an orange for a long time may perhaps induce this effect, by focusing perception on highly granular properties of the object.

An object may fail to match a schema if it involves the aschematic aspects of an episodic memory. Episodic memories are memories of events, and have unique properties, alongside manifesting features which fit into our long-term schematic memory for types of events. Episodic memories can include an autonoetic component, the feel of having been there, and can be vivid and distinctive as in the subtype of episodic memory which is a flashbulb memory. It is possible that the aschematic aspects of episodic memories, if they involve objects, can make those objects distinctive in how they are perceived, as aschematic relative to the schemata we know.

Another possible explanation for why objects appear distinctive can be developed from Kang et al.'s (2017) discussion of what it is for us to become conscious of an object. One way of knowing an object is by what Gibson (1979) called its affordances, which are the ways we interact with the object. My knowledge of the object through its affordances is an unconscious knowing in which the object is interpreted usually relative to me, subjectively. It is however possible for me to come to know the object independently of my subjective relation to it, so that it can be represented as an independent entity. This happens when I talk about the object, which is a conscious way of knowing the object, and involves a change in the perceptual relation to the object. Kang et al. note: 'For example, the location of the object transcends my personal frame of reference, and the object itself seems to possess qualities that are independent of my actions – an essence, as it were'. Perhaps this is one of the ways in which we change in our perception of an object, such that it produces epiphany. In this regard, Kang et al.'s use of the term 'essence' is tantalizing as it suggests some potential profundity in this shift of perception. When we view an object via its affordances, we view the object as it is for us. James's account of strong experience suggests that we can become passive when confronted by an object, and this may correlate with our no longer seeing the object in terms of its affordances. By passivity James means that 'the mystic feels as if his own will were in abeyance, and indeed sometimes as if he were grasped and held by a superior power'. In religious experience generally, McNamara (2009: 143) suggests that there is a feeling of reduction in personal agency which is mediated by a reduction in serotonergic activity which correlates with an increase in dopaminergic activity. Further, perhaps passivity is related to the delusions of control as found for example in schizophrenia, where the body appears to be under the control of another, and which Frith (2005: 171) suggests arises from false prediction error and again correlates with increased dopaminergic activity. All of this suggests that one of the reasons for an object taking on distinctive significance is that we no longer perceive it as under our subjective control. The idea that the object of epiphany is stripped of affordances relates to the possibility that it is also stripped of its context, as in déjà vu, discussed next.

Déjà vu is 'any subjectively inappropriate impression of familiarity of a present experience with an undefined past' (Neppe 1983). The effect resembles epiphanies, because it involves an unusual perception of an ordinary object, and it produces a strange feeling as a result. What is also unusual is that the experience goes against a general schema for experience which tells us that we cannot have exactly the same experience twice, and so the experience is metacognitively surprising. Déjà vu may come from a momentary dissociation of two aspects of memory which are normally combined: familiarity and recall. Cleary (2008: 55) describes an instance of déjà vu where a person enters a room and sees a lamp that has previously been seen in another location, and the sight of the object produces déjà vu. The feeling of familiarity is triggered by the lamp but because the lamp is now in a different context, that exact lamp is not recalled. The experience of familiarity without recall produces déjà vu.

Perhaps some of the epiphanies which are triggered by objects work in the same way; an object may be seen in a way such that it is familiar but unrecalled, perhaps because of its context. To explore this for a moment, consider Stephen's epiphany of the clock in *Stephen Hero*. One way of describing Stephen's experience of the clock is that the clock is defamiliarized, hence strange. But equally we might ask whether it is not the object but the context which is defamiliarized, so that Stephen sees it in a way which takes away the context, leaving the clock as familiar but not recalled. Brown (2003: 404) suggests that if an object is particularly fluently processed, then this will produce a sense of familiarity, but the changed context will prevent its being recalled. Perhaps the clock is fluently processed, making it feel familiar, and perhaps separating it from the background familiarity of the context. Further, the background may be for a moment unattended to, so that the object itself may be harder to retrieve out of its normal context. In all these ways, the perception of the clock might arise from mechanisms similar to déjà vu. A connection with déjà vu may come from their both involving a high prediction error, which arises for example when a familiar object is in an unfamiliar context (van Kesteren et al. 2012), exactly the context for déjà vu.

Déjà vu is a surprising experience, and though it may have a different cause, the feeling of déjà vu is often grouped with the other strong experiences. In his 1902 book, James (1982) included it as a mystical experience, as the feeling 'which sometimes sweeps over us of having "been here before"'. Freud thought that déjà vu was a type of the uncanny (Brown 2004: 13), which I have suggested is a type of strong experience. Cleary (2008: 356) describes the related experience of presque vu ('almost seen') as a feeling that 'one is on the verge of an epiphany'.

Déjà vu is also a rather clear example of an experience whose psychological basis means that it should arise in all humans, but it is not always reported or even apparently known. In this, it is perhaps like other types of strong experience, which may also arise from general human psychology of surprise, but which are not always reported or known. Déjà vu has been reported over the same historical period as other strong experiences, from at least Walter Scott onwards, though the term itself was first used late in the nineteenth century and came into general use from the mid twentieth (Brown 2004: 11). But Enfield and Zuckerman (2024) show that Lao speakers (in Laos) do not recognize the experience when it is described to them. Borrowing from Levy (1973: 324), they suggest that this is an instance of hypocognition where a concept is 'underthought'. So, like strong experiences, déjà vu has a specific history, but it is also a psychological universal always potentially capable of appearing and being recognized and reported.

Empathy

Empathy is a response to another person, animal or object and may play a role in some strong experiences. As Decety (2009) notes, it has two parts, emotional and cognitive, consisting of an emotional response to the other and perhaps a sharing of their emotion, and the cognitive ability to take someone else's perspective, drawing on metarepresentational capacity.

Empathy is part of our experience of being transported into a narrative, where we are both in and not in the fictional space, and both part and not part of the fictional events. Koopman (2015: 74, following Mar) suggests that trait empathy is a personality variable which may have developed more strongly because of exposure to narratives. An important finding about empathy is that we seem to be as capable of empathy with a fictional character as with a real person (Koopman 2015: 76), and this relates to Gerrig's point that we do not have a special psychology for fiction as opposed to fact. Tangerås (2020: 179) notes that Emily, one of his readers whose life has been changed by a book is 'saying that first you experience empathy from the book, and then that makes you more empathic towards others', and Emily replies 'Yes. Empathy with oneself and with other'.

We can however also relate to characters in narratives without empathizing with them. For example, we can understand characters by taking their perspective but without taking on their emotions. Magliano et al. (2013: 79) discuss our ability to understand a character's goals, without necessarily empathizing with them, though empathy can play a role. Understanding goals involves understanding when goals are reached, and this is important for establishing narrative boundaries. Strong experiences can cluster around narrative boundaries. Radvansky and Zacks (2014: 21) say that a reader will create richer conceptualizations of fictional characters which are interconnected with many other characters, drawing on the assumption that entities with many causal connections are more important for understanding the narrative. That richer conceptualization involves a conceptualization of the characters' emotions, at least to sympathetically understand them, if not to empathize with them. Our ability to sympathize involves our metacognitive and metarepresentational abilities, which I have already argued play a role in strong experiences. Gerrig (1993) describes 'participatory responses', in which the subject relates to the action as a side-participant, which means that they feel as though they are a character within the fiction but suppress any actual behaviour such as jumping onto a theatre stage to intervene. In this case, the subject has their own emotional responses, not those of the characters. Bezdek et al. (2013: 409) argue that participatory responses influence one's expectations about goals, such that for example dispreferred outcomes for a character are read more slowly, perhaps indicating greater processing effort, and we have seen that changes in processing effort can play a role in generating strong experiences. Thus in many ways, empathy has characteristics which are shared with strong experience.

Empathy seems to play a specific role in triggering some strong experiences. Strong experiences often begin with surprise, and so it is worth asking whether there is a relation between empathy and surprise. Perhaps our experience of empathy is a contradictory experience of being both oneself and another person. This should be an experience which is discrepant relative to our deeply embedded schemata for experience, and so surprising and schematically discrepant. If this is correct, then it suggests that though we have evolved the capacity for empathy, we are not born with knowledge about it: the possibility of empathy has not yet been embedded as one of the basic schemata for experience.

As Kuiken and Douglas (2017) and others have argued, empathy is thus a bit like metaphor, because it involves a gap between two items, here between the self and the other, where there is an apparent bridge between the two, where one both *is and is not* the other. This non-identity, the *is and is not*, cannot be resolved or schematized; it remains ineffable. This is similar to some theories of the sublime, where the sublime comes from a dangerous event or object viewed from a place of safety, where there is relation between us and the sublime object, but it cannot be bridged. In Kant's terms, we have access to it through the application of reason (i.e., metacognition), but it cannot be understood, not accommodated to a schema, and so not taken into ourselves. There is also evidence that empathy is sensitive to narrative surprises. Hein et al. (2016: 80) use a prediction error account to show that a subject's empathy for an out-group member is increased if the out-group member behaves in a way which is both surprising and positive. In their experiment, empathy is a positive behaviour towards the experiencing subject. However, we might wonder whether empathy towards a fictional character is significantly increased if they behave in a surprisingly positive way, if for example a villain is transformed. In this case, empathy is a consequence of the surprise and is appraised as part of the elaboration of the surprise into a strong experience.

The pleasure in a strong experience may sometimes depend in part on the pleasures of empathy which in turn can involve oxytocin, a neurotransmitter brain chemical which is rewarding. Oxytocin functions to increase prosocial behaviours such as social cognition and empathy (Bos et al. 2012: 24), and is involved in sexual and romantic love. Zak (2015: 2–3) says that 'if you treat me well, in most cases my brain will synthesize oxytocin and this will motivate me to treat you well in return'. Zak (2015) argues that a viewer's changing concern for characters in a story correlates with the changes in the neurotransmitter oxytocin in the brain, which is known to be involved in empathy with real people, but seems also be involved in empathy for represented people. Injection of oxytocin has been shown to increase concern for represented characters and can lead for example to prosocial behaviour such as giving to a charity after viewing a narrative about a child with cancer. In an experiment, Barraza et al. (2015) found that the degree of a viewer's autonomic arousal, both sympathetic and parasympathetic, was in an experiment found to correlate positively with whether they were likely to take empathetic action (such as giving money away). Oxytocin may be particularly implicated in female social behaviour and may be involved in the tend-and-befriend pattern, an alternative response pattern to fight–flight–freeze. This all raises the possibility that an increase in oxytocin might also correlate with having a strong experience.

In Thomas Weiskel's psychoanalytically inspired approach to the sublime, the experience of the sublime involves the disruption of normal perception by a surprising excess, which leads the mind to form a new relationship with the excessive object (Weiskel 1976: 23–24). For Morley (2010: 17), 'the sublime defines the moment when thought comes to an end and we encounter that which is "other"'. There is a longstanding tradition of allowing that distinctive kinds of experience might involve empathy with inanimate objects; the English word 'empathy' is a translation of German *Einfühlung*, a term which can describe bodily mimicry of a work of art which becomes an emotional response, for example when people imitate statues when looking at them (Kreitler and Kreitler 1972). Oatley (1994: 56) notes that Eliot's 'objective correlative... the formula of that *particular* emotion' is a development of these ideas, whereby the reader projects themselves into the artwork. Alfred Gell (1998) noted that sometimes people respond to artworks, particularly those which represent living beings such as statues, as though they are alive. Gell says that these artworks have 'agency' without being animate, which Van Eck (2010) argues is a paradoxical combination which produces the effect of the sublime. In our terms this is because it is metacognitively surprising, because of the violation of deeply embedded schematic knowledge about the world. The sublime arises from the combining of two things which are both different and the same, on an uncertain ground which connects them. Van Eck refers back to Burke and claims that the sublime comes from 'the struggle of the mind to reconcile conflicting ideas that are presented in poetry as a unity, or comprehend something that surpasses its understanding'. The experience of what Gell called the 'agency' of artworks is thus itself a type of the sublime.

Freedberg (1989) presents a discussion of intense responses to visual art, manifested by emotion, as well as by acts, such as violently attacking the artwork. His fundamental claim is that the power of the artwork which causes these effects comes from the fact of representation itself, where for example an image resembles a person. The power can be made stronger by acts of ritual consecration, but it is there in the image itself; and Freedberg argues that a copy of an original can also have deep power. In this, Freedberg disagrees with Benjamin (1969), who thought that the copy loses its essential aura. The possibility of profound experience in front of the image depends on 'an attentiveness particularized in terms of the intimate experience of the beholder [... who ...] directs his meditations to those aspects which are most likely to rouse a strong sense of fragility or tragedy'. So Freedberg traces the strong response to an artwork to external attention, and emotion framed within a narrative which is both social in the consecration of the artwork and part of the personal emotional life. However in his book and in his neuroaesthetic work (e.g., Freedberg and Gallese 2007), Freedberg emphasizes automatic emotion responses and de-emphasizes cognition. His claim that the mimicry of the image is itself experientially strange fits with my general proposal that aesthetic and representational practices are inherently odd, and generally metacognitively surprising, in a way which can result in strong experience.

Why Do People Vary in Whether and When They Get Strong Experiences?

Whether someone gets a strong experience in a particular situation, and what kind of experience it is, is subject to a great deal of variation. In this section, I consider some of the relevant factors which lead to this variation. The following are the three major dimensions of variation: within the same individual at different times, between different individuals and between individuals who belong to different cultures and time-periods. As an example of variation within the same individual, here is the painter Graham Sutherland's description of an experience of the 'epiphany' type (it was quoted earlier in Kenneth Clark's account of moments of vision):

> When one goes for a walk there is everything around one; but one reacts to certain things only, as in response to some personal need of the nerves. The reaction varies; I may have noticed a certain juxtaposition of forms at the side of a road, but on passing the same place next time, I

might look for them in vain. It was only at the original moment of seeing that they had significance for me. (Sutherland 1953)

As an example of variation between individuals, there is extensive evidence from the experimental study of thrills that the same piece of music can cause thrills in one person and not in another and that the thrill is manifested as different arousals in different people. As another example, in Joyce's novel *Stephen Hero*, Stephen gets epiphanies from ordinary objects but Cranly does not. As an example of variation between cultures, we might note that the various kinds of strong experience are more commonly reported in the eighteenth century than before; this is when people start talking more about the sublime, and when certain physical sensations such as chills are more widely mentioned. Epiphanic experiences of ordinary objects become more widely reported in fictions of the nineteenth century and even more in the twentieth century. It is generally possible, and strongly implied by what we know of cultural variation in concepts of experience, that some of the kinds of strong experience are more recognizable in some cultures than in others, and may be divided differently into kinds in different cultures. It may be that the notion of a strong experience, or a particular kind of strong experience such as the sublime, is in a specific culture what Levy (1973) calls 'hypocognized', that is, not generally reported or discussed, and without a terminology.

This variation needs to be set against the basic claim of this book, which is that strong experiences are the result of surprise, where surprise has the same psychological structure for all humans. Other relevant aspects such as the ability to engage in metacognition and metarepresentation or the ability to think about other people and imagine how they are thinking and feeling (i.e., theory of mind and empathy) are also general human abilities. Everyone in our species has the basic psychological components which make strong experience possible. So the problem is to explain why, given the same basic components, the experiences which are built on those components can nevertheless be so variable.

Consider the trigger of a strong experience, which must be perceived if the experience is to occur. But if for example that trigger is an object, then different people may perceive the same object in different ways, some of which may be more likely to trigger strong experience. The Dublin Ballast Office clock triggers Stephen's epiphany (Joyce 1944: 188). This same object can trigger an epiphany once for Stephen, but not for him at another time, and never for another person such as his friend Cranly. Why these differences? Perhaps the object is seen differently, or the context might be different. The clock might be mentally represented in any of a number of different ways, some invoking the powerful symbolic associations of time, and any of which different perspectives on the clock might be the actual trigger, rather than the object in itself. Perhaps some other factor, not mentioned in the description, also plays a role in the epiphany, such as the location of the real-life clock above a doorway, an important liminal trigger for strong experiences, but not mentioned in the text. Furthermore, though one trigger is named, there may be multiple components which together constitute the trigger. Turpin and Fabb (2018) hypothesize a cause for the epistemic feeling of 'brilliance' caused by ritual practices in Australian Aboriginal culture (Morphy 1989). We noted that in many cases, a ritual event involves the simultaneous presentation of many discrete component parts, and that the attempt to attend to all at the same time, hence with high processing effort, might produce an epistemic experience, here the effect of brilliance. It is not one element which is the trigger but the combination of factors which constitutes the trigger.

The second point to consider is the role of context in whether a strong experience is triggered. This might be environmental context, textual context, cognitive context including what the subject has been thinking about, and bodily context such as a background arousal state of alertness or sleepiness. Another factor is whether the person is alone, or in a crowd, or even alone while in a crowd, for example moving in the opposite direction through a moving crowd. Any of these might play a factor, though some theorists have argued that aloneness is crucial. Thus Laski (1961: 177) says that people are more likely to get ecstasies when they are alone and that crowds are an 'anti-trigger'; she cites Gerard Manley Hopkins, 'even with one companion ecstasy is almost banished; you want to be alone to feel that'. On the other hand, crowds – including crowds of objects – are a common motif in literary descriptions of strong experience.

People also differ from one another, and it is possible that individual characteristics play a role in whether someone will get a strong experience, just as these characteristics play a role in whether someone experiences an emotion (Scherer 2009b: 1329). Polito et al. (2010: 919) comment on this:

> In shamanic rituals such as the sweat lodge some participants may describe profound emotional or even visionary experiences while others report experiencing little more than slight relaxation or agitation. Factors which might explain this variation include any of the myriad of psychological concepts that have been used to describe the enduring characteristics of a person; beliefs, affect, personality, attachment, intelligence, health, or physical conditioning, for example.

Dixon and Bortolussi (2015) discuss why two people will read the same text in different ways, attending to different things, mind-wandering to a greater or lesser extent and at different places, being differentially able to construct the represented world, and so on; and that this can be both an individual variation, but also a variation just depending on contextual factors. There is also extensive evidence that level of expertise can affect experience of literary texts (Hanauer 1995), the granularity of our perceptions (Cohen 2000: 11), and the pleasure we get from objects (Kirk et al. 2009: 314). Expertise might thus potentiate strong experience. Further, the narrative of the self and the self-construct (Rathbone et al. 2011) may play a role in making an experience into a strong experience.

Biological differences between people might be relevant in whether and when they get strong experiences. This includes genetic differences relating to dopaminergic and serotonergic activity, which contribute to the trait of religiosity (McNamara 2009), and perhaps might contribute to the potential to have strong experiences. Individuals have stable patterns of heart rate variability as controlled by the parasympathetic and sympathetic systems across time, which may be biological markers of personality traits. Čukić and Bates (2014) note the correlation between a certain component of heart rate variability and openness to experience and add that this correlates with the experience of chills. They comment on Blood and Zatorre's (2001) finding that there is increased blood flow in brain areas associated with reward and motivation, emotion and arousal, in correlation with the intensity of chills, and indirectly suggest that this might relate to sympathetic heart rate variation.

Another relevant factor is the level of respiratory sinus arrhythmia (RSA). This is a variability in heart rate, controlled by the parasympathetic system, which depends on whether the subject is inhaling or exhaling; inhalation causes an increase in heart rate, and exhalation a decrease in heart rate. RSA is inversely correlated with changes in external attention; decreased RSA correlates with increased external attentional engagement (Ravaja 2004: 221). Individuals differ in the degree of variation in RSA when in a resting state, as one part of their resting physiological arousal. Having a high RSA correlates with swift modulation of cardiac activity and emotional response and is 'indicative of physiological flexibility and a greater capacity for adaptive regulation and social engagement' (Mori and Iwanaga 2014: 220). Mori and Iwanaga show that people with a low RSA more frequently experience music-induced chills. Possibly people with low resting RSA can anticipate the structure of familiar music but have difficulty changing external attention quickly and sudden acoustic changes consequently violate their expectations. A similar correlation exists for people with a higher resting skin conductance level (SCL), who more frequently experience music-induced chills. A higher resting SCL correlates with persistent anxiety, and so is seen generally as negative. The theory is that higher SCL decreases activation in the prefrontal cortex, which leads to tonic disinhibition of the amygdala. The amygdala in turn has a bias towards negative arousing responses to uncertainty, novelty and threat. One interest of these findings is to raise again the question of whether chills and more generally strong experiences are underlyingly negative phenomena, which become positive. Sachs et al. (2016) argue that the volume of white matter connectivity between areas of the brain correlates with the experience of chills in response to music; these three areas are 'the auditory perceptual regions (posterior superior temporal gyrus) and regions of the brain important for emotional and social processing (anterior insula, and medial prefrontal cortex)'.

Gender may be relevant. Panksepp (1998: 278) claims that females are more likely to get chills from sad triggers and builds this into his theory. One theoretical reason for thinking that there might be a difference at least in terms of arousal between men and women relates to the proposal that while males respond with fight and flight responses which emphasize sympathetic autonomic activity, females respond with tend-and-befriend responses which downregulate sympathetic autonomic activity (Taylor et al. 2000), and in principle this might affect strong experiences by gender. However, evidence for gender-based differences is not very extensive. I do not know of any evidence that age plays a role in getting a strong experience; Laski (1961: 136) explores Wordsworth's view that children are more likely to have ecstasies than adults and finds no evidence for it in the data she gathered.

Personality traits may differentiate people in terms of whether they get strong experiences, such as the trait of openness to experience (McCrae 2007; Nusbaum et al. 2014; Colver and El-Alayi 2016). Getting chills is the best single marker of openness to experience, according to McCrae and Costa (1997). Mar et al. (2009: 409–410) associate openness to experience with imaginative tendencies, curiosity, intellectual endeavours and creativity. Sachs et al. (2016) similarly found that measures of openness to experience correlated with chills in their experiment. Grewe et al. (2007: 211) characterize chill responders as showing a preference for less intensive stimuli, they are not thrill and adventure seekers, and they are more reward dependent: they especially like approval and positive emotional input from their environment. Maruskin et al. (2012: 140) suggest that different impression management tendencies may make people overstate or understate their subjective experience of chills. Appel and Richter (2010) describe what Maio and Esses (2001) call 'the need for affect' as a personality trait; the magnitude of a person's need for affect determines whether and to what extent the person experiences transportation into the story world and is persuaded by the information presented in the narrative. Another personality type is the high sensation seeker (Jensen et al. 2011: 541). High sensation seekers 'have a low baseline level of arousal and appear to be drawn to dramatic, novel, explicit, and emotionally complex stimuli and experiences'. On the other hand, this trait also correlates with low empathy, and yet empathy is involved in some of these experiences. Sumpf et al. (2015: 3–4) found higher levels of the personality trait of extraversion in the group of people who experienced more chills. Conway and Pleydell-Pearce (2000) discuss the role of the construction of the self and cite McAdams et al. (1997) on different trait types relative to how they understand peak experience.

The Problems with Introspection

Almost everything we know about strong experiences comes from the experiencer's own report, which is based on introspection. For fictional versions of the experiences, authors might in some cases be drawing on their own experiences, and so these have some inherited authenticity as reports of actual experience. However, we are not always correct when we report our own experience, our own feelings or our own mental processes (Wildman and McNamara 2010; Whaley et al. 2009: 458–459). As I. A. Richards (1926: 126) said in his pioneering account of problems in literary reading 'the facts which introspection yields are notoriously uncertain, and the special position of the observer may well preclude success'. Nisbett and Wilson (1977) argue that we have poor introspective access to the causal sequences by which we produce judgements, while noting that we have reasonably good introspective access to our mental states. This means that people do not have good introspective access into how they make inferences, either what the critical stimuli are or how they have responded to these stimuli, or even whether they have engaged in inferences at all. They suggest that we observe our own mental processes in the same way we observe other people's mental processes, as though we do not have a privileged access to our own mental processes (Nisbett and Wilson 1977: 250). Schwitzgebel (2016) says that 'both psychologists and philosophers now tend to accept Nisbett's and Wilson's view that there is at best only a modest first-person advantage in assessing the factors influencing our judgements and behavior'. This is the first of several unresolvable problems which are faced by any study of strong experiences, or indeed for the study of experience in general including aesthetic experience and the experience of literature, and there are more of the same kind as I now discuss.

Confirmation bias is a subject's unconscious bias towards selecting facts which support her pre-existing beliefs, particularly in reasoning (Nickerson 1998), and it presents another problem for the reliability of reports of strong experience. It derives from an innate heuristic, which works against hesitation and so helped our prey ancestors survive any predator which one hunted us (Mercier and Sperber 2011). We are not consciously aware of confirmation bias and have difficulty avoiding it, though it is more likely to have an effect in some circumstances than others. Related psychological factors are the primacy and recency effects where information which is acquired either early or late (but not in the middle) carries more weight (Bower 2000: 16). Another is belief persistence: even compelling counter-evidence cannot change beliefs once they are formed. Experimental studies (Nickerson 1998) have shown that the confirmation bias can arise when a person restricts the information they use to that which fits with a favoured hypothesis, as well as preferential treatment of evidence supporting one's beliefs, looking mainly for positive cases, giving too great a weight to positive confirmatory instances, and in general, seeing what one is looking for. Confirmation bias is relevant here because many cited examples of strong experience come from people who know or are told what to look for, for example via a questionnaire, and who may have a pre-existing theory of what a strong experience is. Evidence from authors also falls into this category, because an author's representation of an experience will to some extent be intertextual with and influenced by other authors' representation of experience, or draws on their own already-formed theory. This is an example of how we are subject to the influence of implicit a priori theories of how stimulus and response are connected, where those theories may be culturally learned, and may be incorrect. The further removed in time from the experience, the more stereotyped the account of it.

Robert Levy's (1973) notion of hypercognition is relevant: 'A hypercognitive concept is salient and woven extensively, perhaps too much, into people's explanatory schemes of objects and events' (Wu et al. 2018: 30). Similarly, Laski (1961: 20) uses William James's term 'over-belief' to characterize the culturally specific interpretations of ecstasies. James (1982: 431) says that over-beliefs are 'buildings-out performed by the intellect into directions of which feeling originally supplied the hint', such that we start with a feeling and develop a religion from it. For example, when a subject says that they feel 'as if being borne into heaven itself', Laski suggests that the 'heaven' part of the experience is part of the overbelief, the interpretation of a particular emotion by someone who has particular religious beliefs and uses them to interpret the experience. Strong experiences are not reported to the same extent in all cultural contexts, and different kinds of strong experience are more commonly reported at some times than others. This suggests that the absence of strong experiences in many contexts may be a result of hypocognition, where the lack of a coherent concept of the experience means that the experience does not occur in a coherent way which is culturally recognizable. Most of the examples in this book come from a narrow cultural and historical range. The variability in reporting strong experiences may arise partly because of the role of culture in shaping our schematic knowledge, and hence our memories and our assessment of our own emotions. Cultural difference will also influence the extent to which we report our experiences, and what we report of them. Almost all the evidence we have of strong experience, with the possible exception of some thrills, is heavily determined by cultural context.

Another reason for worrying about the reliability of accounts of strong experiences comes from the classic study of mis-remembering by Bartlett (1932), from which the notion of 'schema' as used in this book was developed. Bartlett argued that memories are new constructions based on our schematic knowledge. Our memories are not direct copies of our experience of past events which we have retrieved from a memory store, even though this is how a memory introspectively feels. Because we construct our memories anew, this means that our knowledge of past events can change without our being aware of it. It might mean that when people report on their strong experience, they do so partly based on schematic expectations about what these experiences should be and how they are structured. The specificities of the event may be absorbed into a generic narrative. Furthermore, strong experiences are emotional events, and Robinson and Clore (2002) show that there are discrepancies between reports of emotions at the moment of experience as opposed to emotions as remembered, as well as prospective or hypothetical reports of emotion. This is because 'an emotional experience can neither be stored nor retrieved' (Robinson and Clore 2002: 935). The further in time we are from the remembered emotion, the greater the role of biases, heuristics and beliefs in constructing what that emotion was. Furthermore, even while we are experiencing an emotion, we have comparably poor access to our own bodily reactions, and so will draw on schematic beliefs about emotion and arousal in describing our own arousal: 'reports of physiological responding are largely constructed on the basis of situation-specific beliefs' (Robinson and Clore 2002: 925).

A further problem for the reliability of reports of strong experience comes from the fact that that we are constitutionally poor at judging causation, and so are liable to misattribute an experience to a trigger which did not in fact cause it. Edmund Burke (1987: 45) describes a kind of misattribution:

> I am afraid it is a practice much too common in inquiries of this nature, to attribute the cause of feelings which merely arise from the mechanical structure of our bodies, or from the natural frame and constitution of our minds, to certain conclusions of the reasoning faculty on the objects presented to us; for I should imagine, that the influence of reason in producing our passions is nothing near so extensive as it is commonly believed.

Similarly, we make incorrect judgements of how mood is caused (Robinson and Clore 2002: 9). A classic psychological account of misattribution is by Dutton and Aron (1974), in which they showed that subjects attributed arousal to a trigger which was almost certainly not the actual trigger. This is a problem for the reliability of self-report and has consequences for the reporting of strong experiences, though it also produces its own interesting effects.

Thus Huron (2006: 138), following Dutton and Aron's experiment, argues that misattribution plays an important role in how we judge causation and identify triggers of arousal when listening to music. For example, if we are expecting a certain pitch, and we hear that pitch, we experience pleasure because our expectation is met, but we attribute the pleasure to the pitch itself as the trigger, rather than to its actual triggering role in satisfying our expectations. Huron cites the music psychologist Carl Seashore, writing in 1938, who noted that listeners hear things which are not in the music and fail to hear things which are. Huron (2011: 147) concludes that 'psychological research suggests that introspection can be highly inaccurate, especially when people are asked to identify the causes of feeling states'. One of the interesting errors we characteristically make in attribution of causes is that we find it difficult to accept that trivial causes can lead to major effects. But literary epiphanies are apparently major effects from trivial causes, and perhaps our metacognitive reflection on this in itself produces a schematic discrepancy, a feeling of surprise at a causal sequence which should not exist. Thus the experience of having an epiphany could in itself be a cause of a further strong experience.

Evidence for arousal comes from subjective report and from objective observation. Objective observation of arousal in the body almost always involves measurement from organs such as skin or heart, some more invasive than others. Objective observation is possible for easily stimulated arousal experiences such as chills in response to music, but almost impossible for the significant epistemic aspects of strong experiences, both because there is little to measure, and because these experiences are rare. Subjective report is not necessarily reliable either, and there is a further issue which is that symbolic imaginings of the body come into play. Housman's claim that he cannot shave properly because his hair raises when he thinks of a line of Keats is also a demonstration of his masculinity. When Emerson (1850) says 'we cannot read Plutarch without a tingling of the blood' it is unclear whether blood in this sense is metaphorical rather than a physiological description. The same might be said of Nabokov's notion of reading with the spine as 'the true reader's main organ' (Nabokov 1972: 72):

Although we read with our minds, the seat of artistic delight is between the shoulder blades. That little shiver behind is quite certainly the highest form of emotion that humanity has attained with evolving pure art and pure science. Let us worship the spine and its tingle. (Nabokov 1982: 64)

Here we might wonder whether 'spine' is also used in a more metaphorical or symbolic sense, particularly as Nabokov explicitly opposes it to the brain, with the hardness of bone against the softness of brain. As another example, here is Helen Maria Williams, looking at a cataract, where it is unclear to what extent the heart is symbolic and to what extent her real bodily organ:

Never, never can I forget the sensations of that moment! when with a sort of annihilation of self, with every past impression erased from my memory, I felt as if my heart were bursting with emotions too strong to be sustained. – Oh, majestic torrent! which hast conveyed a new image of nature to my soul, the moments I have passed in contemplating thy sublimity will form an epocha [sic] in my short span! – thy course is coeval with time, and thou wilt rush down thy rocky walls when this bosom, which throbs with admiration of thy greatness, shall beat no longer! (Helen Maria Williams *A Tour in Switzerland* 1798: 60–61, cited in Ashfield and de Bolla 1996: 304)

The heart is certainly involved in some strong experiences, for example, where heart rate increases or decreases, but descriptions involving the heart are subject to a heavy symbolic load relating to ideas about the heart and emotion. Thus Albertus Magnus's *Metaphysics* (c.1260) says that wonder is 'shocked surprise [*agoniam*] and a suspension of the heart in amazement [*stupore*] before the sensible appearance of a great prodigy, so that the heart experiences systole. Thus wonder is somewhat similar to fear in the motion of the heart' (cited in Daston and Park 2001: 112). But to what extent is this a description of arousal and to what extent a symbolic account of the body?

The research discussed in this section has shown that we must rely on introspection in order to know about strong experiences, whether our own or other people's. There are many reasons to be cautious about the evidence that introspection can produce. There is no way to escape this, however, if we want to try to understand our experiences, including our strong experiences.

Summary of Chapter

This chapter has explored various aspects of ordinary psychology and suggested ways in which an ordinary experience can occasionally become a strong experience. We have seen that aspects of processing effort, in working memory, and involving also focused attention, may play a role in strong experiences. Of the three basic kinds of strong experience, the sublime and the thrill are the two which are easiest to explain in terms of emotional responses, but the epiphany is the most puzzling. We have seen that there are various ways in which the epiphanic experience of ordinary objects can arise. The object may be perceived as not fitting into its schema, perhaps because it is perceived as unique and thus not having a schema to fit into. This uniqueness in turn might involve its being perceived at some level of granularity below the level of generalization, or by false prediction error, or as stripped of its affordances or stripped of other contextual characteristics in a way reminiscent of déjà vu. Empathy appears to play a role in some strong experiences, and again there are various routes by which this could arise. The chapter concludes by noting that evidence for any kind of experience, given its subjective and introspective basis, is unreliable; and by noting some of the factors which might make a strong experience arise for one person but not another.

Chapter 6

HOW LITERATURE TRIGGERS STRONG EXPERIENCES

In this chapter, I show that the ordinary characteristics of literary texts have the capacity to set in motion the various triggers for strong experience. These same characteristics which peak in strong experiences also give literary texts their continuous epistemic characteristics and produce feelings of mild arousal.

Literature and Strong Experiences

Literature is relevant for the study of strong experiences for two reasons. First, people can have strong experiences triggered by literary texts. Emily Dickinson defined poetry by its ability to cause a thrill:

> If I read a book [and] it makes my whole body so cold no fire can warm me I know that is poetry. If I feel physically as if the top of my head were taken off, I know that is poetry. These are the only way I know it. (Johnson and Ward 1958: L342a/1870)

Second, literary texts can represent characters as having strong experiences. Here for example is a fictionalized account by Kate Chopin of a character responding to music with thrills:

> The very first chords which Mademoiselle Reisz struck upon the piano sent a keen tremor down Mrs. Pontellier's spinal column. It was not the first time she had heard an artist at the piano. Perhaps it was the first time she was ready, perhaps the first time her being was tempered to take an impress of the abiding truth.
>
> She waited for the material pictures which she thought would gather and blaze before her imagination. She waited in vain. She saw no pictures of solitude, of hope, of longing, or of despair. But the very passions themselves were aroused within her soul, swaying it, lashing it,

as the waves daily beat upon her splendid body. She trembled, she was choking, and the tears blinded her. Chopin (1899: ch.9).

Sometimes an author will describe a character's experience, and this may also be a kind of indirect report if the character's experience is based on a real experience known to the author. Because all reports of strong experience are unverifiable, the distinction between real and fictional reports is not as important as it might be.

The two sides of literature as 'trigger of strong experience' and literature as 'representation of strong experience' may combine when a character has a strong experience which triggers a strong experience in the reader. This is an example of the 'catching' of the strong experience. Beja (1971: 231–232) says that 'the artist attempts not merely to record epiphanies but also to produce or reproduce them too – in James's phrase, to "render" them; "to produce the most momentary illusion"'. Losey (1999: 379) says that 'to convey this magical power, the writer must not only dramatize it within his narrative but also transform it so that the reader can share the revelation'.

The Inherent Surprisingness of Literature

Strong experiences always emerge suddenly from our ongoing experience, and it is worth asking whether the ongoing experience already has the component elements which make the suddenly different strong experience possible. In particular, we might ask whether aesthetic objects including literary texts have characteristics which increase the probability of strong experiences in the reader or experiencer. All of the possible triggers in literature which are discussed in this chapter are quite common in literary texts. But there are some general characteristics of literary texts which are discrepant relative to our schematic knowledge of the world, and this discrepancy may play a role in making literary texts affect us as they do, not just in the moments of strong experience but more generally. It may be that the minor discrepancies which are continuous features of literary language give us an ongoing mild sense of surprise, a kind of mood of surprise as opposed to a sudden burst of surprise.

The language of literature is often unlike the everyday language which we find outside literature. For example, literary language can have forms added to it, such as lineation in poetry, rhyme or metre, and these can further alter the language by forcing changes in word order or omission of words. In Fabb (2009) I suggest that the language of poetry is sometimes not language at all, but a mimicry of language. These aspects all suggest that the language of literature is discrepant relative to our schematic knowledge of language in general. The schemata we learn about literary language are superficial in comparison with more deeply rooted schemata for ordinary (non-literary) language. This means that literary language is discrepant in a way that we can never quite accommodate to, and so it always slightly surprises us.

Consider also the slightly strange content of literature, for example in literary narratives, though the same is true of many kinds of narrative. Literary narratives are fictional sequences of events which resemble what we know of sequences of events in the world, involving human agency and causation. But there is usually a difference: the literary narratives have simple and easy-to-understand causal sequences and they may follow arcs from beginning to end, such that narratives have closure, but this is unlike many real-life sequences of events. Again, though we can learn schemata for features of literary narrative including for closure, these schemata may be in competition with more deeply rooted schemata which constitute our knowledge of event sequences in reality, so that literary narratives are always slightly discrepant relative to our basic knowledge of the world. Furthermore, literary narratives may be guided by, or allude to, other literary narratives, in which case the relation between the narrative and any real world is further distanced and made strange.

A related characteristic of literary and other aesthetic narrative is that it can take its events and characters from another pre-existing narrative. This is a further source of discrepancy, both from the mismatches between the new narrative and the pre-existing narrative and from the inherent mismatches between both narratives and our schemata for reality. I can illustrate this from a film narrative, Sally Potter's *The Roads Not Taken* (2020) whose narrative and characters both belong to Homer's *Odyssey* and to Joyce's *Ulysses*. The film, though it appears to tell a potentially true story about a day in a life of a man (Leo) with limited capacity after a stroke, accompanied by his daughter (Molly), is also all of these other narratives and characters at the same time, and thus multiply distanced from any possibly real narrative. The events of the film are matched to schemata drawn from other texts, as well as to schemata drawn from our knowledge of reality, and so discrepancies abound. In this way, the film generates an aesthetic from the multiple discrepancies which an aesthetic narrative makes possible.

A further characteristic of the schematic discrepancy of any fiction relates to fictional characters (or indeed any object within a fiction). Fictional characters are similar to real people in certain ways, but there are at least two key differences. First, fictional characters are much less interconnected with other characters/people than real people are, and with events, and places, and exist within small and clearly bounded contexts (Abraham and von Cramon 2009). Second, we know things about fictional characters, notably what they are thinking, which are impossible to know about real people. Fictional characters are thus discrepant if we compare them with our schematic knowledge of real people.

Literary texts tend towards repetition and parallelism. This is true for some of the common forms of poetry, such as lines which repeat the same metre or the same rhyme pattern. Jakobson (1960) thought that principles of parallelism were manifested in many aspects of poetic language. Songs tend towards repetition, including in choruses. We find parallel plots in narratives, or paired characters. These modes of repetition loosely resemble the multiples and doubles which are described as triggers of the sublime and of the uncanny.

Another of the modes of repetition is the way in which verbal art is 'entexualized', which applies even to oral verbal art, which enables a narrative to have characteristics that survive different performances. What survives repetition is the entextualized forms (Bauman and Briggs 1990: 72). We thus have a language-based object which is somewhat independent of both speaker and hearer, and context, and this is another strangeness of literature.

Finally, literary texts often fit into genres by virtue of conforming to rules of composition. The same is true of all artworks. The conformity to rules allows complexity to arise at all points in a literary text or other aesthetic object. From Wundt (1874) onwards and notably in Berlyne's (1971) psychological aesthetics, aesthetic objects and practices are often theorized as optimally at a middle level of complexity, neither too simple nor too complex. This middle level of complexity constitutes a mild but continuous type of discrepancy which is continuously, at a low level, surprising.

Literature is inherently surprising in all these ways, and as I have noted, the same can be said of most aesthetic practices, particularly those with narrative content.

Formal Changes

We can extend this account of literature into aesthetic practices that have a limited or non-existent narrative content, such as music. Musical form can cause thrills in people, and this has been extensively demonstrated in the experimental psychology of music. Because musical form is similar in some ways to poetic form, it is possible that they share similar kinds of trigger such that aspects of poetic form can trigger thrills for similar reasons. Sloboda (1991) elicited self-reports about formal changes in music which can trigger tears, shivers or heart-racing, and many other studies have reproduced these results (Huron and Margulis 2010). It is also true that psychoacoustic effects which have no equivalent in literature, such as crescendos, play an important role in triggering thrills in music. However, Gabrielsson and Lindström (2010: 368) argue that in music, composed structure is more powerful than performed structure, thus placing an emphasis on more complex cognition, rather than the immediate processes of reacting to raw acoustic events such as sudden loudness. Sloboda (1991: 119) says that 'it is clear that the ability to experience these responses in connection with specific musical structures is learned', with the appeal to learning suggesting that a fairly high level of musical cognition, and not just psychoacoustic effects, is responsible for the thrill response.

If this is true, then it suggests that literature could trigger thrills by formal devices analogous to those of music. The musical formal devices include manipulations of our expectations about musical form, either a generic form such as sonata form or the specific form of any musical piece about which a listener has come to build expectations while listening to it. There might be a sudden change in texture, where fewer (or more) instruments are suddenly used or certain kinds of melodic or harmonic change. Expectations can be satisfied but at an unexpected time; an important and anticipatable note such as the tonic might arrive later than expected because of the insertion of another note as an appoggiatura or an expected harmonic change might arrive earlier than expected. Sometimes the thrill-inducing changes are anticipatable but nevertheless produce a thrill, as when there is a descending cycle of fifths to the tonic; here the satisfaction of expectation seems to produce the response. Sometimes systematic complexity seems to produce a thrill, as when there are repeated syncopations.

The notion of 'processing effort' was explored in Chapter 5, where I discussed fluency of processing, difficulty of processing and shifts between these. Any of these might be relevant in triggering a strong experience. Any formal change may cause an increase in processing effort. The formal change might relate to expectations, either satisfying those expectations or failing them. An increase in processing effort can arise from making the change earlier or later than expected. As Labov and Waletzky (1967) showed, when we read or listen to a story we can recognize its narrative form, and so we can anticipate how and when the narrative will change, for example at its turning point or in how it resolves its initial complications. These anticipations can be met or violated, and in principle, these are places where a strong experience can be triggered. For example, absence of closure could thus in itself be a source of strong experience, or some problem in the way closure happens as in the arrival of the boat party at the lighthouse in Woolf's *To the Lighthouse*, a text to which I return. We expect changes in a text as part of our schematic knowledge, and so the location and kind of change can satisfy or disappoint expectations, or otherwise manipulate expectations, all of which might constitute a trigger for a strong experience. Hogan (2013: 324; 2016: 25–30) argues that we gain a particular aesthetic pleasure when a narrative outcome is unanticipated but recognizable once it has occured, a type of surprise which he calls 'nonanomalous suprise', and which we might take to be another contributing factor in the strong experience.

Schoeller and Perlovsky (2015: 2101) say that narrative chills often occur when the narrative tension reaches its peak and the plot resolves itself. When a strong experience is written in as a part of the narrative, and experienced by a character, this can also create the turning point in the narrative. Leypoldt (2011: 533) says that '[t]he sudden illumination, then, becomes a seminal narrative device with which not only to structure plot but also to provide it with a narrative climax (marked by the pathos of sudden illumination) and a logical resolution'. We might add that unlike music, in literature, form is always accompanied by referential meaning, and the formal changes can also be changes in meaning. Presumably, the changing meanings also function as triggers, along with other meaning-related triggers such as empathy with characters. But it may be that by putting these triggering meanings also at points of formal change such as a narrative turning point or closure, this placement makes the meanings more likely to trigger a strong experience.

Metre and Rhythm

A poem is a text divided into lines, and lines are 'added form' because ordinary language does not have lines. Lines are not the same as the constituent structures which are inherent to language, these being syntactic constituents and prosodic constituents. Once a text is divided into lines, it can also have metre. A metre is a type of added form, specific to poetry because it depends on the division of a text into lines (Fabb and Halle 2008). The English metres regulate the number of syllables in the line, permitting some variation, and they can also control aspects of the prosody of the language in the line, such as the distribution of stressed syllables. Thus, for example, the English iambic pentameter specifies 10 syllables to the line. But it also allows for variations, such as an extrametrical eleventh syllable at the end, and additional line-internal syllables where there are adjacent vowels by synaloepha, and very occasionally a catalectic missing first syllable. As to the rhythmic control, iambic pentameter specifies that where a syllable has strong stress as part of the word's sound-structure, that stressed syllable should normally be in an even-numbered position, but with permitted variations such as allowing the line-initial syllable to be strongly stressed in a so-called 'trochaic inversion'. Iambic pentameter thus controls both the number of syllables and the pattern of stressed syllables, but allows for a great deal of variation, so that in a poem, every line can be in the same metre even if every line is different in rhythm or length. Thus variation in itself may be a source of aesthetic experience. Wordsworth and Coleridge (1802) in the Preface to *Lyrical Ballads* discuss the 'small, but continual and regular impulses of pleasurable surprise from the metrical arrangement' in Shakespeare's verse. There is thus a relation between the fixed rules of the metre and the variable linguistic rhythm of the line which has the consequence that lines can be more regular in matching rhythm to metre, or less regular in matching rhythm to metre. This in turn allows for formal change, when for example a poem matches rhythm to metre more closely at its end (making the rhythm more regular), which is one of Smith's (1968) markers of closure, or in a contrary way also where the rhythm becomes more irregular at the end. An example of irregularity as closure comes at the end of Robert Browning's poem 'Childe Roland to the Dark Tower Came' (1855), of which the final stanza is quoted here:

> There they stood, ranged along the hill-sides, met
> To view the last of me, a living frame
> For one more picture! in a sheet of flame
> I saw them and I knew them all. And yet
> Dauntless the slug-horn to my lips I set,
> And blew 'Childe Roland to the Dark Tower came'.

This poem ends with its hero's sudden epistemic experience when he discovers that he has arrived at his goal. I personally find it a trigger of thrill – in this case, catching a strong experience from the character as represented in the text. Nichols (1987: 109) discusses the epiphany of the ending, saying, '[t]hough still unclear in its meaning, the power of the experience cannot be doubted'.

This poem throughout is in iambic pentameter, a metre in which we generally expect stressed line-internal syllables to be in even-numbered positions. But occasionally in this poem, odd-numbered syllables are stressed, and sometimes three syllables in sequence all carry stress. These are all normal aperiodic variations in iambic pentameter, allowed because this is rhythmically quite a flexible metre. However, the last line is different in being more rhythmically irregular than other lines, in a specific way. It is unique in being the only line with two separate sequences of triple stresses. One is the three-syllable sequence 'blew Childe Ro-', and the other is the three-syllable sequence 'Dark Tower came' (here, 'tower' is treated as a monosyllable by convention). The reason for suggesting that this increases processing effort starts from the assumption that when we listen to a metrical poem, we keep checking the rhythm of the line against the metre as part of the normal process of evaluating poetic performance against poetic rules. This assumption fits with Bauman's (1975) notion that verbal art, including written literature, is defined by evaluation. Thus Browning's last line will require more effort to check, because it is rhythmically further from the metrical template. This may not be enough on the own to generate a thrill, but the increased processing effort may be part of a collection of other characteristics of our reading of the line which contribute to the thrill. For example, this line also includes the title of the poem, now heard for the first time in the poem, and so the last line is a fragment which stands for the whole, one of the triggers in strong experience. Other triggers include the liminal zone of the hill-side as frame, and the crowd. Finally, and as an aside, the poem has an interesting relation to the 'flashbulb memory' discussed earlier, which is a bit like a strong experience; Kreilkamp (2006: 426) suggests that the ending might mimic a flash photograph, recently developed as a technology as described in a just-published essay by Fox Talbot which Browning might have read when he composed the poem.

Browning's text shows that changes in regularity might help a text trigger strong experience. Another way in which metre might trigger strong experience is just by the poetry being metrical. Blair (1996: 220) thinks that Milton shows that 'the boldness, freedom, and variety of our blank verse [unrhymed iambic pentameter], is infinitely more favourable than rhyme [rhymed iambic pentameter couplets], to all kinds of sublime poetry'. Longinus (1998: 181–182) quotes a prose passage by Demosthenes where the sublime effect 'depends as much on the harmony as on the thought. The whole passage is based on dactylic rhythms, and these are very noble and grand'. Friedrich (2001: 236) argues poetry produces lyric epiphany when there is 'greater sound texture through, for example, internal rhyme, alliteration, anaphora, onomatopoeisis and phonetic chiasmus within the line'. These may all be ways in which literary language is in itself surprising.

A relevant factor in understanding rhythmic variation might be 'tension'. This is a term long used in aesthetics and more generally in psychology. Wundt (1874) introduces the dimension of feeling, *Spannung-Lösung*, translated as tension-relaxation. However, as a term, 'tension' has its faults: it is used with different meanings and sometimes with no clear meaning. (For a summary of some of the problems this presents for music, see Fredrickson 1997; Keller and Schubert 2011: 134; Lerdahl and Krumhansl 2007: 329; Farbood and Price 2017; Temperley 2018: 144.) In the analysis of poetry, the term 'tension' is sometimes used to describe the relation between metre and rhythm. For example, Jakobson (1960: 80) discusses the iambic pentameter line from *Hamlet* 'No, let the candied tongue lick absurd pomp', and notes that the ninth syllable '-surd' in the line can only be pronounced as stressed, even though it is in a metrical position which normally does not permit stress. He describes this as 'the tension between the ictus [a metrical peak] and the word stress'. In the study of poetry, music, painting and other arts, the term 'tension' is sometimes used to describe aspects of the form. There is often an underlying idea, perhaps covert, that when the form has tension this produces some corresponding kind of tension in the listener, for example when tension correlates with arousal (Farbood and Price 2017: 420). In an unusually literal exploration of the notion of tension, Nielsen (1983) conducted an experiment in which subjects squeezed spring-loaded tongs in response to listening to music to show that musculo-skeletal tension correlates with musical tension. Lanz (1926: 1020), discussing 'the physical basis of rhyme' claims that, compared with rhyming couplets, in our experience of alternating rhymes 'the expectation becomes more tense'. Not everybody uses 'tension' with a psychological meaning. In a different approach, Halle and Keyser (1971) treat metrical tension as synonymous with metrical complexity, thus avoiding any specific psychological claim.

If formal tension produces experiential tension, then this tension might perhaps correlate with or be the same as arousal, which is one of the components of a strong experience, and it might correlate with increased processing effort that may be a trigger of strong experiences. We might ask what in a text makes it complex in ways which correlate with psychological effects. Consider Donne's iambic pentameter as compared with Marvell's, and specifically the fact that Donne often counts two syllables with adjacent vowels as metrically one unit (synaloepha). This means that his iambic pentameter lines can vary to be longer than the standard 10 syllables, and so longer than Marvell's lines, who uses synaloepha less. Which kind of line is more inherently complex than the other, specifically when it comes to its metricality? Is Donne being 'loose' with the metrical rules, and if so, does that make his poetry metrically simpler than Marvell who is stricter with the syllable counting? Or, since Donne's looseness is all regulated by its own rule system, and not really loose at all on its own terms, does this make the line more complex as a legitimate and radical variation on the rules? The answer is not objectively clear. And whatever the answer is, does Donne's line show more 'tension' than Marvell's, in any meaningful way which is different from just saying that Donne's has more syllables, while in the same metre?

These questions are difficult to answer, but it is a reasonable assumption that texts differ in complexity and that there is a correlation between textual complexity and processing effort, which might provide a way by which textual complexity can trigger strong experience.

Narrative

Strong experiences often begin with surprises, where a perception fails to match a schematic expectation. Narratives are laid out sequentially and so they should be able to produce surprises which in principle might trigger strong experience. Narrative schemata can characterize large-scale events which contain predictable sequences of small-scale events, making it possible to predict when an event might occur. Schematic discrepancy will then be perceived if an event occurs before it is predicted to occur or after it is predicted to occur. Huron (2006) and Sloboda (1991) show that both are true of the ways in which music can surprise us, and narratives can produce strong experiences by manipulating our expectations in a similar way.

Brewer and Lichtenstein (1982) propose a 'structural affect theory' that readers can be surprised by a significant event if the causal sequence that leads to it is concealed. In this type of 'surprise discourse organization', the reader comes to reinterpret the event sequence covered but concealed by the text already read, resulting in 'a sharp rise on the surprise scale at the point where the crucial information was introduced into the discourse' (Brewer and Lichtenstein 1982: 480). Hoeken and van Vliet (2000: 280) note that surprise discourse organization can sometimes improve recall of preceding events because it requires readers to reassess their understanding of the story and that this can increase appreciation for the story. Tobin (2009: 160, drawing on Camerer et al. 1989) shows that in surprise discourse organization an author may exploit an inherent bias, called 'the curse of knowledge', which is 'a pervasive cognitive bias that makes it very difficult for us accurately to imagine, once we know something, what it is like not to know it'. This means that though we are surprised by a narrative event, we come to feel that we already knew it, such that the event was obvious. Griffiths and Tenenbaum (2007: 184) suggest that coincidences grab our attention 'because they suggest the existence of hidden causal structure in contexts where our current understanding would suggest no such structure should exist'. In other words, coincidences are analogous to surprise discourse organizations. In these various ways, narratives have the potential to surprise a reader, and a surprise can become a strong experience.

Gerrig (1993) and Green and Brock (2000) have proposed that a reader of a fictional or factual narrative can enter a state of 'transportation', which involves a vivid mental simulation of the events described in a narrative and has the consequence of making the reader have a greater sense that the narrated events really happened. Johnson et al. (1993) note that fictional events experienced under transportation can be mis-remembered as if they were actual experiences. Transportation is not by itself a strong experience, and indeed may be a variant of the (not 'strong') experience which is 'flow' (Csikszentmihalyi 1990; Appel and Richter 2010: 105; Tal-Or and Cohen 2010: 405; Jensen et al. 2011: 542). However, one of the side effects of transportation is the production of suspense (Tal-Or and Cohen 2010: 405). The expectation–resolution pattern of suspense is a possible trigger of strong experience, and we know that psychological affect may significantly increase at a surprise ending (Dijkstra et al. 1995: 145). It is worth noting, incidentally, that defamiliarization, which is also a possible trigger of strong experience, is incompatible with transportation and disrupts suspense (Dijkstra et al. 1995: 141). Again, we see that there are different routes by which strong experiences can arise. Jensen et al. (2011) link increased transportation to increased arousal, as do Visch et al. (2010: 1442), where higher immersion correlates with higher viewer emotions (see also Jacobs 2015 on immersion). Mar et al. (2011: 828) suggest that empathetic involvement with a character slows reading, producing a more elaborate simulation of the events described; thus, empathetic involvement may increase processing effort. In sum, we might say that the reader's transportation by a narrative makes a strong experience possible by contributing features such as empathy, suspense and arousal.

Event Segmentation in Everyday Experience and in Narrative

Our ability to understand narratives depends on our basic cognitive ability to perceive our experience as divided into events (Radvansky and Zacks 2014). This 'event structure perception' is exploited by literary authors, who can manipulate this basic ability when they represent events and their relations in the literary text. Specific events have a relation to types of events, where each type is stored in memory as an event schema (Radvansky and Zacks 2014: 27). These event schemata help us organize our perceptions of ongoing reality into events, and this carries over to readers who can draw on their probabilistic knowledge of actors and goals and kinds of event, in order to determine when an event has come to an end (Zacks et al. 2007: 281). Event schemata, like other aspects of our schematic knowledge, constitute semantic memories and involve schematic expectations. Event perception allows for the possibility of a discrepancy to arise between a perceived event and its associated schema, which might trigger a strong experience.

The boundaries between events, both in life and in fictions, are locations where strong experiences can be triggered. Zacks and Tversky (2001: 3) define an event as 'a segment of time at a given location that is conceived by an observer to have a beginning and an end', and the observer does this by event structure perception. Events are thereby distinguished from one another, and boundaries set between them. The process by which this is achieved is described by the event-indexing model of Radvansky et al. (1998), and Zwaan, Langston and Graesser (1995a), in which 'event models' are psychological constructs which represent particular events as perceived in the world. Zacks et al. (2007: 274) argue that our interpretation of our perceptions is determined by our finding event models in the perceptual stream, where 'an event model is a representation of "what is happening now" which is robust to transient variability in the sensory input'. A specific event lasts for a while, and then changes; the stable period is perceived as an event and the change as an event boundary. Events have situational continuity such that they are coherent in 'time, space, intentionality, causality and protagonist'. There are more long-term associations between items when they are within the same event than when they are in different events (Sargent, et al. 2013: 242). Events in narratives are largely driven by character intentions and the achievement of goals. The reader's empathetic engagement with characters may play a role in triggering strong experience, which makes it relevant that a character's perceived intentions are relevant in understanding how events form around them, and the character's achievement of a goal can signal the end of the event: 'moments of maximal feature changes tend to correspond to the satisfaction of goals' (Zacks and Tversky 2001: 10). Changes in any of these can signal an event boundary, and so there is a special role for empathy at event boundaries because empathy enables us better to recognize these changes. This is another reason why event boundaries might trigger strong experience. There is also increased processing effort at an event boundary (Zacks et al. 2007: 278), which improves recall for material near an event boundary; for example, a sentence at an episode boundary may be read more slowly (Garnham and Mason 1987: 134). This is relevant because increased processing effort might itself be a trigger of strong experience.

Event boundaries are places of raised prediction error, the neural signal that there is a discrepancy between perception and expectation (Zacks et al. 2009: 307; Magliano and Zacks 2011: 1492; Sargent et al. 2013: 242). Because a new event can include new people, new objects, new surroundings and/or new time, its components are less predictable. This means that prediction errors increase at an event boundary, and so an increase in prediction errors is evidence that there is an event boundary. After the event boundary passes, the prediction errors are not as significant. Once the new event is in its early stage, predictions can generally be made with less confidence, so prediction errors will be less strongly weighted. The two different models of surprise might work differently here. The Meyer-Reisenzein (2009) expectation-based model of surprise would explain surprise at the end of an event, when prediction errors rise. The Foster and Keane (2015) sense-making model of surprise could explain surprise at the beginning of an event because expectations should be weaker. In either case, a strong experience might arise at an event boundary or just after an event boundary. Where events appear to be surprising or confusing or less coherent, the subject may choose to focus on more fine grained segmentations of events, which are likely to remain intact as events even if the higher-level organization does not seem to be (Zacks et al. 2007: 278). This might connect to the possibility that ordinary objects trigger epiphanies when they are perceived at a high level of granularity, which I discussed in Chapter 5.

Event structure is both sequential and hierarchical. In the sequential dimension, one event follows another, with a boundary between them. In the hierarchical dimension, events are hierarchically organized, so that one or more lower-level events are completely contained within a higher-level event: events are thus organized like boxes which contain boxes (for general discussion of hierarchy in cognition see Cohen 2000). Humans are sensitive to events at both smaller and larger scales (Zacks and Tversky 2001: 7). Real-world events lasting between 10 and 30 seconds are understood as intentional acts, events lasting from a few minutes to hours can be understood in terms of participants' goals and plans and form narrative plots, and over long timescales events are characterized thematically. As noted in the previous paragraph, Zacks et al. (2007: 278) suggest that it is possible to perceive event boundaries at different levels in the hierarchy, but that at a specific time, the subject selectively attends to a particular level of events, whether at the large-scale coarse organization of events or at the small-scale fine grain of events. Though it is possible to perceive events at different levels, human cognition may be particularly fluent at a particular level, that of the 'behaviour episode' (Zacks and Tversky 2001: 6). The kinds of change we expect at the boundary of a behaviour episode include for example a shift between speaking, acting and thinking, or a change in physical direction or setting, or a change in which part of the body is involved.

Event boundaries need not be well defined. Zacks and Tversky (2001: 18) note that many events have fuzzy edges, but also that we are nevertheless able to find hierarchical structure in events, when that structure is available. Events can also be interrupted, with other events inserted into them after which the original event continues, as in a meeting interrupted by a fire alarm (Zacks and Tversky 2001: 3). The disruption of event boundaries might play a role in strong experience, but like the other triggers for strong experience this disruption is ordinary: events are disrupted in all kinds of ways in ordinary life as well. Hence, disruption by itself is not enough to cause a strong experience and may need to combine with other triggers to produce a strong experience.

When we imagine a world as a result of reading a literary text, that world is divided into events, organized hierarchically. The text's description is necessarily sparse and can be filled in by the reader with additional detail to build up a richer imagining of the event than is literally given on the page. Some interesting questions arise when it comes to the boundaries of the event as represented, compared with the event as imagined, and in particular when the imagined event extends before or after the boundaries of the event as represented. The event as represented can be incomplete, in ways which might possibly stimulate strong experience. This is further complicated by another kind of sectioning, by the dividing of the text into formal sections, such as paragraphs, chapters, lines, stanzas, and so on, which can also be organized hierarchically. In principle the boundaries of a whole section can match with the boundaries of a represented event and also with the boundaries of the event as imagined. An example of this matching would be when a whole chapter describes a whole event. But the boundaries can also be violated, with the event overlapping the chapter's edge. The same in principle can be true of other sectional divisions of literary texts: they can reinforce represented and imagined event structure, or mismatch with them. As an example of strong experience arising at a boundary, Chard (1996: 117) describes the sublime ending of Sterne's *Sentimental Journey* 'within the liminal space of the Alps' where 'the reader is left to speculate indefinitely as to what might take place once the boundary is crossed'. Another example of the mismatch of events to literary sections comes when a narrative opens on an imagined world which in principle already exists. Consider for example Charlotte Brontë's *Jane Eyre*, where the novel begins as though it is mid-way through some larger event, with its first sentence addressing us as though we were already there and knew the represented world.

> There was no possibility of taking a walk that day. We had been wandering, indeed, in the leafless shrubbery an hour in the morning; but since dinner (Mrs. Reed, when there was no company, dined early) the cold winter wind had brought with it clouds so sombre, and a rain so penetrating, that further out-door exercise was now out of the question. (Brontë 2016: 9).

This is a very striking beginning, and the strikingness comes in part from the way that textual and event boundaries fail to match.

Another clear example of boundary manipulation in a text which Beja (1971: 144) identifies as epiphanic is the end of the penultimate chapter of Woolf's *To the Lighthouse*.

> They watched him, both of them, sitting bareheaded with his parcel on his knee staring and staring at the frail blue shape which seemed like the vapour of something that had burnt itself away. What do you want? they both wanted to ask. They both wanted to say, Ask us anything and we will give it you. But he did not ask them anything. He sat and looked at the island and he might be thinking, We perished, each alone, or he might be thinking, I have reached it. I have found it, but he said nothing.

Then he put on his hat.

'Bring those parcels,' he said, nodding his head at the things Nancy had done up for them to take to the Lighthouse. 'The parcels for the Lighthouse men,' he said. He rose and stood in the bow of the boat, very straight and tall, for all the world, James thought, as if he were saying, 'There is no God,' and Cam thought, as if he were leaping into space, and they both rose to follow him as he sprang, lightly like a young man, holding his parcel, on to the rock. (Woolf 2006: 169)

Mr Ramsay and his two children arrive at the island where the lighthouse is, and he steps off the boat and they rise to follow him but this event is never concluded in the text's representation because the chapter just ends. As Speidel (2007: 325) describes it, '[h]ere we have at once the implied completion of the journey, and a breaking-off at precisely the moment of fulfilment, so that the impression the reader is left with is the lighthouse trip forever suspended in this moment, with Mr Ramsay caught (as if in cinematic freeze-frame) jumping on to the rock'. Thus the arrival which is implied by the title both does and does not happen; this is Ricoeur's metaphorical mode of the *is and is not*. It is worth noting something else about this passage, which is the six-word penultimate paragraph; as Emmott et al. (2006) show, these unusually short paragraphs draw the reader's attention and increase depth of processing, hence requiring greater processing effort, and the increase of processing effort may also be contributing to a reader's strong experience here.

There is a further interesting aspect to this organization of events, which relates to the theoretical claim made by Zacks and Tversky (2001), that over small timescales events are characterized by their physical form and over larger timescales by the intentions of the participants. In *To the Lighthouse*, we witness the end of the defining event of the novel, which has been driven in part by the initially frustrated intention to go to the lighthouse. But this main event comes to an end by cutting into the small event of physical movement which is all physicality, not intention; in fact, the intentions of Mr Ramsay are unclear at the end. Perhaps concealment of intention occurs in other cases where strong experiences are triggered at event boundaries. Thus consider the potential for triggering strong experience at the famous end of John Ford's (1956) film *The Searchers*, which reaches the end of its main narrative with the return of the 'sought' girl to the house, but where the other narrative centred on the searcher character of Ethan Edwards does not end, and his event of leaving is intersected and ended by the closing of the liminal final door. It is notable that this event is defined also by gesture as he grasps his arm, which implies intention but does not tell us what it is. We might recall the role of empathy in strong experiences; in these strong experiences any attempt at empathy with the character is blocked by the text.

Texts can also be organized so that sections overlap, such that the final part of a sequence of events can be the first part of another sequence of events. Hymes (1987) calls this a 'pivot' in his discussion of the oral narratives of North America, where an event is both the concluding event of a sequence and the initiating event of the next sequence. Overlaps of this kind arise at important moments in Australian Aboriginal ceremony, as Ellis (1984: 183) shows in her discussion of the overlap of forms in a song where 'in order to maintain power at its optimum, overlapping/interlocking/cyclical processes must occur. These tie together a large body of musical material, the intent of which is to alter perceptions of time in order to re-evaluate real time and the individual's place within it'. The events in this case are the structural components of the song. Barwick et al. (2007: 21) explore this for a particular song in the Australian language Murrinh Patha, where the song is in five sections but divided into two large parts, with the third section belonging to both the first and second part (i.e., Hymes's pivot). They say that '[t]he aesthetic gestures described here seem fitting for ceremonies that concern themselves with the social negotiation of liminality, as the deceased person's spirit turns away from the living and joins the world of the dead, or as boys turn away from their mothers and become men. Indeed, this particular song is often performed at significant points in ceremonies'. Here, again, we have a version of Ricoeur's metaphorical *is and is not* as a potential trigger of strong experience.

In our experience of the world, events are contained within other events as part of a hierarchical structure where at each level the events are sequenced in time. One of the ways of disrupting this in a literary text is by inserting an event which does not belong to the sequence or does not belong to the hierarchy. This can be done by the device of flashback, a device which Beja (1971: 22) relates to the literary epiphany. We find another type of interruption in Philip K. Dick's science fiction novel *The Man in the High Castle* (1962), when Mr. Tagomi has a strong experience which is produced by an interruptive intrusion of events from the true world to which he ordinarily has no access, into the sequence formed by the untrue events of the novel (Dick 1965: 222). An intrusion into another event is important for Auerbach in his study of *Mimesis*, and his book begins with an example of intrusion from the *Odyssey* and ends with a similar example from *To the Lighthouse*. Here the exterior time of the containing narrative contains the interior time of the interruption, where the two times are different: 'This entirely insignificant occurrence is constantly interspersed with other elements which, although they do not interrupt its progress, take up far more time in the narration than the whole scene can possibly have lasted' (Auerbach 1953: 529). Here, as elsewhere in modernist texts, the relations between events, both in sequence and in hierarchy are 'loosely joined so that the reader has no definite thread of action which he can always follow'. Though Auerbach does not claim this as a source of epiphany or other strong experience, I think it is legitimate to suggest that it might have this effect, by its disruption of the event structure.

While this embedding takes an event and places another event inside it, it is also possible to cut a part out of an event, splicing together the remaining parts to produce a jump in time or place, for example where a person departs and arrives at adjacent textual moments, as though the intervening journey is cut; for example, one moment we see them leave and the next moment we see them arrive. These juxtapositions somewhat resemble the practice of parallelism, a source of the sublime for Burke and others, where items which are related are put together, but without the relation between them made clear. In spliced narratives, the relation is sequential, and what is missing is the causal sequence. It is a way of creating a relation between two events, which are made to be adjacent because of the jump in time but where there is no obvious causal relation between them. Another way to disrupt the sequence of events is to have two events represented in a fiction as separated by a gap which does not clearly contain any event. Thus 'nothing happens' while waiting for events to occur in Beckett's *Waiting for Godot* (1953) and Stoppard's *Rosencrantz and Guildenstern Are Dead* (1966). Consider also the transitional section between the two narrated days in *To the Lighthouse* which is titled 'Time Passes'. Events occur within this section that include Mrs. Ramsay dying, and the First World War, but this section can be also interpreted as a gap between the events of the first day and the last day. Henke (1999: 263) describes it as the 'interchapter in which nature and the universe are seen without a self and the human eye/I has been obliterated' and says that Spivak calls this section of the novel a copula or 'hinge' (again, Hymes's pivot). These examples of disruptions to the event structure are potentially triggers of strong experience.

Events in themselves may be a trigger of strong experience in a manner similar to significant objects. The major theorist of this is Walter Benjamin and his notion of 'tableau', which is found in the theatre, where characters are arranged spatially at a moment of narrative significance. In his account of German drama, the image produced by the tableau 'becomes the key to historical understanding' (2009: 92), and I return to his account of Brecht's tableaux shortly. Brecht himself describes the tableau as a source of 'astonishment'. Beja (1971: 23) calls 'a frozen tableau' epiphanic. Zemka (2012: 36) says that the tableau is a point of equilibrium. The tableau can be interpreted as a way of making an event significant in the way that an epiphanic object is significant; the event is a bounded and whole entity which is somehow special, and so a trigger of strong experience. Time is also altered, appearing to stop. It is a moment when the viewer might be expected to pay great attention, and increase processing effort.

The endings of texts are typical locations for strong experience. Beja (1971: 94) says of Joyce's *Dubliners* (1914) that 'the epiphany almost invariably comes at or toward the end'. Sloboda (1991: 120) suggests that tears in response to music may relate to emotions provoked by endings. Langbaum (1999: 48) discusses 'short poems and stories where the epiphany occurs at the end, reordering and rendering static all that has preceded'. He quotes Joseph Frank: 'Modern poetry asks its readers to suspend the process of individual reference temporarily until the entire pattern of internal references can be apprehended as a unity'; Langbaum adds 'as in my terms, a static retrospective flash'. In her account of poetic closure, Smith says something similar:

> Poetic structure is, in a sense, an inference which we draw from the evidence of a series of events. As we read the poem, it is a hypothesis whose probability is tested as we move from line to line and adjusted in response to what we find there [...] the conclusion of a poem has special status in the process, for it is only at that point that the total pattern – the structural principles which we have been testing – is revealed. (Smith 1968)

Sometimes there are good narrative reasons why endings might trigger strong experiences, because of the characteristic contents of endings. For example, Tigges (1999: 30) discusses the epiphany of the ultimate moment, such as dying, and endings can offer these ultimate moments. Endings also allow for mismatches or matches between text and event, as a possible trigger for strong experiences. And endings can be interpreted as liminalities, between the world of the text and our world.

Another aspect of endings is the possibility of a coda, as discussed by Labov and Waletzky (1967). The coda can be a summary of what has preceded which comes at the end of the text, like a part which stands for the whole, or it can be a stepping out of the narrative to reflect on it, in a kind of liminal space at the end. In folktales this can be a way of bringing the listener back from the displaced world of the narrative to the world of now, from the fictional to the real world, and this shift might be the kind of cognitive shift which might trigger strong experience. Ramey (2011: 620) says about *Beowulf*, 'these scenes of performance function as portals that lead out from the main narrative, allowing for sudden shifts in time and place, offering alternative narratives and themes, and as a whole helping to situate the story of the hero

Beowulf within a wider poetic web of traditional song'. The coda in a text might trigger strong experience for various reasons, and in part because of the uncertain status of the coda relative to the rest of the narrative, so that it is not quite in the narrative or quite outside it. This is another example of Ricoeur's metaphorical *is and is not*.

Boundaries and Boundlessness

Events are bounded (they have boundaries) and in this they are like many objects, such as bodies. Boundedness is what we schematically expect, and for this reason boundlessness might in principle be surprising, and a source of strong experience. Boundlessness is a characteristic trigger of the sublime. Burke discussed why bounded objects prevent us reaching a sense of infinity, and hence why buildings which are rotundas have a profound effect because they have no boundaries and hence produce the perception of infinity (Burke 1987: 75). Etlyn (2012: 226) discusses Étienne-Louis Boullée's architecture and specifically his design for Newton's tomb: 'At the moment of epiphany, the viewer becomes one with nature through the endless circumferences of the spherical cavity or with the impression of boundless space that the vast interior conveys, especially in darkness. At the same time the viewer becomes one with Newton through the tomb thereby participating in the "sublimity of [Newton's] genius"' (note that 'epiphany' and 'sublime' are used here together). Following the same theme, Etlyn (2012: 263) says that 'on entering the chapel [of the Château d'Anet], a visitor is not merely confronted with a rotating swirl of forms in the dome and on the floor but undergoes a more powerful, visceral experience of being aspirated upward into the dome, while simultaneously being sucked downward into an abyss'. Kant talks of 'the boundless ocean rising with rebellious force' (Kant 1952: 111). Smith (2013) says of Turner that 'his works have been widely recognized as the most successful in capturing the effect of boundlessness which Burke and Kant saw as a prerequisite for the sublime in verbal and visual representation – the sublime being something that can be evoked but not achieved'. Coleridge says that the sublime involves 'boundless or endless allness' (cited Brady 2013: 107). Laski (1980) analyses an ecstasy experienced by Mary Wilson, alone on a beach in the Isles of Scilly, who talks about 'a mystical experience [...] a most extraordinary experience as if I was dissolving'. Laski comments: 'The physical circumstances surrounding its occurrence are, as we shall see, among the most common: being alone by the sea after a period of worry and stress'. Here Mary Wilson is dissolving but is also at the boundary of a life-period, and on a beach, a boundary between the zones of land and sea. Some of these boundaries can be interpreted as 'liminal zones'.

Liminality

A liminality, also called a liminal zone, is a boundary between two distinctly different zones. Liminalities are motifs in strong experiences, some of which for example occur in the liminal zones of the beach, in a doorway or on stairs. Bishop (1959: 49) says of Wordsworth's 'spots of time' that '[i]n these experiences the other world is literally beyond the limits of this; the grim shape emerges from behind the horizon, from under the surface of the water, at the crest of a road. To pass a boundary is to evoke the unknown'. Liminal zones can be spatial, temporal, personal, social, or some combination of these. People can pass through a liminal zone, or be in a liminal zone such as the architectural liminalities of doors, windows and stairs, and natural liminalities of shore, horizon and ground surface. A liminality can also be created by movement, where the liminal zone is created by being travelled through. People can also pass through symbolic, personal or socio-cultural liminal zones.

Arnold Van Gennep (1909) described 'rites of passage', associated with a person's passage through the liminal zone from one status to another. In his theory a pre-liminal stage of separation precedes a liminal stage of marginalization in which deviant acts are permitted, ending in a post-liminal stage of reincorporation or reassimilation. Victor Turner (1964) emphasizes the way in which a person in a liminal zone is freed from social obligations and can be deviant, but is also at risk. The person in the liminal state is the 'passenger', whose ambiguous state makes them 'interstructural' relative to the structure of positions which constitutes a society (Turner 1964: 234). The passenger experiences strong emotions and forms of arcane and often ineffable knowledge, which transforms her, and we might see this as a strong experience. Liminalities often provide conventional symbolism in a society. Thus Coldstream (2002: 140, 146) says that medieval rituals were based around processions which crossed liminalities: 'Rites of various kinds were the reason for the continuous spatial flow between interiors and exteriors, and the concomitant significance of thresholds and approaches'.

Many superstitions and cultural practices accrue to liminal zones, particularly to doorways. It is possible that liminal zones are potential triggers for strong experience because of these rich symbolic possibilities. It is also possible to see why a liminal zone might be retrospectively attributed to the strong experience, even if it is not its actual cause, precisely because of this rich symbolism. Barwick (2006: 27) describes the conjunction of aesthetic liminalities and spatial liminalities in Marri Ngarr culture (of Australia):

> It is not too fanciful, I think, to liken the fertile and liminal status of the Kiyirri 1 (moderate) rhythmic mode to Marri Ngarr country's 'liminal

water places' [...] the rhythmic mode's in-betweenness is defined and apparent only in the spaces between songs, in the often non-verbalized contrasts presented to the ears and minds of those who pay attention to them. We are marked by these contrasts: they change our perception of the music.

Also describing an Australian Aboriginal song practice, Treloyn (2009: 61) says that when Scotty Martin 'sings "half way" he may activate a compositional strategy of modifying a text in relation to rhythm to negotiate a fabric of relationships between himself, other singers, dancers, and the ancestral brolga – the ancestral founder of the *jadmi* song tradition'.

Schemata often have bounded objects and events as their contents. The boundary between two adjacent schemata can thus be conceptualized as a liminal zone. For example, the schema for land and the schema for the sea can be conceptualized as adjacent bounded domains, with the beach as a liminal zone between them. The beach has its own schema, but a beach can also be conceptualized as belonging both to the schema of land and the schema of sea, and thus, like the pivots and overlaps between sections discussed earlier, the beach is schematically discrepant. The potential schematic discrepancy of the beach may potentiate it as a place of strong experience, when for example a person is on a beach. The same could be said of dawn and dusk, the new year, marriage, stairways, windows, doors or other liminalities. Ziolkowski (2014: 8, 14) discusses Petrarch's climbing of a mountain, while he was also in a liminality between two epochs (*Epochenschwelle*), and the shift that Petrarch manifests from Dante's vertical vision to a new horizontal vision: 'his awareness of the epochal tension was triggered not by his experience of the landscape itself but by a subsequent epiphany of the book that resulted in a total change of perception that [...] reflected the spirit of the times'. Virginia Woolf's characters have a tendency to be in liminal zones when strong experiences arise. An example is Mr Ramsay's leap from boat to land in *To the Lighthouse*, an event cited by Northrop Frye as an example of what he calls a 'point of epiphany'. Here, there is a movement from the natural to the symbolic world, and hence which we could call a type of liminal zone (though Frye does not use the term):

> This is the symbolic presentation of the point at which the undisplaced apocalyptic world and the cyclical world of nature come into alignment, and which we propose to call the point of epiphany. Its most common settings are the mountain-top, the island, the tower, the lighthouse and the ladder or staircase. Folk tales and mythologies are full of stories

of an original connection between heaven or the sun and earth. (Frye 1957: 203)

William Wordsworth's *The Prelude* includes various 'spots of time' which Nichols (1987: 49) treats as kinds of epiphany and which we can classify as strong experiences.

> There are in our existence spots of time,
> which with distinct pre-eminence retain
> A vivifying virtue, whence...
> ...our minds are nourished and invisibly repaired;
> A virtue, by which pleasure is enhanced,
> That penetrates, enables us to mount,
> When high, more high, and lifts us up when fallen
> (Wordsworth *Prelude* 1850 book XII, Maxwell 1986: 479)

Many of these spots of time occur in liminal zones or while travelling. While nesting (1805, I: 333–350) the young Wordsworth is hanging off a cliff edge. The stolen skiff (1805, I: 372–427) involves a huge cliff rising from the liminality of 'the bound of the horizon'. When he stops skating (1805, I: 452–489) he is both on the liminal zone of the surface of the water, and 'the solitary cliffs / Wheeled by me'. The travellers cross the liminal zone of the Alps (1805, VI: 488–572) without realizing it. The blind beggar (1805, VII: 592–622) is propped against a wall. In another episode (1805, XI: 345–389) Wordsworth sits on a 'highest summit', liminal between earth and sky, and looks down at the two roads along one of which will come the horses to take him home for the holidays; he is by a wall. He has an experience of climbing Mount Snowdon (1805, XIII: 1–65) with the intention of watching the liminal moment of sunrise; high on a mountain is a liminality between earth and sky, and metaphorically he is 'on the shore [...] of a huge sea of mist'.

James Joyce made a personal list of his own epiphanies, and again liminalities are prominent. In this posthumously published list (Joyce 1956), we find that many of them involve transition or bodies in transitional spaces. Sometimes this is implicit and sometimes explicit. The following epiphanies from the list (numbered as in the published form) involve entrance or exit:

> 1 'comes in', 7 from chapel into street, 25 'they are leaving shelter [...] returning to the convent', 28 'The ship is entering a harbour', 31 'What moves upon me from the darkness subtle and murmerous as a flood, passionate and fierce with an indecent movement of the loins? What

HOW LITERATURE TRIGGERS STRONG EXPERIENCES   163

leaps, crying in answer, out of me, as eagle to eagle in mid air, crying to overcome, crying for an iniquitous abandonment?'

People stand in entrances in these epiphanies:

> 5 the woman who appears to be a skull, or monkey, 17 'even now the rabblement may be standing at the door', 19 a very significant one: 'do you know anything about the body? [...] There's some matter coming away from the hole in Georgie's stomach', 38 takes place at the garden gate: sexuality introduced to 'the little male child'.

People are on steps or stairs in these epiphanies:

> 3 'we seem to listen, I on the upper step and she on the lower. She comes up to my step many times and goes down again, between our phrases, and once or twice remains beside me, forgetting to go down, and then goes down [...] Let be, let be [...]', 20 'I will go up now [...] He lies on my bed where I lay last night': up the stairs to death.

They are between land and water in these epiphanies:

> 8 takes place 'where three roads meet and before a swampy beach', 16 'an arctic beast [...] rises out of the water.'

I have focused on spatial liminalities. But there are also other types of liminality or mixing or transition in the epiphanies. Some include mixed creatures: 5 the woman/monkey in the doorway, 6 half-men, half-goats; 'confused forms'. In 18 the stars come out, and in 27 there is the passing sound of hoofs, heard through 'the dark windows'. And the inside and the outside are referenced in 13 'it looks all right from the outside ... to those who don't know' and 24 'her eyes have revealed her – secret, vigilance, an enclosed garden'.

Liminality might be associated with strong experience because of its schematic discrepancy, which is a trigger of surprise. But in a simple way also, liminality makes surprise possible because if we move from one place to another by crossing a liminality this is a change, particularly for our perceptions, and this has the potential to surprise us. It can also be dangerous to move through a liminality, such as stepping out of, or into, an unknown place, and perhaps this plays a role in generating the thrill arousals associated with fear. One of the types of strong experience involves the surprising blocking of a path or interrupting of a journey, thus producing a surprise which can be elaborated into a strong experience. In the New Testament, Saul/Paul received his epiphany at a moment of blockage while travelling to Damascus. The epiphany while travelling is common, and the inherent liminality of travelling must play a role in this. Beja (1971: 213) notes that in Baldwin and other writers, a passenger on a train experiences fleeting moments of epiphany. The traveller may observe a range of events and objects passing by, thus being surprised by juxtapositions not usually found. Perhaps by moving relative to the object, in different ways at different times, the object occasionally appears in a juxtaposition which produces strong experience. Bell and Lyall (2002: 93) say that 'when Hackett [bunjee-] jumped off the Eiffel Tower, it was the moment at which the inverted sublime turned the nineteenth-century-built sublime into its pedestal'. When the spacecraft Voyager 1 moved out of the heliopause into empty space, 'we have an event of the technological sublime encountering the vast horizontality of intergalactic space, where it will exist in a condition of more absolute stillness and silence than ever before achieved' (Bell and Lyell 2002: 192). Chard (1996: 126, 130) describes the sublime as transgressive and destabilizing and suggests that the sublime readily becomes entangled with the needs and desires that prompt transgressive travel.

Notions of liminality have an association with a philosophical tradition of sedentarism, associated with Heidegger's (1927) dwelling (*das Wohnen*) in the world. They also have an association with psychological approaches which suggest that our human psychology leads us to perceive stable domains, whether in Gestalt theory or in theories of episodic memory or event segmentation theory. But there are alternative approaches in which the between-ness of liminality becomes central, and stable domains dissipate. These include Deleuze and Guattari's (1987) extended notion of nomadism whereby we are all in various ways nomads, the time-space compression of Massey (1991) where places are processes produced from social combinations, or the 'mobilities paradigm' of Sheller and Urry where instead of sedentarism the basic metaphors are those of travel and flight (Sheller and Urry 2006: 210). These approaches have little use for the special notion of liminality. For Sheller and Urry, what might otherwise have been liminal zones now become 'nodes' where people come together. The airport would be one such place. The airport can be conceived as a non-space through which we transit (Augé, cited Küpers 2011: 47) or as a central, nodal kind of space (for Sheller and Urry) in which we come together. This is relevant for our purposes because of 'airport syndrome' (Bar-el et al. 2000: 89) which is interpreted as a pathology arising from not being in a psychologically properly defined place, instead being in-between, and there may be a relation between airport syndrome and Stendhal's syndrome, the psychologically and physically overwhelming response to art characteristic particularly of tourist visitors, mentioned in

Chapter 4 as related to strong experience. Thus even though we live now in a world of extensive mobility, nevertheless our psychology still requires us to be in stable domains. This brings us back to the possibility that locational and transitional liminalities do have a distinct psychological status, making them a trigger for strong experience.

Metaphor

Metaphor is one of the modes of communication in which what we say has an indirect relation to what we mean. Longinus (1998: 174) says that 'metaphors conduce to sublimity', and Van Eck (2010: 651) suggests that Longinus approaches the sublime as an 'experience of extreme vividness' and by the exercise of metaphor 'speech appears to dissolve into what it describes'. In particular, metaphor is able to make the inanimate animate, and the blurring of this distinction is the source of the sublime. Shaftesbury, writing in 1711, saw the sublime style as 'formed by the variety of figures, the multiplicity of metaphors, and by quitting as much as possible the natural and easy way of expression, for that which is most unlike to humanity or ordinary use' (quoted Costelloe 2012: 51). Shaw (2006: 47) says that for eighteenth-century thinkers 'what the sublime embodies is nothing less than the transformational power of language, its ability to link disparate entities (both physical and mental objects) by analogy'. Metaphors thus have the potential to produce strong experience, and this applies also to literary practices which involve similar indirectness, such as allegory. A metaphor can be conceptualized as involving at least two meanings, the literal meaning and the implied meaning. Metaphor can be a straightforward part of any communicative act. Following a relevance theory perspective (Sperber and Wilson 1995), we can say that in every communicative act, the literal meaning of the words cannot be guaranteed to be the intended meaning, and metaphor is one of the ways in which the intended meaning can differ from what is literally said. One way in which metaphor might work is by taking a schema and altering it. For example, Rumelhart and Ortony (1977: 126) suggest that the communicated meaning of a metaphor can involve generalizing a schema. Wilson and Carston (2006) suggest that metaphors involve the broadening and other altering of concepts (i.e., of schemata).

Kuiken et al. (2012: 8) explain the sublime in terms of a personal transformation through the process of 'experiencing', a term adapted from Wilhelm Dilthey's term *Erlebnis* (Dilthey 1976: 215). Experiencing begins with a sense of something more than can be currently known. This leads to a transformation of schematic thinking and self-understanding. It can produce knowledge which is ineffable. Kant's two kinds of the sublime are reinterpreted psychologically: the mathematical sublime is wonder via sublime enthrallment, while the dynamic sublime is sublime disquietude or discord, manifested in inexpressible realizations, disquietude and self-perceptual depth. A crucial part of Kuiken et al.'s argument is that there are formal devices such as metaphor, or simile, or parallelism in which two entities are put into a situation where they are both different and the same: 'The crossings or correspondences created by metaphor give rise to conjunctive units that capture more than can be immediately said' (Kuiken and Oliver 2013: 300). Two entities or events are alike, but in a way which the reader cannot at first understand; the ontological crossing involves the gap between them: 'Sublime feeling is embodied in the crossed ontological categories of the text' (Kuiken et al. 2012: 30). They cite Ricoeur's theory of a living metaphor in which there is both identity and difference, a relation between the expression (vehicle) and its communicated meaning (tenor) of *is and is not*. Kuiken and Douglas (2017: 10) suggest that empathy with a character works in the same way: the reader *is and is not* the character. The idea that the metaphor can transform the self, as one of the modes of the sublime, is discussed by Pelowski and Akiba (2011: 91, citing Burch-Brown 1993).

Indirectness is part of the 'poetic effects' as proposed by Sperber and Wilson, where a large number of possible meanings are derived from the metaphor, but with only weak confidence that any specific meaning was particularly implied by the metaphor's creator. Perhaps this large number of meanings contributes to an epistemic feeling of significance. Kaeppler (2008: 7) describes the value placed on indirectness in ritual language, noting that terms such as Hawaiian *kaona* and Tongan *heliaki* 'refer to hidden or veiled meanings that must be unravelled layer by layer until the metaphors on which they are based can be understood'.

The synechdochic relation of part standing to whole is one of the types of metaphor and might trigger strong experience because of its compression, where a small part generates significant knowledge. It may also be an example of perfection as an uncanny relation between two representations, as when a part of a narrative is a perfect instance of the whole narrative which contains it. Robert Louis Stevenson describes narratives in which there are moments 'which put the last mark of truth upon a story, and fill up, at one blow, our capacity for sympathetic pleasure'. Character, thought or emotion are embodied in an act or attitude, as in 'Crusoe recoiling from the footprint, Achilles shouting over against the Trojans, Ulysses bending the great bow, Christian running with his fingers in his ears' (Stevenson 1882). A variant of synecdoche is Lessing's characterization of artworks such as the Laocoon sculpture as expressing a 'pregnant moment', the moment from which a sequence of preceding and subsequent events can be reconstructed

(Arnheim 1967: 408). Brecht's notion of the *Grundgestus* (Brecht 1964: 246) as the expression of the basic attitude of a play is similarly synechdochic. The *Gestus* itself is 'a number of related gestures expressing such different attitudes as politeness, anger and so on'.

> Splitting such material into one gestus after another, the actor masters his character by first mastering the 'story'. It is only after walking all round the entire episode that he can, as it were by a single leap, seize and fix his character, complete with all its individual features. Once he has done his best to let himself be amazed by the inconsistencies in its various attitudes knowing that he will in turn have to make them amaze the audience, then the story as a whole gives him a chance to pull the inconsistencies together; for the story, being a limited episode, has a specific sense, i.e. only gratifies a specific fraction of all the interests that could arise. (Brecht 1964: 200)

The *Gestus* is thus associated with surprise, and is perhaps a form of strong experience. Benjamin brings out this meaning more clearly, adding a mystical element: 'The damming of the stream of real life, the moment when the flow comes to a standstill, makes itself felt as reflux: this reflux is astonishment. The dialectic at a standstill is its real object' (Benjamin 1983a: 13).

We have seen that there is some reason to think that increased processing effort might potentiate a strong experience, while noting that changes in processing effort are very common, so the change presumably needs to be combined with something else for it to be effective. Do metaphors increase processing effort? Though it seems plausible that they should, the evidence is not straightforward. Evidence that metaphors increase processing effort comes from Rapp et al. (2011: 203), who suggest that increased activation in the left inferior frontal gyrus of the brain is observable during the processing metaphors, metonyms, idioms and irony, suggesting that they all involve 'an increased cognitive processing demand to integrate nonliteral meanings into the overall sentence meaning'. Bohrn et al. (2009: 2681) correspondingly claim that literal language is processed more easily. However, there is also evidence that metaphorical meanings are processed as quickly as literal meanings, meaning perhaps that metaphors do not demand increased processing effort. Glucksberg (2003: 92) argues that metaphorical interpretation does not follow an initial stage of literal interpretation; this is demonstrated by the metaphor interference effect which shows that a metaphorical meaning is automatically activated rather than slowly derived, as demonstrated by the fact that the metaphorical meaning can slow down any judgement that the metaphor is literally false (Pierce et al. 2010: 400; Glucksberg et al. 1982). Similarly,

Gibbs and Tendahl (2006: 383) note that nonliteral statements may be as easy to process as literal statements. It is for example possible for an idiom to produce a wider range of cognitive effects than are produced by a paraphrase of the idiom, even though the idiom is processed more quickly; here, greater cognitive effects seem to arise from lesser processing effort. Nevertheless, they say that '[i]n general it is impossible to predict the processing effort needed to comprehend metaphors given the number, or types of cognitive effects that may arise from interpreting these statements' (Gibbs and Tendahl 2006: 392). They agree with relevance theory (Sperber and Wilson 1995) that metaphors have the potential for even more cognitive effects, if more processing effort is put in. The general principle of relevance which underlies communication is that the effort put into processing the utterance is rewarded by the cognitive effects which result; more effort guarantees more cognitive effects. Metaphors have at least the potential to demand increased processing effort, and this might help them trigger strong experiences.

Parallelism and Repetition

In literary texts, parallelism is a repetition in which there is also a variation. Parallelism is found in English literary texts and is common in the poetry of Dryden and Pope. However, in English, parallelism is not a fundamental structural principle of poetry; metre plays this role instead. In contrast, in other traditions, parallelism is a fundamental structural principle and may for example tie adjacent lines together in couplets in a poem. There are detailed and extensive accounts of these practices in Fox (1988, 2014), Frog (2014) and Fabb (1997 chapter 6, 2015 chapter 6). In parallelism, words or sequences of words may be paired, with matching meanings and syntactic structures.

There are various reasons for thinking that parallelism might trigger strong experiences. First, some kinds of parallelism are like metaphor, because they communicate the same meaning with two different sets of words, which means that neither set of words literally expresses the meaning, but rather must be somewhat metaphorical. Second, parallelism is a type of double or multiple, and these can be triggers of strong experience. Third, parallelism is often quite dense within a text, with parallel elements juxtaposed. Given the interpretative complications of parallelism, this puts the reader to a lot of processing effort over a short stretch, and processing effort potentiates strong experience. Fourth, parallelism may be a mode of defamiliarization. Jakobson (1960) thought that parallelism performed the poetic function of drawing attention to the form of the text. Defamiliarization may be a source of strong experience.

Burke illustrates how parallelism might work as a trigger of strong experience, in his example of a parallelistic text as sublime.

> There are also many descriptions in the poets and orators, which owe their sublimity to a richness and profusion of images, in which the mind is so dazzled as to make it impossible to attend to that exact coherence and agreement of the allusions, which we should require on every other occasion. I do not now remember a more striking example of this, than the description which is given of the king's army in the play of Henry the fourth:
>
>   All furnished, all in arms,
>   All plumed like ostriches that with the wind
>   Baited like eagles having lately bathed:
>   As full of spirit as the month of May,
>   And gorgeous as the sun in Midsummer,
>   Wanton as youthful goats, wild as young bulls.
>   I saw young Harry with his beaver on
>   Rise from the ground like feathered Mercury;
>   And vaulted with such ease into his seat
>   As if an angel dropped down from the clouds
>   To turn and wind a fiery Pegasus.
>   (Burke 1987: 78, quoting loosely from
>   Shakespeare *Henry IV.1*, IV: i, 97–109)

The distinctive formal characteristic of this text is its parallelism, based mainly around adjacent similes. The soldiers are like ostriches and like eagles, like May and midsummer, and like goats and bulls; and Harry Hotspur is like Mercury and like an angel. Each of the individual similes, such as the soldiers like ostriches, needs to be interpreted, finding a meaning which is not literally expressed; and then the pairing of the similes needs to be interpreted because ostriches are not like eagles, and by comparing the soldiers to both, we need to find yet another implied set of meanings. This is a doubling of the indirectness, a kind of metaphor of a metaphor.

The example given by Burke manifests a variant of Longinus's amplification (*amplificatio*) where 'you wheel up one impressive unit after another to give a series of increasing importance', and also manifests the rhetorical device of *accumulatio*, which is 'heaping up praise or accusation to emphasize or summarize points or inferences already made' (Lanham 1991). Here we might note Dorter's (1990: 48) claim that a Shakespearian metaphor gets its power from 'the running together of diverse images ... in defiance of conceptual clarity. The greatest metaphors are of this kind, too pregnant with associations to be reduced to conceptual analogies'. But this sort of density also accelerates the text, as when Blair (1996: 219) says that Ossian 'throws forth his images with a rapid conciseness, which enable them to strike the mind with the greatest force'. Margulis (2013) argues that in songs when a word is repeated many times, attention is shifted away from its meaning to its form, and specifically to its sound. We might say that the word thus becomes something which is not really a word, in the sense that it is no longer a combination of sound and meaning, and metacognitively we might be surprised by this discrepancy relative to our schema of what a word is. Margulis suggests further that this experience of losing the meaning and focusing on the sound relates to the experience of being moved by music, which we can relate to strong experience. The artist Max Ernst (1968: 427) had a strong experience after an experience of repetition when reading an illustrated catalogue of scientific instruments, when the pictures of unconnected objects 'provoked a sudden intensification of the visionary faculties in me and brought forth an illusive succession of contradictory images, double, triple and multiple images, piling up on each other with the persistence and rapidity which are peculiar to love memories and visions of half-sleep'. It is possible that the densely packed adjacent elements, which must be interpreted relative to each other, are a source of strong experience. It is worth asking whether they increase processing effort, and whether the strong experience is also enabled by this.

Other writers on the sublime have used parallelism as an example of the sublime. Longinus cites a parallelistic example of the sublime from Xenophon: 'They slung their shields together, closed ranks, fought, killed, perished', and another from Demosthenes:

> For when someone is on the offensive he can employ many things that the offended party cannot even recount; gestures, glances, and things he says, in part as a daredevil, in part as an enemy, in part with the fist, in part with the face.

Here is an example from Lord Kames from 1765, where the parallel items are not themselves similes or fully formed metaphors (though there is some metaphoricity).

> I shall produce but one instance, from Shakespeare, which sets a few objects before the eye, without much pomp of language: it operates its effect, by representing these objects in a climax, raising the mind higher and higher till it feel the emotion of grandeur in perfection:

> The cloud-capt tow'rs, the gorgeous palaces,
> The solemn temples, the great globe itself,
> Yea all which it inherit, shall dissolve, &tc.

> *The cloud-capt tow'rs* produce an elevating emotion, heightened by the *gorgeous palaces*; and the mind is carried still higher and higher by the images that follow. Successive images, making thus stronger and stronger impressions, must elevate more than any single image can do. (Kames 1996: 231)

Shaw (2006: 9, 30) says of Wordsworth's use of connectives as in 'And the round ocean, and the living air, / And the blue sky' that it is a way 'to make the connection between objects and ideas' and that these multiplied connectives are a manifestation of the sublime. Friedrich (2001: 226) suggests that the epiphany at the beginning of Tolstoy's *Hadji Murat* (1912) is enabled by the list of flowers, with the catalogue as 'a particular kind of linearity that gets commuted and telescoped into one aesthetical point'. These lists, concatenations and parallelisms may all work in a similar way, demanding that the reader find some ground to connect the parts, to produce the implied meaning, but also presenting the component parts very rapidly. Parallelism thus may enable the sublime both in the way that the increased processing effort enables the sublime, as well as in the way that metaphor enables the sublime.

This is the place to mention another very common aesthetic practice which may function as a trigger of strong experience, when various discrete elements in an aesthetic practice are put in parallel, and may become identical with one another. An example of this would be choral singing, or dancing, both of which involve a coordination between voices or bodies, but where we would normally expect variation and where the identity between the performers may be experienced as metacognitively surprising for reasons explained earlier. Choral singing and dancing have something in common with the uncanny double or Moses Mendelssohn's sublime repetitions. This is a variant of the multiple as a trigger of strong experience, and it shows up also in the motif of the individual in the crowd, which is seen for example in Wordsworth's 'Daffodils' poem, and also in his 'spots of time' in *The Prelude* (Bishop 1959: 47). There may be a shift between the various parts being different and then all being the same, for example in a polyphonic song where the voices momentarily come together in harmony, or when dancers momentarily align so that they are all making the same bodily gestures. This is a type of parallelism. But it is also related separately to metaphor, because dancing is itself a kind of metaphor for walking, and singing a kind of metaphor for speaking. In these regulated aesthetic practices, the bodily movements or voices resemble their ordinary forms of walking, running, jumping and speaking but by being regulated and controlled, they can be taken as evidence of meanings beyond themselves. This is another way in which the ordinary aspects of an aesthetic practice potentiate strong experience.

Fragments and Small Texts

Fragments and short texts are sometimes triggers. Housman says that 'if a line of poetry strays into my memory, my skin bristles so that the razor ceases to act' (Housman 1933: 46). Woolf's 1928 story 'Moments of Being: "Slater's Pins Have No Points"' begins when the narrator hears an utterance 'Slater's pins have no points – don't you always find that?' This single utterance triggers a strong experience in her. William James describes 'that deepened sense of the significance of a maxim or formula which occasionally sweeps over one'. James thinks that sometimes just a single word may be enough, and cites the wondrous name 'Philadelphia', 'chalcedony', the names of ancient heroes, 'hermit', 'woods' and 'forest', each of which may trigger a strong experience. John Bunyan has a strong experience which he describes in *Grace Abounding*: 'One day, as I was passing in the field, this sentence fell upon my soul: Thy righteousness is in heaven; and methought withal I saw with the eyes of my soul, Jesus Christ, at God's right hand' (Bunyan 1666, cited Nichols 1987: 17, discussed also in Kim 2012: 54). We have seen that strong experiences sometimes are attached to fragments, which may be separated from their original contexts, or may just stand out against the foil of their original context. Why might fragments trigger strong experiences? It is possible that fragments push beyond the normal range of variation the relation between token in the form of the perceived fragment and type/schema to which it belongs. This might be because a fragment is a very bad tokening of a type, because of its fragmentariness, hence above the normal range of variation and so in principle surprising and triggering a strong experience. On the other hand, metacognition may play a role, with the fragment perceived with a high degree of granularity, such that it no longer seems to be a token of a very general type, but is a unique token with no type, another trigger of strong experience via metacognitive surprise. A further possibility is that the fragment has a synechdochic relation to the whole and so draws on the ways in which synecdoche as a kind of metaphor can trigger strong experience.

Fragments of speech trigger Joyce's first epiphany in the novel *Stephen Hero* (written early, but first published after his death).

He was passing through Eccles' St one evening, one misty evening, with all these thoughts dancing the dance of unrest in his brain when a trivial incident set him composing some ardent verses which he entitled a 'Vilanelle of the Temptress'. A young lady was standing on the steps of one of those brown brick houses which seem the very incarnation of Irish paralysis. A young gentleman was leaning on the rusty railings of the area. Stephen as he passed on his quest heard the following fragment of colloquy out of which he received an impression keen enough to afflict his sensitiveness very severely.

> The Young Lady – (drawling discreetly) ... O, yes ... I was ... at the ... cha ... pel. ...
> The Young Gentleman – (inaudibly) ... I ... (again inaudibly) ... I ...
> The Young Lady – (softly) ... O ... but you're ... ve ... ry ... wick ... ed ...

This triviality made him think of collecting such moments together in a book of epiphanies. By an epiphany he meant a sudden spiritual manifestation, whether in the vulgarity of speech or of gesture or in a memorable phase of the mind itself. He believed that it was for the man of letters to record these epiphanies with extreme care, seeing that they themselves are the most delicate and evanescent of moments.

(Joyce 1944: 188)

As an example of a strong experience, this has significance in its 'spiritual manifestation' and an arousal response in its being 'keen enough to afflict his sensitiveness very severely'. The fragmentariness of the speech may be part of the trigger, and there are other contributing factors. As in many strong experiences, there may be overdetermination. For example, he is walking, there are spatial liminalities in the steps and railings, and the speech is perhaps slowed down. It is further worth considering whether there is some failure in multisensory integration here, if the people as seen do not fit with the people as heard; a failure of multisensory integration may correlate both with overattention to detail and with a failure to match token to type, both of which may be part of the experience of epiphany.

An overheard fragment of speech also has a key role in Augustine's life-transforming strong experience which begins after he throws himself down below a fig tree, tears flowing in 'rivers' (*et dimisi habemas lacrimis, et proruperunt flumina oculorum meorum*) and calling out to God.

> As I was saying this and weeping to the bitter agony of my heart, suddenly I heard a voice from the nearby house chanting as if it might be

a boy or a girl (I do not know which), saying and repeating over and over again 'Pick up and read, pick up and read.' At once my countenance changed, and I began to think intently whether there might be some sort of children's game in which such a chant is used. But I could not remember having heard of one. I checked the flood of tears and stood up. I interpreted it solely as a divine command to me to open the book and read the first chapter I might find. [...] So I hurried back to the place where Alypius was sitting. There I had put down the book of the apostle when I got up. I seized it, opened it and in silence read the first passage on which my eyes lit: 'Not in riots and drunken parties, not in eroticism and indecencies, not in strife and rivalry, but put on the Lord Jesus Christ and make no provision for the flesh in its lusts.' (Rom. 13: 13–14).

I neither wished nor needed to read further. At once, with the last words of this sentence, it was as if a light of relief from all anxiety flooded into my heart. All the shadows of doubt were dispelled.

(Augustine VIII.xii, 28–29 in
O'Donnell 1992: 152)

Augustine experiences a sudden emotional change, followed by intense metacognitive speculation about the apparent cause. What he perceives is schematically discrepant: the chanter has no clear gender, and the chant belongs to a children's game which does not fit into a schema in his memory. The repeated might be seen as an example of the uncanny double. Of particular relevance here, he hears a small text, the fragment perhaps of something larger; and then he goes and reads another apparently arbitrarily found fragment, a small text from the Bible. Then he gets a strong epistemic feeling of significance. It is also worth noting that he starts in the physical posture of lying down, and this posture, perhaps associated with hypoarousal, seems to play a role in some strong experiences. There is also extensive water imagery throughout, which is a common motif in strong experiences. Ziolkowski (2014: 6) emphasizes particularly the role of the fragment of the book in generating the strong experience, citing for example bibliomancy, manifested as 'the practice of opening the books of Virgil at random, placing one's finger on a passage, and then reading it as prophetic'.

Sometimes the trigger of a strong experience is a visual fragment, as in Barthes's *Camera Lucida* (1982) where a part of a photograph pierces him in a '*punctum*'. Panzarella (1980: 83) notes that a fragment of a work may produce an aesthetic peak experience, particularly in visual art, where a colour or a shape might trigger it. In Proust's *The Captive*, the critic Bergotte dies from a strong experience, focused on a fragment. Teive et al. (2014) suggest that this fictional incident might be an example of Stendhal's syndrome and may reflect Proust's own experience of the painting at the Jeu de Paume in 1921. The fictional character of Bergotte goes to see Vermeer's *View of Delft*, painted in about 1661, which is at that time on exhibition in Paris. He is already giddy as he climbs the liminal zone of the steps into the exhibition, and after viewing other paintings comes to the Vermeer. He already associates this painting with one of its details, a beautifully painted little patch of yellow wall.

> At last he came to the Vermeer which he remembered as more striking, more different from anything else that he knew, but in which, thanks to the critic's article, he remarked for the first time some small figures in blue, that the ground was pink, and finally the precious substance of the tiny patch of yellow wall. His giddiness increased; he fixed his eyes, like a child upon a yellow butterfly which it is trying to catch, upon the precious little patch of wall.

He speculates, remembers his life, and then:

> He repeated to himself: 'Little patch of yellow wall, with a sloping roof, little patch of yellow wall'. While doing so he sank down upon a circular divan; and then at once he ceased to think that his life was in jeopardy and, reverting to his natural optimism, told himself: 'It is just an ordinary indigestion from those potatoes; they weren't properly cooked; it is nothing'. A fresh attack beat him down; he rolled from the divan to the floor, as visitors and attendants came hurrying to his assistance. He was dead. (Proust 2006: 600)

Fragments are present here in this strong experience: the fragment of speech in his repeated utterance, and a fragment of colour in a representation of a liminal zone. It is also worth noting that the three-word sentence 'He was dead' (*Il était mort*) is by far the shortest sentence compared with previous sentences in the same paragraph; in the French original most of the sentences are quite long. As a short sentence, it may draw the reader's attention, increasing processing effort via increased depth of processing as argued by Emmott et al. (2006). This in itself might help contribute to the strong experience. In Proust's account of what Bergotte saw, an opposition between water and land reappears in the opposition of paint and dryness, including the dryness of Bergotte's own work. There is also perhaps the motif of the individual in the crowd at the end of the passage.

I went to see this painting where it now hangs in the Mauritshuis in The Hague, and I spent a long time with it, also watching other visitors to the museum looking at it. Bergotte is described as focusing intensely on scale, mentioning the small figures, and when I looked at the painting, I thought that there was something visually odd about the perspective relating to the two sides of the canal; the figures on the proximal side and on the distal side are out of scale relative to the distance between the shores. This is a schematic discrepancy. Second, though the spatial locations of water and land and sky are clear in the painting, they form visual echoes so that land and water and sky are mixed through the reflections, and in the characteristic shine or brilliance of a Vermeer painting. This is a mixing of distinct schemata, representing different kinds of place, like 'the outline against the watery sky' in the ecstasy at Culross discussed earlier in this book (Laski 1961). As I walked out of the room at the end of my viewing, my back was overtaken by a tremendous shudder.

Motifs

We can find themes or motifs which recur in descriptions of strong experiences. Compare for example Joyce's unpublished 'epiphany 28', quoted below and followed by an extract from Tennyson's 'Audley Court' (1842) which Nichols (1987: 151) called 'one of Tennyson's strikingly modern epiphanies'.

> A moonless night under which the waves gleam feebly. The ship is entering a harbour where there are some lights. The sea is uneasy, charged with dull anger like the eyes of an animal which is about to spring, the prey of its own pitiless hunger. The land is flat and thinly wooded. Many people are gathered on the shore to see what ship it is that is entering their harbour.
>
> (Joyce 1956)

>   but ere the night we rose
> And saunter'd home beneath a moon, that, just
> In crescent, dimly rain'd about the leaf
> Twilights of airy silver, till we reach'd
> The limit of the hills; and as we sank
> From rock to rock upon the glooming quay,
> The town was hush'd beneath us: lower down
> The bay was oily calm; the harbour-buoy,
> Sole star of phosphorescence in the calm,
> With one green sparkle ever and anon
> Dipt by itself, and we were glad at heart.
>   (Tennyson 'Audley Court' ll. 78-88, in Roberts 2000: 95)

We can identify in both cases the motif of water and more specifically of the sea. This appears also in Longinus, whose sublime passages include descriptions of the sea, where he compares the sublime Homer to the sea, and he says that 'we admire not the small streams, useful and pellucid though they may be, but the Nile, the Danube or the Rhine, and still more the Ocean' (Longinus 1998: 146). In Joyce's epiphany there is the motif of the crowd of people. Liminalities are motifs in both. In Joyce's epiphany there is the motif of the shore. In Tennyson there is 'the limit of the hills'. And in both cases there is a crossing of a liminality, which might remind us of other liminal crossings: Kant entering St. Peter's or Mr Ramsay leaping from boat to shore in *To the Lighthouse*.

Laski (1961) and others have noted that motifs appear in descriptions of strong experiences, and we might ask why. I now briefly consider some explanations which relate motifs to the triggers we have already seen. The first is the metaphorical possibilities of these motifs; for example, Illich (1986: 24) says of water that it 'has a nearly unlimited ability to carry metaphors'. The second is that the motifs might be stereotyped examples of triggers; crowds can be treated as multiples, which we have seen are metacognitively surprising. Third, the motifs seem to be capable of transforming one into another as when the crowds are also the water.

> They were moved involuntarily from street to street by the crowds ebbing and flowing. The whole nation seemed to have expanded into a huge family in a moment, and a *frisson* of brotherhood, in face of the invader, passed through the hearts of rich and poor, and linked them electrically. (Swift 1898: 114)

The crowd motif and the water motif are sometimes combined in triggers of strong experience. The association is conventional: the OED cites 'waves of populations' and 'wave of democratic equality' from the mid-nineteenth century. Benjamin (1983b, 61, 64) cites Hugo saying that the 'the depths are crowds' (*Les profondeurs sont des multitudes*):

> When on his seventieth birthday the population of the capital pressed toward his house on Avenue d'Eylau, this meant the realization of the image of the wave surging against the cliffs as well as the realization of the message of the spirit world.

Laski notes that motifs are associated with ecstasies both as external features and as metaphorical ways of describing the experience itself, and this is clearly true of the water motif. Thus the motifs are also found in the metacognition about the experience. Consider for example Schopenhauer, for whom something suddenly 'raises us out of the endless stream of willing' (cited Collinson 1992: 127). As Barthes (1967: 56) notes, Saussure uses a metaphor of waves in the sea to express how meaning emerges from the floating realm of thought (*ce royaume flottant*). We earlier saw that Benjamin says of Brecht's tableaux that 'we gaze down into the stream of things'. We might think of motifs as crystallizations of the general kinds of trigger which have been considered in this chapter, and this book.

Summary of Chapter

Laski (1961) argues that ecstasies have 'triggers'. In this chapter, I explored some of the ways in which aspects of literary texts may function as triggers for strong experience. The general principle is that these triggers come from the ordinary and general characteristics of literary texts, some of which are shared with other aesthetic practices, and some of which are shared with other uses of language. In the right circumstances these ordinary characteristics can become triggers of strong experience. The right circumstances involve textual and extra-textual context, the co-presence of other triggers, the right subjective state and a cultural context which allows for a discourse of strong experiences. The triggers all work because they are ways of producing surprise by pushing the relation between the perceived token and the known schematic type beyond the normal range of variation, either by creating discrepancy between token and type, or by creating an identity between token and type which is metacognitively discrepant. We have seen that narratives work with our expectations and by encouraging us to empathetically immerse ourselves in the actions of the characters. Narratives are also divided into bounded and hierarchically structured events and this allows for various kinds of complexity which can trigger strong experience. Boundaries are also liminalities, and liminality appears both in the contents and forms of many literary texts. Literary texts have form and when form changes, which can produce strong experience, perhaps in part through demanding increased processing effort. In poetry, metrical and rhythmic forms can produce complex effects in combination. Metaphor has long been considered a potential trigger of the sublime, and I argued that parallelism can also be interpreted as a type of metaphor, along with the kinds of uncanny multiplicity found in parallelism and repetition in literary texts, along with other aesthetic objects and practices. Whole texts are sometimes substituted by their fragments, and both the fragment in itself and relation between fragment and whole seem to be triggers of strong experience. The chapter concludes by noting that repeated motifs, such as water and crowds, can be triggers and that this may be because the motifs have significant metaphorical force. Literary texts thus have many components that make them liable to trigger strong experience.

Chapter 7
CONCLUSIONS

How the Strong Experience Is Triggered

A strong experience involves a sudden experience characterized by a strong feeling. One kind of strong feeling is an epistemic feeling of coming to know something highly significant, though what is known may be ineffable. The other kind of strong feeling is a sudden phasic arousal such as a chill or tears or some other bodily feeling that can otherwise be associated with emotion. The strong experience can involve both of these feelings, but sometimes just one is felt. In this book I have put strong experiences into three groups. One is the 'thrill' which is often just the arousal. The second is the 'sublime' which is often both the epistemic feeling and the arousal. The third is the 'epiphany' which is often just the epistemic feeling. Neither the strong experience in itself nor these three subtypes are natural kinds of experience. Rather, they are a way of grouping certain experiences which might be related, with the goal of understanding why they arise.

I have suggested that strong experiences all start as surprise. This explains why they are sudden and brief, like surprise. It also explains why they can be triggered, like surprise, and by triggers which are surprising. It explains why they involve an epistemic feeling, because surprise is basically an epistemic event of coming to know something not previously known. Why the feeling of significance arises is discussed in Chapter 3, as is the feeling of ineffability. And strong experiences involve arousal because surprise involves arousal, as discussed in Chapter 4. There are various ways in which surprise can arise, but in this book I focus on the way by which 'if a discrepancy between schema and input occurs, surprise is elicited' (Meyer et al. 1991: 296). I have proposed two ways in which a discrepancy might generate a strong experience. The first is when the perception of events or objects or characters, whether directly perceived or represented, is discrepant relative to a schema. Expectation plays an important role, by making schemata available which are then checked against the perceptions. Narratives and the sequential aspects of texts often depend on expectation to play this role in enabling schematic discrepancy. Perceptions of extreme tokenings of certain types, as in the sublime, may also be a discrepancy between perception and schema, and so surprising. The second kind of discrepancy involves metacognition, in the matching of our perception of our own experience to our schemata for experience. I have said that discrepancies here produce 'metacognitive surprise', while noting that this is really just ordinary surprise, directed at cognition itself. I suggest that this kind of metacognitive surprise is what we see in some of the epiphanic experiences of ordinary objects (but with other possible routes discussed in Chapter 5). A reading of Kant suggests that the sublime also involves metacognitive surprise. And one reason we can catch a strong experience by recalling one, or reading about one, is that strong experiences are in themselves metacognitively surprising.

Not Every Surprise Is a Strong Experience

Thrill experiences are common for some people. Experiences of the sublime are less common, though they have sufficiently predictable triggers that the experience of the sublime can be sought out. Epiphanies seem to come unexpectedly and rarely. If the experiences all begin with surprise, then we might ask why only some surprises turn into strong experiences. A related point is that what seems to be the same trigger may cause a strong experience in one person and not another.

We must assume that other factors, probably a great number and variety of factors, contribute to turning a surprise into a strong experience. The experiencer's physical, psychophysical and mental states, including prior knowledge and experience, all play a role. Personality traits and levels of expertise in a particular kind of perception and schema play a role. The cultural, environmental, natural and social contexts play a role. These variations are discussed in Chapter 5.

All of us have the capacity to be surprised. A reason why every surprise does not turn into a strong experience may also relate to culture. Cultural difference may affect the possibility of both having and reporting a strong experience, as well as what kinds of strong experience arise. Levy's (1973) notion of hypocognition is useful here, the notion that a kind of experience might arise within someone, but not be recognized within their culture, and so made invisible. The opposite possibility of hypercognition represents how a kind of experience can be made prominent in a culture, named and discussed and represented in fiction, as happens to strong experiences such as the sublime and the epiphany, which are extensively talked about in the modern Western tradition.

General Aesthetic Experience and the Strong Experience

Strong experiences are sudden and brief. In this section I discuss ways in which the extended experience of aesthetic objects might share, at a lower level, some of the characteristics of strong experiences. This possibility arises because strong experiences are explained in this book as ordinary psychological events, but which are experienced for contextual or other reasons as distinctive. Strong experiences are just surprises that are experienced in a distinctive way. Metacognitive surprise, which is one source of strong experience, is just surprise, triggered by our own metacognitions. Though strong experiences are rare, the perceptions and thoughts which trigger them are often variants of what we normally perceive. Similarly, when literary texts trigger strong experiences, they exploit general characteristics of textual practice. Literary triggers of strong experience are just ordinary aspects of literary texts.

This suggests that the triggers might have a more common but low-level experiential effect, not usually peaking into a strong experience, and that this might in part be how aesthetic experience is generated. In particular, and as discussed in Chapter 6, literature has many aspects that are potentially surprising. This can relate to the way literary texts, and particularly narratives, can generate expectations that can be met or violated. The notion that literary texts 'defamiliarize' is relevant here. The language of literature is strange relative to ordinary language, more regulated and more repetitive and otherwise altered. This might generate a low level of metacognitive surprise relative to our knowledge of language in general. And similarly the narratives and characters in literary texts resemble but are not fully like our knowledge of sequences of events and people in reality, and so are discrepant relative to our deeply embedded schemata for reality itself. This should also be metacognitively surprising. Furthermore, literary texts are each unique in their bounded completeness and organic unity (or are imagined to be), and thus literary texts can appear to be perfect objects, the kind of object from which we gain an epiphany. Thus literary texts might generate a low level of surprise throughout, and with it, a low-level epistemic feeling of significance, and perhaps a low level of arousal.

By related formal devices, other types of artwork may produce surprise either directly or metacognitively, but in a rather low level and general way, as a way of generating aesthetic experience. One of the fundamental themes of this book is that strong experiences have a connection to ordinary experience and can be explained by using the same psychological notions as ordinary experience. Artworks including literature make more systematic but still generic use of surprise, in order to produce the general aesthetic experience that can on occasion peak into strong experience.

The Basic Claims of the Book, Summarized

The various kinds of strong experience include thrills, sublime and epiphany. Strong experiences begin as surprises, and surprise is a response to a discrepancy relative to our schematic knowledge which we bring to our ongoing experience of the world. In some of these experiences, the new perception (or thought) is very divergent from the schema, and this is surprising. In other experiences, the new perception is of something which is identical with its schema, or identical with other tokenings of the same schema. This violates the principle of variation that perceptions are variations on a basic schema and not identical to it, and the perception of this violation is surprising relative to the schemata which we have for experience, knowledge and perception itself. This is a metacognitive surprise, and a trigger of strong experience. Strong experiences in themselves are discrepant relative to ordinary experience, and so strong experiences are metacognitively surprising and themselves a trigger for strong experience, and this is how we catch a thrill. Literature, along with other aesthetic forms, is made from materials that are inherently discrepant and so surprising, and our aesthetic experience in general is a mild form of the experience which peaks in a thrill, epiphany or feeling of the sublime.

This book makes some new claims, but without introducing any new mechanisms and it makes new claims by drawing on previous theories, and a standard psychology. I do not claim that there is a single type of experience, 'strong experience', but rather that a range of experiences which are in specific ways 'strong' are related by arising from surprise and by sharing other aspects of their psychology. The proposal that some of the strong experiences are a response to discrepancy is close to many other accounts of the sublime, and of the thrill, particularly in the psychology of music. I propose that strong experiences are infectious because we perceive them as themselves discrepant. The most radical proposal of the book, which draws on Dan Sperber's account of the strangeness of perfect animals, is that a strict nondiscrepancy, in the form of identity, is in itself discrepant at a higher level, in metacognition. This is because the perception of identity contradicts our knowledge that a perfect match of perception to schema is impossible. This is fundamental to my account in particular of the epiphanies of ordinary objects. These are the connections which mean that in their own ways, all these experiences are experiences of discrepancy, of surprise and so of strong experience.

BIBLIOGRAPHY

Abraham, Anna, and D. Yves von Cramon. 2009. "Reality=Relevance? Insights From Spontaneous Modulations of the Brain's Default Network When Telling Apart Reality from Fiction (Reality and Personal Relevance)." *PLoS One* 4, no. 3: E4741.

Adelman, Steven, C. Richard Taylor, and Norman C. Heglund. 1975. "Sweating on Paws and Palms: What Is Its Function?" *American Journal of Physiology* 229, no. 5: 1400–1402.

Adler, Jonathan E. 2008. "Surprise." *Educational Theory* 58, no. 2: 149–173.

Aggleton, John P., and Mortimer Mishkin. 1986. "The Amygdala: Sensory Gateway to the Emotions." In *Biological Foundations of Emotion*, edited by Robert Plutchik and Henry Kellerman, 281–299. Cambridge, MA: Academic Press.

Allen, Philip A., Kevin P. Kaut, and Robert R. Lord. 2008. "Emotion and Episodic Memory." In *Handbook of Episodic Memory: Handbook of Behavioral Neuroscience Vol. 18*, edited by Ekram Dere, Alexander Easton, Lynn Nadel, and Joe P. Huston, 115–132. Amsterdam: Elsevier.

Amos, India. 2019. "'That's What They Talk About When They Talk About Epiphanies': An Invitation to Engage With the Process of Developing Found Poetry to Illuminate Exceptional Human Experience." *Counselling and Psychotherapy Research* 19, no. 1: 16–24.

Appel, Markus, and Tobias Richter. 2010. "Transportation and Need for Affect in Narrative Persuasion: A Mediated Moderation Model." *Media Psychology* 13, no. 2: 101–135.

Armstrong, Thomas, and Brian Detweiler-Bedell. 2008. "Beauty as an Emotion: The Exhilarating Prospect of Mastering a Challenging World." *Review of General Psychology* 12, no. 4: 305–329.

Arnheim, Rudolf. 1967. *Art and Visual Perception*. London: Faber and Faber.

Arnold, Magda B. 1960. *Emotion and Personality*. New York: Columbia University Press.

Ashfield, Andrew, and Peter De Bolla, eds. 1996. *The Sublime: A Reader in British Eighteenth-Century Aesthetic Theory*. Cambridge: Cambridge University Press.

Auerbach, Erich. 1953. *Mimesis: The Representation of Reality in Western Literature*. Translated by Willard R. Trask. Princeton, NJ: Princeton University Press.

Augustine. 1991. *Confessions*. Translated With an Introduction and Notes by Henry Chadwick. Oxford: Oxford University Press.

Baddeley, Alan D. 2000. "Short-Term and Working Memory." In *The Oxford Handbook of Memory*, edited by Endel Tulving and Fergus I. M. Craik, 77–92. Oxford: Oxford University Press.

Baddeley, Alan D., and Graham J. Hitch. 1974. "Working Memory." In *The Psychology of Learning and Motivation: Advances in Research and Theory*, edited by Gordon H. Bower, 47–89. New York: Academic Press.

Baillie, John. 1996. "An Essay on the Sublime." In *The Sublime: A Reader in British Eighteenth-Century Aesthetic Theory*, edited by Andrew Ashfield and Peter De Bolla, 87–100. Cambridge: Cambridge University Press.

Ballard, Elise. 2014. *Epiphany: True Stories of Sudden Insight to Inspire, Encourage and Transform*. New York: Harmony Books.

Bar-El, Yair, Rimona Durst, Gregory Katz, Josef Zislin, Ziva Strauss, and Haim Y. Knobler. 2000. "Jerusalem Syndrome." *British Journal of Psychiatry* 176: 86–90.

Barfoot, C. C. 1999. ""Milton Silent Came Down My Path": The Epiphany of Blake's Left Foot." In *Moments of Moment: Aspects of the Literary Epiphany*, edited by Wim Tigges, 61–84. Amsterdam: Rodopi.

Barraza, Jorge A., Veronika Alexander, Laura E. Beavin, Elizabeth T. Terris, and Paul J. Zak. 2015. "The Heart of the Story: Peripheral Physiology During Narrative Exposure Predicts Charitable Giving." *Biological Psychology* 105, no. 2015: 138–143.

Barrett, Lisa F. 2011. "Constructing Emotion." *Psychological Topics* 20, no. 3: 359–380.

Barthes, Roland. 1967. *Elements of Semiology*. Translated by Annette Lavers and Colin Smith. New York: Hill and Wang.

Barthes, Roland. 1982. *Camera Lucida: Reflections on Photography*. London: Fontana.

Bartlett, Frederick C. 1932. *Remembering: A Study in Experimental and Social Psychology*. Cambridge: Cambridge University Press.

Barwick, Linda. 2006. "Marri Ngarr Lirrga Songs: A Musicological Analysis of Song Pairs in Performance." *Musicology Australia* 28, no. 1: 1–25.

Barwick, Linda, Allan Marett, Joe Blythe, and Michael Walsh. 2007. "Arriving, Digging, Performing, Returning: An Exercise in Rich Interpretation of a Djanba Song Text in the Sound Archive of the Wadeye Knowledge Centre, Northern Territory of Australia." In *Oceanic Music Encounters: The Print Resource and the Human Resource: Essays in Honour of Mervyn Mclean*, edited by Richard Moyle, 13–24. Auckland, NZ: Department of Anthropology, University of Auckland.

Bauman, Richard. 1975. "Verbal Art as Performance." *American Anthropologist* 77: 290–311.

Bauman, Richard, and Charles L. Briggs.1990. "Poetics and Performance as Critical Perspectives on Language and Social Life." *Annual Review of Anthropology* 19: 59–88.

Beatty, Jackson. 1982. "Task-Evoked Pupillary Responses, Processing Load, and the Structure of Processing Resources." *Psychological Bulletin* 91: 276–292.

Beckett, Samuel. 2006. *Novels of Samuel Beckett: The Grove Centenary Edition, Volume 1*. New York: Grove Press.

Beja, Morris. 1971. *Epiphany in the Modern Novel*. Seattle, WA: University of Washington Press.

Bell, Claudia, and John Lyall. 2002. *The Accelerated Sublime: Landscape, Tourism, and Identity*. Westport, CT: Praeger.

Benedek, Mathias, and Christian Kaernbach. 2011. "Physiological Correlates and Emotional Specificity of Human Piloerection." *Biological Psychology* 86, no. 3: 320–332.

Benjamin, Walter. 1969. "The Work of Art in the Age of Mechanical Reproduction." In *Illuminations*, edited by Hannah Arendt. Translated by Harry Zohn, From the 1935 Essay. New York: Schocken Books.

———. 1983a. *Understanding Brecht*. Translated by Anna Bostock. London: Verso.

———. 1983b. *Charles Baudelaire. A Lyric Poet in the Era of High Capitalism*. Translated by Harry Zohn. London: Verso.

———. 2009. *The Origin of German Tragic Drama*. Translated by John Osborne. London: Verso.

Berenson, Bernard. 1948. *Aesthetics and History in the Visual Arts*. New York: Pantheon.

Bergson, Henri. 1911. *Creative Evolution*. Translated by Arthur Mitchell. New York: Henry Holt and Company.

Berlyne, Daniel E. 1954. "An Experimental Study of Human Curiosity." *British Journal of Psychology* 45, no. 4: 256–265.

———. 1971. *Aesthetics and Psychobiology.* New York: Appleton Century Crofts.
Bernstein, Alvin S., Kenneth Taylor, Burton G. Austen, Martin Nathanson, and Anthony Scarpelli. 1971. "Orienting Response and Apparent Movement Toward or Away From the Observer." *Journal of Experimental Psychology* 87, no. 1: 37–45.
Bezdek, Matthew A., Jeffrey E. Foy, and Richard J. Gerrig. 2013. "'Run for It!': Viewers' Participatory Responses to Film Narratives." *Psychology of Aesthetics, Creativity, and the Arts* 7, no. 4: 409–416.
Bharucha, Jamshed J. 1994. "Tonality and Expectation." In *Musical Perceptions*, edited by Rita Aiello and John A. Sloboda, 213–239. New York: Oxford University Press.
Biddle, Jennifer L. 2007. *Breasts, Bodies, Canvas: Central Desert Art as Experience.* Sydney: University of South Wales Press.
Bidney, Martin. 1997. *Patterns of Epiphany: From Wordsworth to Tolstoy, Pater, and Barrett Browning.* Carbondale, IL: Southern Illinois University Press.
———. 2004. "Epiphany in Autobiography: The Quantum Changes of Dostoevsky and Tolstoy." *Journal of Clinical Psychology* 60, no. 5: 471–480.
Biederman, Irving, and Edward A. Vessel. 2006. "Perceptual Pleasure and the Brain: A Novel Theory Explains Why the Brain Craves Information and Seeks It Through the Senses." *American Scientist* 94, no. 3: 247–253.
Bindra, Dalbir. 1972. "Weeping: A Problem of Many Facets." *Bulletin of the British Psychological Society* 25, no. 89: 281–284.
Bishop, Jonathan. 1959. "Wordsworth and the "Spots of Time"." *ELH* 26, no. 1: 45–65.
Blair, Hugh. 1996. "Lectures on Rhetoric and Belles Lettres." In *The Sublime: A Reader in British Eighteenth-Century Aesthetic Theory*, edited by Andrew Ashfield and Peter De Bolla, 213–223. Cambridge: Cambridge University Press.
Blood, Anne J., and Robert J. Zatorre. 2001. "Intensely Pleasurable Responses to Music Correlate With Activity in Brain Regions Implicated in Reward and Emotion." *PNAS* 98, no. 20: 11818–11823.
Blood, Benjamin Paul. 1874. *The Anaesthetic Revelation and the Gist of Philosophy.* Amsterdam, NY: B. P. Blood.
Bloom, Harold. 1981. "Freud and the Poetic Sublime: A Catastrophe Theory of Creativity." In *Freud: A Collection of Critical Essays*, edited by Perry Meisel, 211–231. Eaglewood Cliffs, NJ: Prentice-Hall.
Bohrer, Karl Heinz. 1994. *Suddenness: On the Moment of Aesthetic Appearance.* Translated by Ruth Crowley. New York: Columbia University Press.
Bohrn, Isabel C., Ulrike Altmann, and Arthur M. Jacobs. 2009. "Looking at the Brains Behind Figurative Language: A Quantitative Meta-Analysis of Neuroimaging Studies on Metaphor, Idiom, and Irony Processing." *Neuropsychologia* 50, no. 11: 2669–2683.
Bohrn, Isabel C., Ulrike Altmann, Oliver Lubrich, Winfried Menninghaus, and Arthur M. Jacobs. 2012. "Old Proverbs in New Skins: An fMRI Study on Defamiliarization." *Frontiers in Psychology* 3, no. 204: 1–18.
Bohrn, Isabel C., Ulrike Altmann, Oliver Lubrich, Winfried Menninghaus, and Arthur M. Jacobs. 2013. "When we Like What we Know – A Parametric FMRI Analysis of Beauty and Familiarity." *Brain and Language* 124, no. 1: 1–8.
Bonner, Edward T., and Harris L. Friedman. 2011. "A Conceptual Clarification of the Experience of Awe: An Interpretative Phenomenological Analysis." *The Humanistic Psychologist* 39, no. 3: 222–235.
Bornstein, Robert F. 1989. "Exposure and Affect: Overview and Meta-Analysis of Research, 1968–1987." *Psychological Bulletin* 106, no. 2: 265–289.

Bornstein, Robert F., and Paul R. D'Agostino. 1994. "The Attribution and Discounting of Perceptual Fluency: Preliminary Tests of a Perceptual Fluency/Attributional Model of the Mere Exposure Effect." *Social Cognition* 12, no. 2: 103–128.

Bos, Peter A., Jaak Panksepp, Rose-Marie Bluthé, and Jack Van Honk. 2012. "Acute Effects of Steroid Hormones and Neuropeptides on Human Social–Emotional Behavior: A Review of Single Administration Studies." *Frontiers in Neuroendocrinology* 33, no. 1: 17–35.

Botterill, Steven. 1988. "'Quae Non Licet Homini Loqui': The Ineffability of Mystical Experience in *Paradiso I* and the *Epistle to Can Grande*." *The Modern Language Review* 83, no. 2: 332–341.

Bower, Gordon H. 2000. "A Brief History of Memory Research." In *The Oxford Handbook of Memory*, edited by Endel Tulving and Fergus I. M. Craik, 3–32. Oxford: Oxford University Press.

Boyer, Pascal. 1996. "What Makes Anthropomorphism Natural: Intuitive Ontology and Cultural Representations." *The Journal of the Royal Anthropological Institute* 2, no. 1: 83–97.

———. 2001. *Religion Explained: The Human Instincts That Fashion Gods, Spirits and Ancestors*. New York: Basic Books.

Brady, Emily. 2013. *The Sublime in Modern Philosophy. Aesthetics, Ethics, and Nature*. Cambridge: Cambridge University Press.

Brecht, Bertolt. 1964. *Brecht on Theatre*. Edited and Translated by John Willett. New York: Hill and Wang.

Brewer, William F., and Edward H. Lichtenstein. 1982. "Stories Are to Entertain: A Structural-Affect Theory of Stories." *Journal of Pragmatics* 6, no. 5–6: 473–486.

Brison, Susan J. 1993. *Aftermath: Violence and the Remaking of a Self*. Princeton, NJ: Princeton University Press.

Brody, Stuart, and Tillman H. C. Krüger. 2006. "The Post-Orgasmic Prolactin Increase Following Intercourse is Greater Than Following Masturbation and Suggests Greater Satiety." *Biological Psychology* 71, no. 3: 312–315.

Brontë, Charlotte. 2016. *Jane Eyre*. New York: W.W. Norton.

Brooks, Cleanth. 1947. *The Well Wrought Urn*. New York: Harcourt Brace.

Brown, Alan S. 2003. "A Review of the Déjà Vu Experience." *Psychological Bulletin* 129, no. 3: 394–413.

———. 2004. *The Déjà Vu Experience*. New York: Psychology Press.

Brown, Roger, and James Kulik. 1977. "Flashbulb Memories." *Cognition* 5, no. 1: 73–99.

Bruner, Jerome. 1986. *Actual Minds, Possible Worlds*. Cambridge, MA: Harvard University Press.

Bruya, Brian, and Yi-Yuan Tang. 2018. "Is Attention Really Effort? Revisiting Daniel Kahneman's Influential 1973 Book *Attention and Effort*." *Frontiers in Psychology* 9: article 1133.

Bullot, Nicolas J., and Rolf Reber. 2013. "The Artful Mind Meets Art History: Toward a Psycho-Historical Framework for the Science of Art Appreciation." *Behavioral and Brain Sciences* 36, no. 2: 123–137.

Bunyan, John. 1666. *Grace Abounding to the Chief of Sinners*. London: George Larkin.

Burch-Brown, Frank. 1983. *Transfiguration: Poetic Metaphor and the Language of Religious Belief*. Chapel Hill: University of North Carolina Press.

Burke, Edmund. 1987. *A Philosophical Enquiry into the Origin of Our Ideas of the Sublime and Beautiful*. Edited by James T. Boulton. Revised ed. Oxford: Blackwell.

Camerer, Colin, George Loewenstein, and Martin Weber. 1989. "The Curse of Knowledge in Economic Settings: An Experimental Analysis." *Journal of Marketing* 53, no. 5: 1–20.

Chaplin, George, Nina G. Jablonski, Robert W. Sussman, and Elizabeth A. Kelley. 2014. "The Role of Piloerection in Primate Thermoregulation." *Folia Primatologica: International Journal of Primatology* 85, no. 1: 1–17.
Chard, Chloe. 1996. "Crossing Boundaries and Exceeding Limits: Destabilization, Tourism and the Sublime." In *Transports: Travel, Pleasure, and Imaginative Geography: 1600–1830*, edited by Chloe Chard and Helen Langdon. New Haven, CT: Yale University Press.
Charlesworth, William R. 1969. "The Role of Surprise in Cognitive Development." In *Studies in Cognitive Development*, edited by David Elkind and John H. Flavell, 257–314. Oxford: Oxford University Press.
Chater, Nick, and George Loewenstein. 2016. "The Under-Appreciated Drive for Sense-Making." *Journal of Economic Behavior and Organization* 126: 137–154.
Chen, Siyuan, and Julien Epps. 2013. "Automatic Classification of Eye Activity for Cognitive Load Measurement With Emotion Interference." *Computer Methods and Programs in Biomedicine* 110, no. 2: 111–124.
Chopin, Kate. 1899. *The Awakening*. Chicago and New York: Herbert S. Stone and Co.
Chumbley, Justin R., Christopher J. Burke, Klaas E. Stephan, Karl J. Friston, Philippe N. Tobler, and Ernst Fehr. 2014. "Surprise Beyond Prediction Error." *Human Brain Mapping* 35, no. 9: 4805–4814.
Chun, Marvin M., Julie D. Golomb, and Nicholas B. Turk-Browne. 2011. "A Taxonomy of External and Internal Attention." *Annual Review of Psychology* 62: 73–101.
Clark, Andrew, Robert A. Nash, Gabrielle Fincham, and Giuliana Mazzoni. 2012. "Creating Non-Believed Memories for Recent Autobiographical Events." *PLoS One* 7, no. 3: e32998.
Clark, Andy. 2013. "Whatever Next? Predictive Brains, Situated Agents, and the Future of Cognitive Science." *The Behavioral and Brain Sciences* 36, no. 3: 181–204.
Clark, Kenneth. 1981. "Moments of Vision." In *Moments of Vision*, edited by Kenneth Clark, 1–17. London: John Murray.
Cleary, Anne M. 2008. "Recognition Memory, Familiarity, and Déjà Vu Experiences." *Current Directions in Psychological Science* 17, no. 5: 353–357.
Cleary, Anne M., and Alexander B. Claxton. 2018. "Déjà Vu: An Illusion of Prediction." *Psychological Science* 9, no. 4: 635–644.
Clore, Gerald L., and Stanley Colcombe. 2003. "The Parallel Worlds of Affective Concepts and Feelings." In *The Psychology of Evaluation: Affective Processes in Cognition and Emotion*, edited by Jochen Musch and Karl C. Klauer, 335–369. Mahwah, NJ: Erlbaum.
Clore, Gerald L., and W. Gerrod Parrott. 1994. "Cognitive Feelings and Metacognitive Judgments." *European Journal of Social Psychology. Special Issue: Affect in Social Judgments and Cognition* 24, no. 1: 101–115.
Cohen, Gillian. 2000. "Hierarchical Models in Cognition: Do They Have Psychological Reality?" *European Journal of Cognitive Psychology* 12, no. 1: 1–36.
Coldstream, Nicola. 2002. *Medieval Architecture*. Oxford: Oxford University Press.
Collinson, Diané. 1992. "Aesthetic Experience." In *Philosophical Aesthetics: An Introduction*, edited by Oswald Hanfling, 111–178. Oxford: Blackwell.
Colver, Mitchell C., and Amani El-Alayli. 2016. "Getting Aesthetic Chills From Music: The Connection Between Openness to Experience and Frisson." *Psychology of Music* 44, no. 3: 413–427.
Conrad, Joseph. 1986. *Lord Jim*. London: Penguin
Conway, Martin A. 2008. "Exploring Episodic Memory." *Handbook of Behavioral Neuroscience* 18: 19–29.

———. 2009. "Episodic Memories." *Neuropsychologia* 47, no. 11: 2305–2313.
Conway, Martin A., and Christopher W. Pleydell-Pearce. 2000. "The Construction of Autobiographical Memories in the Self-Memory System." *Psychological Review* 107, no. 2: 261–288.
Cook, Guy. 1990. "A Theory of Discourse Deviation: The Application of Schema Theory to the Analysis of Literary Discourse." PhD thesis, University of Leeds.
Coplan, Amy. 2004. "Empathetic Engagement With Narrative Fictions." *Journal of Aesthetics and Art Criticism* 62, no. 2: 141–152.
Corlett, Philip R., Garry D. Honey, Michael R. F. Aitken, Anthony Dickinson, David R. Shanks, Anthony R. Absalom, Michael Lee, Edith Pomarol-Clotet, Graham K. Murray, Peter J. Mckenna, Trevor W. Robbins, Edward T. Bullmore, and Paul C. Fletcher. 2006. "Frontal Responses During Learning Predict Vulnerability to the Psychotogenic Effects of Ketamine: Linking Cognition, Brain Activity, and Psychosis." *Archives of General Psychiatry* 63, no. 6: 611–621.
Cosmides, Leda, and John Tooby. 2000. "Consider the Source: The Evolution of Adaptations for Decoupling and Metarepresentation." In *Metarepresentations: A Multidisciplinary Perspective*, edited by Dan Sperber, 53–115. New York: Oxford University Press.
Costelloe, Timothy M. 2012. "Imagination and Internal Sense: The Sublime in Shaftesbury, Reid, Addison, and Reynolds." In *The Sublime: From Antiquity to the Present*, edited by Timothy M. Costelloe, 50–63. Cambridge: Cambridge University Press.
Coull, Jennifer T., Ruey-Kuang Cheng, and Warren H. Meck. 2011. "Neuroanatomical and Neurochemical Substrates of Timing." *Neuropsychopharmacology* 36, no. 1: 3–25.
Cowan, Nelson. 2000. "The Magical Number 4 in Short-Term Memory: A Reconsideration of Mental Storage Capacity." *Behavioral and Brain Sciences* 24: 87–185.
Craig, Daniel G. 2005. "An Exploratory Study of Physiological Changes During "Chills" Induced by Music." *Musicae Scientiae* 9, no. 2: 273–287.
Craik, Fergus I. M., and Endel Tulving. 1975. "Depth of Processing and the Retention of Words in Episodic Memory." *Journal of Experimental Psychology: General* 104, no. 3: 268–294.
Craik, Fergus I. M., and Robert S. Lockhart. 1972. "Levels of Processing: A Framework for Memory Research." *Journal of Verbal Learning Verbal Behavior* 11: 671–684.
Crichton-Browne, James. 1895. "Dreamy Mental States." *The British Journal of Psychiatry* 43, no. 181: 332–333.
Csikszentmihalyi, Mihaly. 1990. *Flow: The Psychology of Optimal Experience.* New York: Harper Perennial.
Čukić, Iva, and Timothy C. Bates. 2014. "Openness to Experience and Aesthetic Chills: Links to Heart Rate Sympathetic Activity." *Personality and Individual Differences* 64: 152–156.
Cupchik, Gerald C., Garry Leonard, Elise Axelrad, and Judith D. Kalin. 1998a. "The Landscape of Emotion in Literary Encounters." *Cognition and Emotion* 12, no. 6: 825–847.
Cupchik, Gerald C., and Janos Laszlo. 1994. "The Landscape of Time in Literary Reception: Character Experience and Narrative Action." *Cognition and Emotion* 8, no. 4: 297–312.
Cupchik, Gerald C., Keith Oatley, and Peter Vorderer. 1998b. "Emotional Effects of Reading Excerpts From Short Stories by James Joyce." *Poetics* 25: 363–377.
Cupchik, Gerald C., Oshin Vartanian, Adrian Crawley, and David J. Mikulis. 2009. "Viewing Artworks: Contributions of Cognitive Control and Perceptual Facilitation to Aesthetic Experience." *Brain and Cognition* 70: 84–91.

Dalton, Douglas M. 1996. "The Aesthetic of the Sublime: an Interpretation of Rawa Shell Valuable Symbolism." *American Ethnologist* 23, no. 2: 393–415.
Darwin, Charles R. 1965. *The Expression of the Emotions in Man and Animals.* Chicago: University of Chicago Press.
Daston, Lorraine, and Katharine Park. 2001. *Wonders and the Order of Nature: 1150–1750.* New York: Zone Books.
Davies, Stephen. 1994. *Musical Meaning and Expression.* Ithaca, NY: Cornell University Press.
De Chirico, Giorgio. 1968. "Meditations of a Painter." In *Theories of Modern Art: A Source Book by Artists and Critics*, edited by Hershel B. Chipp, 397–401. Berkeley, CA: University of California Press.
De Clerq, Rafael. 2000. "Aesthetic Ineffability." *Journal of Consciousness Studies* 7, nos. 8–9: 87–97.
Decety, Jean. 2009. "Empathy (Neuroscience Perspectives)." In *The Oxford Companion to Emotion and the Affective Sciences*, edited by David Sander and Klaus R. Scherer, 151–153. New York: Oxford University Press.
Deleuze, Gilles, and Felix Guattari. 1987. *A Thousand Plateaus: Capitalism and Schizophrenia.* Translated by Brian Massumi. Minneapolis, MN: University of Minnesota Press.
Deligiorgi, Katerina. 2014. "The Pleasures of Contra-Purposiveness: Kant, the Sublime, and Being Human." *The Journal of Aesthetics and Art Criticism* 72, no. 1: 25–35.
Dewey, John. 1958. *Art as Experience.* New York: Capricorn Books.
Dick, Philip K. 1965. *The Man in the High Castle.* London: Penguin.
Dick, Susan, ed. 1985. *The Complete Shorter Fiction of Virginia Woolf.* London: The Hogarth Press.
Dijkstra, Katinka, Rolf A. Zwaan, Arthur C. Graesser, and Joseph P. Magliano. 1995. "Character and Reader Emotions in Literary Texts." *Poetics* 23, no. 1: 139–157.
Dilthey, Wilhelm. 1976. *Selected Writings.* Edited by H. P. Rickman. Cambridge: Cambridge University Press.
Dixon, Peter, and Marisa Bortolussi. 2015. "Fluctuations in Literary Reading: The Neglected Dimension of Time." In *The Oxford Handbook of Cognitive Literary Studies*, edited by Lisa Zunshine, 541–556. Oxford: Oxford University Press.
Dorter, Kenneth. 1990. "Conceptual Truth and Aesthetic Truth." *Journal of Aesthetics and Art Criticism* 48, no. 1: 37–51.
Douglas, Mary. 1966. *Purity and Danger: An Analysis of the Concepts of Pollution and Taboo.* London: Routledge and Kegan Paul.
Dowden, Wilfred S., ed. 1964. *The Letters of Thomas Moore I (1793–1818)*, Oxford: Clarendon Press.
Dutton, Donald G., and Arthur P. Aron. 1974. "Some Evidence for Heightened Sexual Attraction Under Conditions of High Anxiety." *Journal of Personality and Social Psychology* 30, no. 4: 510–517.
Dyja, Thomas, ed. 2001. *Awake: Stories of Life-Changing Epiphanies.* New York: Marlowe.
Efran, Jay S., and Timothy J. Spangler. 1979. "Why Grown-Ups Cry: A Two-Factor Theory and Evidence From the Miracle Worker." *Motivation and Emotion* 3, no. 1: 63–72.
Eliot, George. 1872. *Middlemarch.* Edinburgh and London: William Blackwood and Sons.
Eliot, T. S. 1972. *The Sacred Wood: Essays on Poetry and Criticism.* London: Methuen.
Elkins, James. 2001. *Pictures and Tears: A History of People Who Have Cried in Front of Paintings.* New York: Routledge.

Ellis, Catherine J. 1984. "Time Consciousness of Aboriginal Performers." In *Problems and Solutions: Occasional Essays in Musicology Presented to Alice M. Moyle*, edited by Jamie C. Kassler and Jill Stubington, 149–185. Sydney: Hale and Iremonger.

Emerson, Ralph Waldo. 1850. *Representative Men: Seven Lectures*. Boston: Phillips, Sampson and Company.

Emmott, Catherine, Anthony J. Sanford, and Lorna I. Morrow. 2006. "Capturing the Attention of Readers? Stylistic and Psychological Perspectives on the Use and Effect of Text Fragmentation in Narratives." *Journal of Literary Semantics* 35, no. 1: 1–31.

Enfield, N. J., and Charles H. P. Zuckerman. 2024. "Moorings: Linguistic Practices and the Tethering of Action, Status, and Experience." Current Anthropology 65, no. 3: 554–576.

Ernst, Max. 1968. "What is the Mechanism of Collage?" In *Theories of Modern Art: A Source Book by Artists and Critics*, edited by Herschel B. Chipp, 427. Berkeley, CA: University of California Press.

Eskine, Kendall J., Natalie A. Kacinik, and Jesse J. Prinz. 2012. "Stirring Images: Fear, Not Happiness or Arousal, Makes Art More Sublime." *Emotion* 12, no. 5: 1071–1074.

Etlyn, Richard A. 2012. "Architecture and the Sublime." In *The Sublime: From Antiquity to the Present*, edited by Timothy M. Costelloe, 230–273. Cambridge: Cambridge University Press.

Fabb, Nigel. 1997. *Linguistics and Literature: Language in the Verbal Arts of the World*. Oxford: Blackwell.

———. 2002. *Language and Literary Structure: The Linguistic Analysis of Form in Verse and Narrative*. Cambridge: Cambridge University Press.

———. 2009. "Why is Verse Poetry?" *PN Review* 189, no. 36: 52–57.

———. 2015. *What Is Poetry? Language and Memory in the Poems of the World*. Cambridge: Cambridge University Press.

———. 2016. "Processing Effort and Poetic Closure." *International Journal of Literary Linguistics* 5, no. 4: 1–22.

———. 2021. "Experiences of Ineffable Significance." In *Beyond Meaning*, edited by Elly Ifantidou, Louis de Saussure, and Tim Wharton, 135–150. Amsterdam: John Benjamins.

Fabb, Nigel, and Morris Halle. 2008. *Meter in Poetry: A New Theory*. Cambridge: Cambridge University Press.

Farbood, Morwaread M., and Khen C. Price. 2017. "The Contribution of Timbre Attributes to Musical Tension." *Journal of the Acoustical Society of America* 141, no. 1: 419.

Feldman, Sandor. 1941. "On Blushing." *Psychiatric Quarterly* 15: 249–261.

Ferri, Sabrina. 2012. "Vittorio Alfieri's Natural Sublime: The Physiology of Poetic Inspiration." *European Romantic Review* 23, no. 5: 555–574.

Fletcher, Paul C., and Chris D. Frith. 2009. "Perceiving is Believing: A Bayesian Approach to Explaining the Positive Symptoms of Schizophrenia." *Nature Reviews: Neuroscience* 10: 48–58.

Fodor, Jerry. 1975. *The Language of Thought*. Cambridge, MA: Harvard University Press.

Folk, Charles L. 2015. "Controlling Spatial Attention: Lessons From the Lab and Implications for Everyday Life." In *The Handbook of Attention*, edited by Jonathan M. Fawcett, Evan F. Risko, and Alan Kingstone, 3–25. Cambridge, MA: MIT Press.

Forsey, Jane. 2007. "Is a Theory of the Sublime Possible?" *The Journal of Aesthetics and Art Criticism* 65, no. 4: 381–389.

Foster, Meadhbh I., and Mark T. Keane. 2015. "Why Some Surprises Are More Surprising Than Others: Surprise as a Metacognitive Sense of Explanatory Difficulty." *Cognitive Psychology* 81: 74–116.

Fox, James. 2014. *Explorations in Semantic Parallelism*. Canberra: Australian National University Press.
Fox, James J., ed. 1988. *To Speak in Pairs. Essays on the Ritual Languages of Eastern Indonesia*. Cambridge: Cambridge University Press.
Fredrickson, William E. 1997. "Elementary, Middle, and High School Student Perceptions of Tension in Music." *Journal of Research in Music Education* 45, no. 4: 626–635.
Freedberg, David. 1989. *The Power of Images: Studies in the History and Theory of Response*. Chicago: University of Chicago Press.
Freedberg, David, and Vittorio Gallese. 2007. "Motion, Emotion and Empathy in Esthetic Experience." *Trends in Cognitive Sciences* 11, no. 5: 197–203.
Freud, Sigmund. 1919. *The "Uncanny"*. Translated by Alix Strachey. First Published in Imago, Bd. V. 1919; Reprinted in *Sammlung*, Fünfte Folge.
Frevert, Ute. 2014. "Defining Emotions: Concepts and Debates Over Three Centuries." In *Emotional Lexicons: Continuity and Change in the Vocabulary of Feeling: 1700–2000*, edited by Ute Frevert, 1–31. Oxford: Oxford University Press.
Frey, William H. 1985. *Crying: The Mystery of Tears*. Minneapolis, MN: Winston Press.
Friedrich, Paul. 2001. "Lyric Epiphany." *Language in Society* 30, no. 2: 217–247.
Frijda, Nico H. 1986. *The Emotions*. Cambridge: Cambridge University Press.
Frith, Chris. 1992. *The Cognitive Neuropsychology of Schizophrenia*. Hove: Lawrence Erlbaum Associates.
———. 2005. "The Neural Basis of Hallucinations and Delusions." *Comptes Rendus Biologies* 328, no. 2: 169–175.
Frog, ed. 2014. *Parallelism in Verbal Art and Performance. Pre-Print Papers of the Seminar-Workshop 26th–27th May. 2014. Helsinki Finland*. Folkloristiikan Toimite. 21. Helsinki: University of Helsinki.
Frye, Northrop. 1957. *Anatomy of Criticism: Four Essays*. Princeton: Princeton University Press.
Gabrielsson, Alf. 2011. *Strong Experiences with Music: Music Is Much More Than Just Music*. Translated by Rod Bradbury. Oxford: Oxford University Press.
Gabrielsson, Alf, and Erik Lindström. 2010. "The Role of Structure in the Musical Expression of Emotions." In *Handbook of Music and Emotion: Theory, Research, Applications*, edited by Patrik N. Juslin and John Sloboda, 367–400. Oxford: Oxford University Press.
Garnham, Alan, and Jenny Mason. 1987. "Episode Structure in Memory for Narrative Text." *Language and Cognitive Processes* 2, no. 2: 133–144.
Garry, Maryanne, and Kimberley A. Wade. 2005. "Actually, a Picture is Worth Less Than 45 Words: Narratives Produce More False Memories Than Photographs Do." *Psychonomic Bulletin and Review* 12, no. 2: 359–366.
Gaver, William, and George Mandler. 1987. "Play It Again Sam: On Liking Music." *Cognition and Emotion* 1, no. 3: 259–282.
Gell, Alfred. 1998. *Art and Agency: An Anthropological Theory*. Oxford: Clarendon Press.
Gendlin, Eugene T. 1997. *Experiencing and the Creation of Meaning*. Evanston, IL: Northwestern University Press.
Genette, Gerard. 1983. *Narrative Discourse: An Essay in Method*. Ithaca, NY: Cornell University Press.
Gerrig, Richard J. 1993. *Experiencing Narrative Worlds: On the Psychological Activities of Reading*. New Haven, CT: Yale University Press.
Ghosh, Vanessa E., and Asaf Gilboa. 2014. "What is a Memory Schema? A Historical Perspective on Current Neuroscience Literature." *Neuropsychologia* 53: 104–114.

Gibbon, John. 1977. "Scalar Expectancy Theory of Weber's Law in Animal Timing." *Psychological Review* 84, no. 3: 279–325.

Gibbon, John, Russel M. Church, and Warren H. Meck. 1984. "Scalar Timing in Memory." In *Timing and Rime Perception*, edited by John Gibbon and Lorraine G. Allan, 52–77. New York: New York Academy of Sciences.

Gibbs, Raymond W., Jr., and Markus Tendahl. 2006. "Cognitive Effort and Effects in Metaphor Comprehension: Relevance Theory and Psycholinguistics." *Mind and Language* 21, no. 3: 379–403.

Gibson, James J. 1958. "Visually Controlled Locomotion and Visual Orientation in Animals." *British Journal of Psychology* 49, no. 3: 182–194.

———. 1979. *The Ecological Approach to Visual Perception*. Boston: Houghton Mifflin.

Gil, Sandrine, and Sylvie Droit-Volet. 2012. "Emotional Time Distortions: The Fundamental Role of Arousal." *Cognition and Emotion* 26, no. 5: 847–862.

Glucksberg, Sam. 2003. "The Psycholinguistics of Metaphor." *Trends in Cognitive Sciences* 7, no. 2: 92–96.

Glucksberg, Sam, Patricia Gildea, and Howard B. Bookin. 1982. "On Understanding Nonliteral Speech: Can People Ignore Metaphors?" *Journal of Verbal Learning and Verbal Behavior* 21, no. 1: 85–98.

Godwin, William. 1996. "The History of the Life of William Pitt, Earl of Chatham." In *The Sublime: A Reader in British Eighteenth-Century Aesthetic Theory*, edited by Andrew Ashfield and Peter De Bolla, XX. Cambridge: Cambridge University Press.

Goldstein, Avram. 1980. "Thrills in Response to Music and Other Stimuli." *Physiological Psychology* 8, no. 1: 126–129.

Graesser, Arthur C., Max A. Kassler, Roger J. Kreuz, and Bonnie McLain-Allen. 1998. "Verification of Statements About Story Worlds That Deviate From Normal Conceptions of Time: What is True About *Einstein's Dreams*?" *Cognitive Psychology* 35: 246–301.

Green, Melanie C., and Timothy C. Brock. 2000. "The Role of Transportation in the Persuasiveness of Public Narratives." *Journal of Personality and Social Psychology* 79, no. 5: 701–721.

Grenier, Sebastien, Anne-Marie Barrette, and Robert Ladouceur. 2005. "Intolerance of Uncertainty and Intolerance of Ambiguity: Similarities and Differences." *Personality and Individual Differences* 39, no. 3: 593–600.

Grewe, Oliver, Björn Katzur, Reinhard Kopiez, and Eckart Altenmüller. 2011. "Chills in Different Sensory Domains: Frisson Elicited by Acoustical, Visual, Tactile and Gustatory Stimuli." *Psychology of Music* 39, no. 2: 220–239.

Grewe, Oliver, Frederik Nagel, Reinhard Kopiez, and Eckart Altenmüller. 2007. "Listening to Music as a Re-Creative Process: Physiological, Psychological, and Psychoacoustical Correlates of Chills and Strong Emotions." *Music Perception: an Interdisciplinary Journal* 24, no. 3: 297–314.

Griffiths, Thomas L., and Joshua B. Tenenbaum. 2007. "From Mere Coincidences to Meaningful Discoveries." *Cognition* 103, no. 2: 180–226.

Gross, James J., Barbara L. Fredrickson, and Robert W. Levenson. 1994. "The Psychophysiology of Crying." *Psychophysiology* 31, 460–468.

Guhn, Martin, Alfons Hamm, and Marcel Zentner. 2007. "Physiological and Musico-Acoustic Correlates of the Chill Response." *Music Perception: An Interdisciplinary Journal* 24, no. 5: 473–484.

Halle, Morris, and Samuel Jay Keyser. 1971. *English Stress: Its Form, Its Growth, and Its Role in Verse*. New York: Harper and Row.

Hanauer, David. 1995. "Literary and Poetic Text Categorization Judgements." *Journal of Literary Semantics* 24: 187–209.

Hanich, Julian, Valentin Wagner, Mira Shah, Thomas Jacobsen, and Winfried Menninghaus. 2014. "Why We Like to Watch Sad Films: The Pleasure of Being Moved in Aesthetic Experiences." *Psychology of Aesthetics, Creativity, and the Art* 8, no. 2: 130–143.

Hart, Joseph Truman. 1965. "Memory and the Feeling-Of-Knowing Experience." *Journal of Educational Psychology* 56, no. 4: 208–216.

Hatfield, Elaine, Lisamarie Bensman, Paul D. Thornton, and Richard L. Rapson. 2014. "New Perspectives on Emotional Contagion: A Review of Classic and Recent Research on Facial Mimicry and Contagion." *Interpersona: An International Journal on Personal Relationships* 8, no. 2: 159–179.

Hatfield, Elaine, and Richard L. Rapson. 2009. "Contagion." In *The Oxford Companion to Emotion and the Affective Sciences*, edited by David Sander and Klaus R. Scherer, 99. New York: Oxford University Press.

Heidegger, Martin. 1927. *Sein Und Zeit*. Tübingen: Max Niemeyer Verlag.

Heilman, Kenneth M. 2016. "Possible Brain Mechanisms of Creativity." *Archives of Clinical Neuropsychology* 31, no. 4: 285–296.

Hein, Grit, Jan B. Engelmann, Marius C. Vollberg, and Philippe N. Tobler. 2016. "How Learning Shapes the Empathic Brain." *Proceedings of the National Academy of Sciences of the United States of America* 113, no. 1: 80–85.

Henke, Suzette. 1999. "Virginia Woolf's *To the Lighthouse*: (En)gendering Epiphany." In *Moments of Moment: Aspects of the Literary Epiphany*, edited by Wim Tigges, 261–278. Amsterdam: Rodopi.

Henry, Home, and Lord, Kames. 1996. "Elements of Criticism." In *The Sublime: A Reader in British Eighteenth-Century Aesthetic Theory*, edited by Andrew Ashfield and Peter De Bolla, 224–243. Cambridge: Cambridge University Press.

Hernandez, Ivan, and Jesse Lee Preston. 2013. "Disfluency Disrupts the Confirmation Bias." *Journal of Experimental Social Psychology* 49, no. 1: 178–182.

Herrington, Tony, ed. 2015. *Epiphanies: Life Changing Encounters With Music*. London: Strange Attractor Press.

Hodges, Donald A. 2010. "Psychophysiological Measures." In *Handbook of Music and Emotion: Theory, Research, Applications*, edited by Patrik N. Juslin and John Sloboda, 281–311. Oxford: Oxford University Press.

Hoeken, Hans, and Mario Van Vliet. 2000. "Suspense, Curiosity, and Surprise: How Discourse Structure Influences the Affective and Cognitive Processing of a Story." *Poetics* 27, no. 4: 277–286.

Hoffman, E. 1992. "Overcoming Evil: An Interview with Abraham Maslow, Founder of Humanistic Psychology." https://www.psychologytoday.com/gb/articles/199201/abraham-maslow.

Hogan, Patrick Colm. 2013. "Literary Aesthetics: Beauty, the Brain, and Mrs. Dalloway". In *Progress in Brain Research* 205, edited by Anne Stiles, Stanley Finger, and François Boller, 319–337. Amsterdam: Elsevier.

Hogan, Patrick Colm. 2016. *Beauty and Sublimity. A Cognitive Aesthetics of Literature and the Arts*. Cambridge: Cambridge University Press.

Holmes, Emily A., Nick Grey, and Kerry A. D. Young. 2005. "Intrusive Images and "Hotspots" of Trauma Memories in Posttraumatic Stress Disorder: An Exploratory Investigation of Emotions and Cognitive Themes." *Journal of Behavior Therapy and Experimental Psychiatry* 36, no. 1: 3–17.

Housman, Alfred E. 1933. *The Name and Nature of Poetry*. Cambridge: Cambridge University Press.

Huron, David. 2006. *Sweet Anticipation: Music and the Psychology of Expectation*. Cambridge, MA: MIT Press.

——. "Why is Sad Music Pleasurable? A Possible Role for Prolactin." *Musicae Scientiae* 15, no. 2: 146–158.

Huron, David, and Elizabeth H. Margulis. 2010. "Musical Expectancy and Thrills?" In *Handbook of Music and Emotion: Theory, Research, Applications*, edited by Patrik N. Juslin and John Sloboda, 575–604. Oxford: Oxford University Press.

Hymes, Dell. 1987. "Tonkawa Poetics: John Rush Buffalo's Coyote and Eagle's Daughter." In *Native American Discourse. Poetics and Rhetoric*, edited by Joel Sherzer and Anthony C. Woodbury, 17–61. Cambridge: Cambridge University Press.

Illich, Ivan. 1986. *H20 and the Waters of Forgetfulness*. London: Marion Boyars.

Inbody, Joel. 2015. "Sensing God: Bodily Manifestations and Their Interpretation in Pentecostal Rituals and Everyday Life." *Sociology of Religion* 76, no. 3: 337–355.

Innocenti, Claudia, Giulia Fioravanti, Raffaello Spiti, and Carlo Faravelli. 2014. "The Stendhal Syndrome Between Psychoanalysis and Neuroscience." *Rivista Di Psichiatria* 49, no. 2: 61–66.

Iser, Wolfgang. 1978. *The Act of Reading: A Theory of Aesthetic Response*. London: Routledge and Kegan Paul.

Ishizu, Tomohiro, and Semir Zeki. 2014. "A Neurobiological Enquiry into the Origins of Our Experience of the Sublime and Beautiful." *Frontiers Human Neuroscience* 8: 891. doi: 10. 3389/Fnhum.2014.00891.

Izard, Carroll E. 1991. *The Psychology of Emotions*. New York: Springer.

Jacobs, Arthur M. 2015. "Neurocognitive Poetics: Methods and Models for Investigating the Neuronal and Cognitive-Affective Bases of Literature Reception." *Frontiers in Human Neuroscience* 9, no. 186.

Jakobson, Roman. 1960. "Closing Statement: Linguistics and Poetics." In *Style in Language*, edited by Thomas A. Sebeok, 350–377. Cambridge, MA: MIT Press.

Jakubowski, Kelly, Andrea R. Halpern, Mick Grierson, and Lauren Stewart. 2015. "The Effect of Exercise-Induced Arousal on Chosen Tempi for Familiar Melodies." *Psychonomic Bulletin and Review* 22, no. 2: 559–565.

James, William. 1884. "What is an Emotion?" *Mind* 9, no. 34: 188–205.

——. 1890. *The Principles of Psychology*. Cambridge, MA: Harvard University Press.

——. 1982. *The Varieties of Religious Experience: A Study in Human Nature*. Edited With an Introduction by Martin E. Marty. New York: Penguin.

Jansen, Karl L. R. 2000. "A Review of the Nonmedical Use of Ketamine: Use, Users and Consequences." *Journal of Psychoactive Drugs* 32, no. 4: 419–433.

Jaspers, Karl. 1963. *General Psychopathology*. Translated by J. Hoenig and Marian W. Hamilton. Manchester: Manchester University Press.

Jeffries, Lesley. 2001. "Schema Affirmation and White Asparagus: Cultural Multilingualism Among Readers of Texts." *Language and Literature* 10, no. 4: 325–343.

Jensen, Jakob, Kristen Imboden, and Rebecca Ivic. 2011. "Sensation Seeking and Transportation: High Sensation Seeking Children's Interest in Reading Outside of School." *Scientific Studies of Reading* 15, no. 6: 541–558.

Jentsch, Ernst. 1906. "On the Psychology of the Uncanny." Translated by Roy Sellars. In *Uncanny Modernity: Cultural Theories, Modern Anxieties*, 2008, edited by Jo Collins and John Jervis, 216–228. Basingstoke: Palgrave Macmillan.

Johnson, Marcia K., Shahin Hashtroudi, and D. Stephen Lindsay. 1993. "Source Monitoring." *Psychological Bulletin* 114, no. 1: 3–28.
Johnson, Thomas H., and Theodora Ward, eds. 1958. *The Letters of Emily Dickinson*. Cambridge, MA: The Belknap Press of Harvard University Press.
Joyce, James. 1944. *Stephen Hero: Part of the First Draft of "A Portrait of the Artist as a Young Man,"* edited by Theodore Spencer. London: Jonathan Cape.
———. 1956. *Epiphanies*. Edited by Oscar Silverman. Buffalo: University of Buffalo, Easy Hill Press.
Juslin, Patrik N. 2013. "From Everyday Emotions to Aesthetic Emotions: Towards a Unified Theory of Musical Emotions." *Physics of Life Reviews* 10: 235–266.
Kaeppler, Adrienne L. 2008. *The Pacific Arts of Polynesia and Micronesia*. Oxford History of Art Oxford: Oxford University Press.
Kahneman, Daniel. 1973. *Attention and Effort*. Englewood Cliffs, NJ: Prentice-Hall.
Kang, Yul H. R., Frederike H. Petzschner, Daniel M. Wolpert, and Michael N. Shadlen. 2017. "Piercing of Consciousness as a Threshold-Crossing Operation." *Current Biology* 27: 2285–2295.
Kant, Immanuel. 1952. *The Critique of Aesthetic Judgement*. Translated With Analytical Indexes by James Creed Meredith. Oxford: Oxford University Press.
Katz, Steven T., ed. 2013. *Comparative Mysticism, an Anthology of Original Sources*. Oxford: Oxford University Press.
Keller, Peter E., and Emery Schubert. 2011. "Cognitive and Affective Judgements of Syncopated Musical Themes." *Advances in Cognitive Psychology* 7: 142–156.
Keltner, Dacher, and Jonathan Haidt. 2003. "Approaching Awe, a Moral, Spiritual, and Aesthetic Emotion." *Cognition and Emotion* 17, no. 2: 297–314.
Kim, Sharon. 2012. *Literary Epiphany in the Novel: 1850–1950: Constellations of the Soul*. Basingstoke: Palgrave Macmillan.
Kirk, Ulrich, Martin Skov, Mark Schram Christensen, and Niels Nygaard. 2009. "Brain Correlates of Aesthetic Expertise: A Parametric fMRI Study." *Brain and Cognition* 69: 306–315.
Kirwan, James. 2005. *Sublimity: The Non-Rational and the Irrational in the History of Aesthetics*. New York: Routledge.
Köhler, Wolfgang. 1921. *Intelligenzprüfungen am Menschenaffen*. Berlin: Springer.
Konečni, Vladimir J., Rebekah A. Wanic, and Amber Brown. 2007. "Emotional and Aesthetic Antecedents and Consequences of Music–Induced Thrills." *American Journal of Psychology* 120, no. 4: 619–643.
Konijn, Elly A., Juliette H. Walma Van Der Molen, and Sander Van Nes. 2009. "Emotions Bias Perceptions of Realism in Audiovisual Media: Why We May Take Fiction for Real." *Discourse Processes* 46, no. 4: 309–340.
Koopman, Eva Maria (Emy). 2015. "Empathic Reactions after Reading: The Role of Genre, Personal Factors and Affective Responses." *Poetics* 50: 62–79.
Koriat, Asher, and Ravit Levy-Sadot. 1999. "Processes Underlying Metacognitive Judgments: Information-Based and Experience-Based Monitoring of One's Own Knowledge." In *Dual-Process Theories in Social Psychology*, edited by Shelley Chaiken and Yaacov Trope, 483–502. New York: Guilford Press.
Korstvedt, Benjamin M. 2000. *Bruckner: Symphony, No. 8*. Cambridge: Cambridge University Press.
Kott, Jan. 1967. *Shakespeare Our Contemporary*. London: Methuen.
Kreilkamp, Ivan. 2006. ""One More Picture": Robert Browning's Optical Unconscious." *ELH* 73, no. 2: 409–435.

Kreitler, Hans, and Shulamith Kreitler. 1972. *Psychology of the Arts*. Durham, NC: Duke University Press.

Kuiken, Don, and Mary Beth Oliver. 2013. "Aesthetic Engagement During Moments of Suffering." *Scientific Study of Literature* 3, no. 2: 294–321.

Kuiken, Don, Paul Campbell, and Paul Sopčák. 2012. "The Experiencing Questionnaire: Locating Exceptional Reading Moments." *Scientific Study of Literature* 2, no. 2: 243–272.

Kuiken, Don, and Shawn Douglas. 2017. "Forms of Absorption that Facilitate the Aesthetic and Explanatory Effects of Literary Reading." In *Narrative Absorption*, edited by Frank Hakemulder, Moniek M. Kuijpers, Ed S. Tan, Katalin Balint, and Miruna M. Doicaru, 217–149. Amsterdam: John Benjamins.

Küpers, Wendelin. 2011. "Dancing on the Limen: Embodied and Creative Inter-Places as Thresholds of Be(Com)Ing: Phenomenological Perspectives on Liminality and Transitional Spaces in Organisation and Leadership." *Tamara – Journal for Critical Organization Inquiry* 9, nos. 3–4: 45–59.

Labov, William, and Joshua Waletzky. 1967. "Narrative Analysis: Oral Versions of Personal Experience." In *Essays on the Verbal and Visual Arts: Proceedings of the 1966 Annual Spring Meeting of the American Ethnological Society*, edited by J. Helm, 12–44. Seattle: University of Washington Press.

Laeng, Bruno, Lise Mette Eidet, Unni Sulutvedt, and Jaak Panksepp. 2016. "Music Chills: The Eye Pupil as a Mirror to Music's Soul." *Consciousness and Cognition* 44: 161–178.

Laidlaw, James. 2004. "Introduction." In *Ritual and Memory: Toward a Comparative Anthropology of Religion*, edited by Harvey Whitehouse and James Laidlaw, 1–9. Walnut Creek, CA: Altamira Press.

Lamb, Jonathan. 1997. "The Sublime." In *The Cambridge History of Literary Criticism: Volume IV: The Eighteenth Century*, edited by H. B. Nisbet and Claude Rawson, 394–416. Cambridge: Cambridge University Press.

Lang, Peter J., Margaret M. Bradley, and Bruce N. Cuthbert. 1997. "Motivated Attention: Affect, Activation, and Action." In *Attention and Orienting: Sensory and Motivational Processes*, edited by Peter J. Lang, Robert F. Simons, and Marie T. Balaban, 97–136. London: Routledge.

Langbaum, Robert. 1999. "The Epiphanic Mode in Wordsworth and Modern Literature." In *Moments of Moment: Aspects of the Literary Epiphany*, edited by Wim Tigges, 37–60. Amsterdam: Rodopi.

Lanham, Richard A. 1991. *A Handlist of Rhetorical Terms*. 2nd ed. Berkeley, CA: University of California Press.

Lanz, Henry. 1926. "The Physical Basis of Rime." *PMLA* 41, no. 4: 1011–1023.

Laski, Marghanita. 1961. *Ecstasy: A Study of Some Secular and Religious Experiences*. London: The Cresset Press.

———. 1980. *Everyday Ecstasy*. London: Thames and Hudson.

Laub, Dori, and Shoshana Felman. 1992. *Testimony: Crises of Witnessing in Literature, Psychoanalysis, and History*. New York: Routledge.

Lazarus, Richard. 1991. *Emotion and Adaptation*. New York: Oxford University Press.

Leder, Helmut, Benno Belke, Andries Oeberst, and Dorothee Augustin. 2004. "A Model of Aesthetic Appreciation and Aesthetic Judgments." *British Journal of Psychology* 95, no. 4: 489–508.

LeDoux, Joseph. 1996. *The Emotional Brain: The Mysterious Underpinnings of Emotional Life*. New York: Touchstone.

Lerdahl, Fred, and Carol Krumhansl. 2007. "Modeling Tonal Tension." *Music Perception* 24, no. 4: 329–366.

Lerdahl, Fred, and Ray Jackendoff. 1983. *A Generative Theory of Tonal Music*. Cambridge, MA: MIT Press.
Lévi-Strauss, Claude. 1962. *Le Totémisme Aujourd'hui*. Paris: Presses Universitaires De France.
Levinson, Jerrold. 2006. "Emotion in Response to Art." In *Contemplating Art*, edited by Jerrold Levinson, 38–55. Oxford: Oxford University Press.
Levy, Robert I. 1973. *Tahitians: Mind and Experience in the Society Islands*. Chicago, IL: University of Chicago Press.
Lewis, Michael J. 2002. *The Gothic Revival*. London: Thames and Hudson.
Leypoldt, Günther. 2011. "Raymond Carver's 'Epiphanic Moments.'" *Style* 35, no. 3: 531–547.
Liddell, Henry George and Scott, Robert 1889. *An Intermediate Greek-English Lexicon*. Oxford: Clarendon Press.
Loddenkemper, Tobias, C. Kellinghaus, J. Gandjour, D. R. Nair, I. M. Najm, W. Bingaman, and H. O. Lüders. 2004. "Localising and Lateralising Value of Ictal Piloerection." *Journal of Neurology, Neurosurgery, and Psychiatry* 75, no. 6: 879–883.
Loewenstein, George. 1994. "The Psychology of Curiosity: A Review and Reinterpretation." *Psychological Bulletin* 116, no. 1: 75–98.
Longinus. 1998. "On Sublimity." In *Classical Literary Criticism*, edited by D. A. Russell and Michael Winterbottom, 143–187. Oxford: Oxford University Press.
Longstaff, Alan. 2011. *Neuroscience*. 3rd ed. New York: Garland.
López-Sintas, Jordi, Ercilia García-Álvarez, and Elena Pérez-Rubiales. 2012. "The Unforgettable Aesthetic Experience: The Relationship Between the Originality of Artworks and Local Culture." *Poetics* 40, no. 4: 337–358.
Losey, Jay. 1999. ""Demonic" Epiphanies: The Denial of Death in Larkin and Heaney." In *Moments of Moment: Aspects of the Literary Epiphany*, edited by Wim Tigges, 375–400. Amsterdam: Rodopi.
Lowth, Robert 1753. *De Sacra Poesi Hebræorum* Oxford: Clarendon.
Lüdtke, Jana, Burkhard Meyer-Sickendieck, and Arthur M. Jacobs. 2014. "Immersing in the Stillness of an Early Morning: Testing the Mood Empathy Hypothesis of Poetry Reception." *Psychology of Aesthetics, Creativity, and the Arts* 8, no. 3: 363–377.
Luhrmann, Tanya M., R. Padmavati, Hema Tharoor, and Akwasi Osei. 2015. "Hearing Voices in Different Cultures: A Social Kindling Hypothesis." *Topics in Cognitive Science* 7, no. 4: 646–663.
MacDowell, Kathleen, and George Mandler. 1989. "Constructions of Emotion: Discrepancy, Arousal, and Mood." *Motivation and Emotion* 13, no.2: 105–124.
Magherini, Graziella. 1995. *La sindrome di Stendhal*. Firenze: Ponte alla Grazie.
Magliano, Joseph P., and Jeffrey M. Zacks. 2011. "The Impact of Continuity Editing in Narrative Film on Event Segmentation." *Cognitive Science* 35, no. 8: 1489–1517.
Magliano, Joseph P., Lester C. Loschky, James A. Clinton, and Adam M. Larson. 2013. "Is Reading the Same as Viewing? An Exploration of the Similarities and Differences Between Processing Text- and Visually Based Narratives." In *Unraveling the Behavioral, Neurobiological, and Genetic Components of Reading Comprehension*, edited by Brett Miller, Laurie E. Cutting, and Peggy McCardle, 78–90. Baltimore, MD: Brookes Publishing Co.
Maio, Gregory R., and Victoria M. Esses. 2001. "The Need for Affect: Individual Differences in the Motivation to Approach or Avoid Emotions." *Journal of Personality* 69, no. 4: 583–615.
Maltby, Paul. 1997. "Postmodern Thoughts on the Visionary Moment." *Centennial Review* 41, no. 1: 119–141.

Mangan, Bruce. 1993. "Taking Phenomenology Seriously: The "Fringe" and Its Implications for Cognitive Research." *Consciousness and Cognition* 2, no. 2: 89–108.
Mar, Raymond A., Keith Oatley, and Jordan B. Peterson. 2009. "Exploring the Link between Reading Fiction and Empathy: Ruling out Individual Differences and Examining Outcomes." *Communications* 34, no. 4: 407–428.
Mar, Raymond A., Keith Oatley, Maja Djikic, and Justin Mullin. 2011. "Emotion and Narrative Fiction: Interactive Influences Before, During, and After Reading." *Cognition and Emotion* 25, no. 5: 818–833.
Margulis, Elizabeth Hellmuth. 2013. "Repetition and Emotive Communication in Music Versus Speech." *Frontiers in Psychology* 4, no. 167.
Maruskin, Laura A., Todd M. Thrash, and Andrew J. Elliot. 2012. "The Chills as a Psychological Construct: Content Universe, Factor Structure, Affective Composition, Elicitors, Trait Antecedents, and Consequences." *Journal of Personality and Social Psychology* 103, no. 1: 135–157.
Maslow, Abraham H. 1976. *Religions, Values, and Peak Experiences*. Middlesex: Penguin.
Massey, Doreen. 1991. "A Global Sense of Place." *Marxism Today* 1991: 24–29.
Maurois, André. 1968. *Illusions*. New York: Columbia University Press.
Maxwell, James Coutts. 1986. *The Prelude by William Wordsworth: A Parallel Text*. London: Penguin.
Maxwell, S. S. 1902. "A Case of Voluntary Erection of the Human Hair and Production of Cutis Anserina." *American Journal of Physiology - Legacy Content* 7, no. 4: 369–379.
McAdams, Dan P., Ann Diamond, Ed De Aubin, and Elizabeth Mansfield. 1997. "Stories of Commitment: The Psychosocial Construction of Generative Lives." *Journal of Personality and Social Psychology* 72, no. 3: 678–694.
McGregor, Ronald Stuart. 1984. *Hindi Literature from its Beginnings to the Nineteenth Century*. Wiesbaden: Otto Harrassowitz.
McCrae, Robert R. 2007. "Aesthetic Chills as a Universal Marker of Openness to Experience." *Motivation and Emotion* 31, no. 1: 5–11.
McCrae, Robert R., and Paul T. Costa, Jr. 1997. "Conceptions and Correlates of Openness to Experience." In *Handbook of Personality Psychology*, edited by Robert Hogan, John A. Johnson, and Stephen Briggs, 725–847. San Diego, CA: Academic Press Inc.
McDonald, Matthew G. 2008. "The Nature of Epiphanic Experience." *The Journal of Humanistic Psychology* 48, no. 1: 89–115.
McGlone, Matthew S., and Jessica Tofighbakhsh. 1999. "The Keats Heuristic: Rhyme as Reason in Aphorism Interpretations." *Poetics* 26: 235–244.
———. 2000. "Birds of a Feather Flock Conjointly? Rhyme as Reason in Aphorisms." *Psychological Science* 11, no. 5: 424–428.
McNamara, Patrick. 2009. *The Neuroscience of Religious Experience*. Cambridge: Cambridge University Press.
Mendelssohn, Moses. 1997. *Philosophical Writings*. Edited by Daniel O. Dahlstrom. Cambridge: Cambridge University Press.
Mercier, Hugo, and Dan Sperber. 2011. "Why Do Humans Reason? Arguments for an Argumentative Theory." *Behavioral and Brain Sciences* 34, no. 2: 57–74.
Meyer, Leonard B. 1956. *Emotion and Meaning in Music*. Chicago: Chicago University Press.
Meyer, Wulf-Uwe, Michael Niepel, Udo Rudolph, and Achim Schützwohl. 1991. "An Experimental Analysis of Surprise." *Cognition and Emotion* 5, no. 4: 295–311.
Meyer, Wulf-Uwe, Rainer Reisenzein, and Achim Schützwohl. 1997. "Toward a Process Analysis of Emotions: The Case of Surprise." *Motivation and Emotion* 21, no. 3: 251–274.

Menninghaus, Winfried, Valentin Wagner, Julian Hanich, Eugen Wassiliwizky, Thomas Jacobsen, and Stefan Koelsch. 2017. "The Distancing–Embracing Model of the Enjoyment of Negative Emotions in Art Reception." *Behavioral and Brain Sciences*. 40: E347.
Miall, David S. 2007. "Foregrounding and the Sublime: Shelley in Chamonix." *Language and Literature* 16, no. 2: 155–168.
Miall, David S., and Don Kuiken. 1994. "Foregrounding, Defamiliarization, and Affect: Response to Literary Stories." *Poetics* 22, no. 5: 389–407.
Miceli, Maria, and Cristiano Castelfranchi. 2003. "Crying: Discussing Its Basic Reasons and Uses." *New Ideas in Psychology* 21, no. 3: 247–273.
Miller, Christopher R. 2007. "Wordsworth's Anatomies of Surprise." *Studies in Romanticism* 46, no. 4: 409–431.
Miller, William R. 2004. "The Phenomenon of Quantum Change." *Journal of Clinical Psychology* 60, no. 5: 453–460.
Miller, William R., and Janet C' De Baca. 2001. *Quantum Change: When Epiphanies and Sudden Insights Transform Ordinary Lives*. New York: Guilford Publications.
Mishara, Aaron L., and Paolo Fusar-Poli. 2013. "The Phenomenology and Neurobiology of Delusion Formation During Psychosis Onset: Jaspers, Truman Symptoms, and Aberrant Salience." *Schizophrenia Bulletin* 39, no. 2: 278–286.
Mohammed, Mazher, Youichirou Ootsuka, and William Blessing. 2014. "Brown Adipose Tissue Thermogenesis Contributes to Emotional Hyperthermia in a Resident R Suddenly Confronted with an Intruder Rat." *American Journal of Physiology-Regulatory Integrative and Comparative Physiology* 306, no. 6: R394–R400.
Monin, Benoît. 2003. "The Warm Glow Heuristic: When Liking Leads to Familiarity." *Journal of Personality and Social Psychology* 85, no. 6: 1035–1048.
Monk, Samuel Holt. 1960. *The Sublime: A Study of Critical Theories in XVIII-Century England*. Ann Arbor, MI: University of Michigan Press.
Mori, Kazuma, and Makoto Iwanaga. 2014. "Resting Physiological Arousal is Associated With the Experience of Music-Induced Chills." *International Journal of Psychophysiology* 93: 220–226.
———. 2017. "Two Types of Peak Emotional Responses to Music: The Psychophysiology of Chills and Tears." *Scientific Reports* 7, no. 1: 1–13.
Morley, Simon, ed. 2010. *The Sublime. Documents of Contemporary Art*. London: Whitechapel Gallery and Cambridge MA: MIT Press.
Morphy, Howard. 1989. "From Dull to Brilliant: The Aesthetics of Spiritual Power among the Yolngu." *Man (New Series)* 24, no. 1: 21–40.
Murdoch, Iris. 1992. *Metaphysics as a Guide to Morals*. London: Chatto and Windus.
Murphy, Gregory L. 2002. *The Big Book of Concepts*. Cambridge, MA: MIT Press.
Nabokov, Vladimir. 1972. *Transparent Things*. New York: McGraw-Hill.
———. 1982. *Lectures on Literature*. Boston: Mariner Books.
Nadal, Marcos, and Marcus T. Pearce. 2011. "The Copenhagen Neuroaesthetics Conference: Prospects and Pitfalls for an Emerging Field." *Brain and Cognition* 76, no. 1: 172–183.
Nadal, Marcos, and Martin Skov. 2013. "Introduction to the Special Issue: Toward an Interdisciplinary Neuroaesthetics." *Psychology of Aesthetics, Creativity, and the Arts* 7, no. 1: 1–12.
Nakamura, Kazuhiro, and Shaun F. Morrison. 2011. "Central Efferent Pathways for Cold-Defensive and Febrile Shivering." *The Journal of Physiology* 589, no. 14: 3641–3658.
Narmour, Eugene. 1990. *The Analysis and Cognition of Basic Melodic Structures*. Chicago: University of Chicago Press.

Nelson, Lowry, Jr. 1956. "The Rhetoric of Ineffability: Toward a Definition of Mystical Poetry." *Comparative Literature* 8, no. 4: 323–336.
Neppe, Vernon M. 1983. *The Psychology of Déjà Vu: Have I Been Here Before?* Johannesburg: Witwatersrand University Press.
Newman, Barnett. 1968. "The Sublime is Now." In *Theories of Modern Art: A Sourcebook by Artists and Critics*, edited by Hershel P. Chipp, 552–553. Berkley, CA: University of California Press.
Nichols, Ashton. 1987. *Poetics of Epiphany: Nineteenth Century Origins of the Modern Literary Moment*. Tuscaloosa, AL: University of Alabama Press.
———. 1999. "Cognitive and Pragmatic Linguistic Moments: Literary Epiphany in Thomas Pynchon and Seamus Heaney." In *Moments of Moment: Aspects of the Literary Epiphany*, edited by Wim Tigges, 467–480. Amsterdam: Rodopi.
Nicholson, Timothy Richard Joseph, Carmine Pariante, and Declan Mcloughlin. 2009. "Stendhal Syndrome: A Case of Cultural Overload." *BMJ Case Reports* 2009: bcr06.2008.0317.
Nickerson, Raymond S. 1998. "Confirmation Bias: A Ubiquitous Phenomenon in Many Guises." *Review of General Psychology* 2, no. 2: 175–220.
Nielsen, F. V. 1983. *Oplevelse of Musikalsk Spending (The Experience of Musical Tension)*. Copenhagen: Akademisk Forlag.
Nisbett, Richard E., and Timothy Decamp Wilson. 1977. "Telling More Than We Can Know: Verbal Reports on Mental Processes." *Psychological Review* 84, no. 3: 231–259.
Noordewier, Marret K., and Seger M. Breugelmans. 2013. "On the Valence of Surprise." *Cognition and Emotion* 27, no. 7: 1326–1334.
Nusbaum, Emily C., Paul J. Silvia, Roger E. Beaty, Chris J. Burgin, Donald A. Hodges, and Thomas R. Kwapil. 2014. "Listening Between the Notes: Aesthetic Chills in Everyday Music Listening." *Psychology of Aesthetics, Creativity, and the Arts* 8, no. 1: 104–109.
O'Connor, Akira R., Colin Lever, and Chris J. A. Moulin. 2010. "Novel Insights into False Recollection: A Model of Déjà Vécu." *Cognitive Neuropsychiatry* 15, nos. 1–3: 118–144.
O'Donnell, James J. 1992. *Augustine Confessions III: Commentary on Books 8–13: Indexes*. Oxford: Clarendon Press.
Oatley, Keith. 1994. "A Taxonomy of the Emotions of Literary Response and a Theory of Identification in Fictional Narrative." *Poetics* 23, nos. 1–2: 53–74.
———. 1999. "Why Fiction May Be Twice as True as Fact: Fiction as Cognitive and Emotional Simulation." *Review of General Psychology* 3, no. 2: 101–117.
Öhman, Arne, and Stefan Wiens. 2003. "On the Automaticity of Autonomic Responses in Emotion: An Evolutionary Perspective." In *Handbook of Affective Sciences*, edited by Richard J. Davidson, Klaus R. Scherer, and H. Hill Goldsmith, 256–275. New York: Oxford University Press.
Ornstein, Robert E. 1977. *The Psychology of Consciousness*. 2nd ed. New York: Harcourt Brace Jovanovich.
Ortony, Anthony, Gerald L. Clore, and Allan Collins. 1988. *The Cognitive Structure of Emotions*. Cambridge: Cambridge University Press.
Otto, Rudolf. 1923. *The Idea of the Holy*. Translated by John W. Harvey. New York: Oxford University Press.
Ouden, H. E. M. Den, Peter Kok, and Floris P. De Lange. 2012. "How Prediction Errors Shape Perception, Attention, and Motivation." *Frontiers in Psychology* 3: 548.
Owen, Stephen. 1992. *Readings in Chinese Literary Thought*. Cambridge, MA: Harvard University Press.

Owen, G., R. Harland, E. Antonova, and M. Broome. 2004. "Jaspers' Concept of Primary Delusion." *British Journal Of Psychiatry* 185: 77–78.
Pahnke, Walter N. 1967. "LSD and Religious Experience." In *LSD, Man and Society*, edited by Richard C. DeBold and Russell C. Leaf. Middletown, CT: Wesleyan University Press.
Panksepp, Jaak. 1995. "The Emotional Sources of 'Chills' Induced by Music." *Music Perception: An Interdisciplinary Journal* 13, no. 2: 171–207.
―――. 1998. *Affective Neuroscience: The Foundations of Human and Animal Emotions*. Oxford: Oxford University Press.
Panzarella, Robert. 1980. "The Phenomenology of Aesthetic Peak Experiences." *Journal of Humanistic Psychology* 20, no. 1: 69–85.
Patel, Aniruddh D. 2008. *Music, Language and the Brain*. Oxford: Oxford University Press.
Pater, Walter. 1910. *The Renaissance*. London: MacMillan.
Pelowski, Matthew, and Fuminori Akiba. 2011. "A Model of Art Perception, Evaluation and Emotion in Transformative Aesthetic Experience." *New Ideas in Psychology* 29, no. 2: 80–97.
Pelowski, Matthew J. 2015. "Tears and Transformation: Feeling Like Crying as an Indicator of Insightful or 'Aesthetic' Experience with Art." *Frontiers in Psychology* 6, no. 1006: 1–23.
Pennebaker, James W. 1997. *Opening Up: The Healing Power of Expressing Emotions*. Revised ed. New York: Guilford Press.
Pierce, Russel S., Rick Maclaren, and Dan L. Chiappe. 2010. "The Role of Working Memory in the Metaphor Interference Effect." *Psychonomic Bulletin and Review* 17, no. 3: 400–404.
Piff, Paul K., Matthew Feinberg, Pia Dietze, Daniel M. Stancato, and Dacher Keltner. 2015. "Awe, the Small Self, and Prosocial Behavior." *Journal of Personality and Social Psychology* 108, no. 6: 883–899.
Polito, Vince, Robyn Langdon, and Jac Brown. 2010. "The Experience of Altered States of Consciousness in Shamanic Ritual: The Role of Pre-Existing Beliefs and Affective Factors." *Consciousness and Cognition* 19, no. 4: 918–925.
Ponder, Eric, and W. P. Kennedy. 1927. "On the Act of Blinking." *Experimental Physiology* 18: 89–110.
Privette, Gayle Hogan. 1983. "Peak Experience, Peak Performance, and Flow: A Comparative Analysis of Positive Human Experiences." *Journal of Personality and Social Psychology* 45, no. 6: 1361–1368.
Proust, Joëlle, and Martin Fortier. 2018. "Metacognitive Diversity Across Cultures: An Introduction." In *Metacognitive Diversity: An Interdisciplinary Approach*, edited by Joëlle Proust and Martin Fortier, 1–22. Oxford: Oxford University Press.
Proust, Marcel. 2002. *In Search of Lost Time: Volume 1: The Way by Swann's*. Translated by Lydia Davis. London: Penguin.
―――. 2006. *Remembrance of Things Past: Volume 2*. Translated by C. K. Scott Moncrieff and Stephen Hudson. London: Wordsworth Editions.
Provine, Robert R. 2017. "Laughter as an Approach to Vocal Evolution: The Bipedal Theory." *Psychonomic Bulletin and Review* 24, no. 1: 238–244.
Radvansky, Gabriel A., and Jeffrey M. Zacks, eds. 2014. *Event Cognition*. New York: Oxford University Press.
Radvansky, Gabriel A., Rolf A. Zwaan, Todd Federico, and Nancy Franklin. 1998. "Retrieval From Temporally Organized Situation Models." *Journal of Experimental Psychology: Learning, Memory, and Cognition* 24, no. 5: 1224–1237.
Raffman, Diana. 1993. *Language, Music and Mind*. Cambridge, MA: MIT Press.

Ramachandran, V. S. 2011. *The Tell-Tale Brain: A Neuroscientist's Quest for What Makes Us Human*. New York: Norton.

Ramey, Peter. 2011. "Beowulf's Singers of Tales as Hyperlinks." *Oral Tradition* 26, no. 2: 619–626.

Rapp, Alexander M., Michael Erb, Wolfgang Grodd, Mathias Bartels, and Katja Markert. 2011. "Neural Correlates of Metonymy Resolution." *Brain and Language* 119, no. 3: 196–205.

Rathbone, Clare J., Martin A. Conway, and Chris J. A. Moulin. 2011. "Remembering and Imagining: The Role of the Self." *Consciousness and Cognition* 20, no. 4: 1175–1182.

Ravaja, Niklas. 2004. "Contributions of Psychophysiology to Media Research: Review and Recommendations." *Media Psychology* 6, no. 2: 193–235.

Reber, Rolf, Norbert Schwarz, and Piotr Winkielman. 2004b. "Processing Fluency and Aesthetic Pleasure: Is Beauty in the Perceiver's Processing Experience?" *Personality and Social Psychology Review* 8, no. 4: 364–382.

Reber, Rolf, Pascal Wurtz, and Thomas D. Zimmermann. 2004a. "Exploring "Fringe" Consciousness: The Subjective Experience of Perceptual Fluency and Its Objective Bases." *Consciousness and Cognition* 13, no. 1: 47–60.

Recanati, François. 1997. "Can We Believe What We Do Not Understand?" *Mind and Language* 12: 84–100.

Reisenzein, Rainer. 2000. "The Subjective Experience of Surprise." In *The Message Within: The Role of Subjective Experience in Social Cognition and Behavior*, edited by Herbert Bless and Joseph P. Forgas, 262–279. Philadelphia, PA: Psychology Press.

———. 2009. "Schachter-Singer Theory." In *The Oxford Companion to Emotion and the Affective Sciences*, edited by David Sander and Klaus R. Scherer, 352–353. New York: Oxford University Press.

Reisenzein, Rainer, and Wulf-Uwe Meyer. 2009. "Surprise." In *The Oxford Companion to Emotion and the Affective Sciences*, edited by David Sander and Klaus R. Scherer, 386–387. New York: Oxford University Press.

Renbourn, Edward Tobias. 1960. "Body Temperature and Pulse Rate in Boys and Young Men Prior to Sporting Contests: A Study of Emotional Hyperthermia: With a Review of the Literature." *Journal of Psychosomatic Research* 4, no. 3: 149–175.

Richards, I. A. 1926. *Principles of Literary Criticism*. 2nd edition. London: Routledge and Kegan Paul.

Richardson, Alan. 2012. *The Neural Sublime: Cognitive Theories and Romantic Texts*. Baltimore, MD: Johns Hopkins University Press.

Rickard, Nikki S. 2004. "Intense Emotional Responses to Music: A Test of the Physiological Arousal Hypothesis." *Psychology of Music* 32, no. 4: 371–388.

Ricoeur, Paul. 1977. *The Rule of Metaphor: The Creation of Meaning in Language*. London: Routledge.

Roberts, Adam. 2000. *Alfred Tennyson: The Major Works*. Oxford: Oxford University Press.

Robinson, Michael D., and Gerald L. Clore. 2002. "Belief and Feeling: Evidence for an Accessibility Model of Emotional Self-Report." *Psychological Bulletin* 128, no. 6: 934–960.

Rollins, Hyder Edward, ed. 1958. *The Letters of John Keats: Volume 1*. Cambridge: Cambridge University Press.

Rooney, Brendan, Ciarán Benson, and Eilis Hennessy. 2012. "The Apparent Reality of Movies and Emotional Arousal: A Study Using Physiological and Self-Report Measures." *Poetics* 40, no. 5: 405–422.

Rubin, David C., and Sharda Umanath. 2015. "Event Memory: A Theory of Memory for Laboratory, Autobiographical, and Fictional Events." *Psychological Review* 122, no. 1: 1–23.

Ruch, Willibald. 1997. "State and Trait Cheerfulness and the Induction of Exhilaration: A FACS Study." *European Psychologist* 2, no. 4: 328–341.
———. 2009. "Amusement." In *The Oxford Companion to Emotion and the Affective Sciences*, edited by David Sander and Klaus R. Scherer, 27–28. New York: Oxford University Press.
Rumelhart, David E. 1980. "Schemata: The Building Blocks of Cognition." In *Theoretical Issues in Reading Comprehension*, edited by Rand J. Spiro, Bertram C. Bruce, and William F. Brewer, 33–58. Hillsdale, NJ: Lawrence Erlbaum.
Rumelhart, David E., and Anthony Ortony. 1977. "The Representation of Knowledge in Memory." In *Schooling and the Acquisition of Knowledge*, edited by Richard C. Anderson, Rand J. Spiro, and William E. Montague, 97–135. Hillsdale, NJ: Erlbaum.
Russell, James A. 1980. "A Circumplex Model of Affect." *Journal of Personality and Social Psychology* 39: 1161–1178.
Ruston, Sharon. 2013. *Creating Romanticism: Case Studies in the Literature, Science and Medicine of the 1790s*. London: Palgrave Macmillan UK.
Sachs, Matthew E., Robert J. Ellis, Gottfried Schlaug, and Psyche Loui. 2016. "Brain Connectivity Reflects Human Aesthetic Responses to Music." *Social Cognitive and Affective Neuroscience* 11, no. 6: 884–891.
Salimpoor, Valorie N., Mitchel Benovoy, Gregory Longo, Jeremy R. Cooperstock, and Robert J. Zatorre. 2009. "The Rewarding Aspects of Music Listening Are Related to Degree of Emotional Arousal." *PLoS One* 4, no. 10: E7487.
Salimpoor, Valorie N., Mitchel Benovoy, Kevin Larcher, Alain Dagher, and Robert J. Zatorre. 2011. "Anatomically Distinct Dopamine Release During Anticipation and Experience of Peak Emotion to Music." *Nature Neuroscience* 14, no. 2: 257–264.
Sander, David, Jordan Grafman, and Tiziana Zalla. 2003. "The Human Amygdala: An Evolved System for Relevance Detection." *Reviews in the Neurosciences* 14, no. 4: 303–316.
Sanford, Anthony J. 2002. "Context, Attention and Depth of Processing During Interpretation." *Mind and Language* 17, nos. 1–2: 188–206.
Santayana, George. 1896. *The Sense of Beauty*. New York: Scribner.
Sargent, Jesse Q., Jeffrey M. Zacks, David Z. Hambrick, Rose R. Zacks, Christopher A. Kurby, Heather R. Bailey, Michelle L. Eisenberg, and Taylor M. Beck. 2013. "Event Segmentation Ability Uniquely Predicts Event Memory." *Cognition* 129, no. 2: 241–255.
Schachter, Stanley, and Jerome Singer. 1962. "Cognitive, Social, and Physiological Determinants of Emotional State." *Psychological Review* 69, no. 5: 379–399.
Scharfstein, Ben-Ami. 1993. *Ineffability: The Failure of Words in Philosophy and Religion*. Albany, NY: State University of New York Press.
Scherer, Klaus R. 2001. "Appraisal Considered as a Process of Multi-Level Sequential Checking." In *Appraisal Processes in Emotion: Theory, Methods, Research*, edited by Klaus R. Scherer, Angela Schorr, and Tom Johnstone, 92–120. New York: Oxford University Press.
———. 2004. "Which Emotions Can Be Induced by Music? What Are the Underlying Mechanisms? And How Can We Measure Them?" *Journal of New Music Research* 33, no 3: 239–251.
———. 2009a. "Emotions Are Emergent Processes: They Require a Dynamic Computational Architecture." *Philosophical Transactions of the Royal Society B* 364, no. 1535: 3459–3474.
———. 2009b. "The Dynamic Architecture of Emotion: Evidence for the Component Process Model." *Cognition and Emotion* 23, no. 7: 1307–1351.
———. 2009c. "Emotion Theories and Concepts; Psychological Perspectives." In *The Oxford Companion to Emotion and the Affective Sciences*, edited by David Sander and Klaus R. Scherer, 145–151. New York: Oxford University Press.

Scherer, Klaus R., and Marcel R. Zentner. 2001. "Emotional Effects of Music: Production Rules." In *Music and Emotion: Theory and Research*, edited by Patrik N. Juslin and John Sloboda, 361–392. New York: Oxford University Press.

Scherer, Klaus R., and Phoebe C. Ellsworth. 2009. "Appraisal Theories." In *The Oxford Companion to Emotion and the Affective Sciences*, edited by David Sander and Klaus R. Scherer, 45–49. New York: Oxford University Press.

Schlipp, Paul Arthur, ed. 1949. *Albert Einstein: Philosopher-Scientist*. Cambridge: Cambridge University Press.

Schmidt, Gwenda L., and Carol A. Seger. 2009. "Neural Correlates of Metaphor Processing: The Roles of Figurativeness, Familiarity and Difficulty." *Brain and Cognition* 71, no. 3: 375–386.

Schoeller, Félix. 2015a. "Knowledge, Curiosity, and Aesthetic Chills." *Frontiers in Psychology* 6: 1546.

———. 2015b. "The Shivers of Knowledge." *Human and Social Studies* 4, no. 3: 26–41.

Schoeller, Félix, and Leonid Perlovsky. 2015. "Great Expectations – Narratives and the Elicitation of Aesthetic Chills." *Psychology* 6: 2098–2102.

Schooler, Jonathan W., Stellan Ohlsson, and Kevin Brooks. 1993. "Thoughts Beyond Words: When Language Overshadows Insight." *Journal of Experimental Psychology: General* 122, no. 2: 166–183.

Schubert, Thomas W., Janis H. Zickfeld, Beate Seibt, and Alan Page Fiske. 2016. "Moment-To-Moment Changes in Feeling Moved Match Changes in Closeness, Tears, Goosebumps, and Warmth: Time Series Analyses." *Cognition and Emotion* 32, no. 1: 174–184.

Schultz, Wolfram. 2002. "Getting Formal with Dopamine and Reward." *Neuron* 36, no. 2: 241–263.

Schurtz, David R., Sarai Blincoe, Richard H. Smith, Caitlin A. J. Powell, David J. Y. Combs, and Sung Hee Kim. 2012. "Exploring the Social Aspects of Goose Bumps and Their Role in Awe and Envy." *Motivation and Emotion* 36, no. 2: 205–217.

Schwan, Stephan, and Bärbel Garsoffky. 2004. "The Cognitive Representation of Filmic Event Summaries." *Applied Cognitive Psychology* 18, no. 1: 37–55.

Schwitzgebel, Eric. 2016. "Introspection." *The Stanford Encyclopedia of Philosophy Winter*. 2016. Edition, Edward N. Zalta Ed. https://Plato.Stanford.Edu/Archives/Win2016/Entries/Introspection/.

Scruton, Roger. 1997. *The Aesthetics of Music*. Oxford: Clarendon Press.

Semino, Elena. 1995. "Schema Theory and the Analysis of Text Worlds in Poetry." *Language and Literature* 4, no. 2: 79–108.

Sharf, Robert H. 1995. "Buddhist Modernism and the Rhetoric of Meditative Experience." *Numen* 42, no. 3: 228–283.

Shaw, Philip. 2006. *The Sublime*. London: Routledge.

Sheller, Mimi, and John Urry. 2006. "The New Mobilities Paradigm." *Environment and Planning A* 38, no. 2: 207–226.

Sikora, Shelley, David S. Miall, and Don Kuiken. 1998. "Enactment Versus Interpretation: A Phenomenological Study of Readers' Responses to Coleridge's "The Rime of the Ancient Mariner."" Paper Presented at the Sixth Biennial Conference of the International Society for the Empirical Study of Literature, Utrecht, the Netherlands.

Silvia, Paul J. 2008. "Interest – the Curious Emotion." *Current Directions in Psychological Science* 17, no. 1: 57–60.

Sircello, Guy. 1993. "How is a Theory of the Sublime Possible?" *The Journal of Aesthetics and Art Criticism* 51, no. 4: 541–550.

Skolnick, Deena, and Paul Bloom. 2006. "What Does Batman Think About Spongebob? Children's Understanding of the Fantasy/Fantasy Distinction." *Cognition* 101, no. 1: B9–B18.

Sloboda, John A. 1991. "Music Structure and Emotional Response: Some Empirical Findings." *Psychology of Music* 19, no. 2: 110–120.

Smallwood, Jonathan. 2015. "Mind Wandering and Attention." In *The Handbook of Attention*, edited by Jonathan Fawcett, Evan Risko, and Alan Kingstone, 233–255. Cambridge, MA: MIT Press.

Smallwood, Jonathan, and Jonathan W. Schooler. 2015. "The Science of Mind Wandering: Empirically Navigating the Stream of Consciousness." *Annual Review of Psychology* 66: 487–518.

Smith, Alison. 2013. "The Sublime in Crisis: Landscape Painting After Turner." In *The Art of the Sublime*, edited by Nigel Llewellyn and Christine Riding. London: Tate.

Smith, Barbara Herrnstein. 1968. *Poetic Closure: A Study of How Poems End*. Chicago: University of Chicago Press.

Smith, Logan Pearsall. 1917. *Trivia*. Garden City, NY: Doubleday, Page and Company.

Speidel, Suzanne. 2007. "The Ending is Out There." In *The X-Files and Literature: Unweaving the Story, Unraveling the Lie to Find the Truth*, edited by Sharon R. Yang, 312–345. Newcastle: Cambridge Scholars Press.

Smith, William. 1996. "Dionysius Longinus on the Sublime." In *The Sublime: A Reader in British Eighteenth-Century Aesthetic Theory*, edited by Andrew Ashfield and Peter De Bolla, 22–29. Cambridge: Cambridge University Press.

Sperber, Dan. 1985. *On Anthropological Knowledge*. Cambridge: Cambridge University Press.

———. 1996. "Why Are Perfect Animals, Hybrids, and Monsters Food for Symbolic Thought?" *Method and Theory in The Study of Religion* 8, no. 2: 143–169.

———. 2005. "Modularity and Relevance: How Can a Massively Modular Mind Be Flexible and Context-Sensitive?" In *The Innate Mind: Structure and Contents*, edited by Peter Carruthers, Stephen Laurence, and Stephen Stich, 53–68. Oxford: Oxford University Press.

———, ed. 2000. *Metarepresentations: A Multidisciplinary Perspective*. New York: Oxford University Press.

Sperber, Dan. 2010. "The Guru Effect." *Review of Philosophy and Psychology* 1, no. 4: 583–592.

Sperber, Dan, and Dierdre Wilson. 1995. *Relevance: Communication and Cognition*. 2nd ed. Oxford: Blackwell.

Stace, Walter Terence. 1960. *Mysticism and Philosophy*. New York: Lippincott.

Stange, Ken, and Shelley Taylor. 2008. "Relationship of Personal Cognitive Schemas to the Labeling of a Profound Emotional Experience as Religious-Mystical or Aesthetic." *Empirical Studies of the Arts* 26, no. 1: 37–49.

Stearns, Peter N., and Carol Z. Stearns. 1985. "Emotionology: Clarifying the History of Emotions and Emotional Standards." *The American Historical Review* 90, no. 4: 813–836.

Stendhal. 1826. *Rome, Naples et Florence*. Vol. 2. Paris: Éditions Delaunay.

Stetson, Chess, Matthew P. Fiesta, and David M. Eagleman. 2007. "Does Time Really Slow Down During a Frightening Event?" *PLoS One* 2, no. 12: e1295.

Stevenson, Robert Louis. 1882. "A Gossip on Romance." *Longman's Magazine* 1, no. 1: 67–79.

Strick, Madelijn, Hanka L. De Bruin, Linde C. De Ruiter, and Wouter Jonkers. 2015. "Striking the Right Chord: Moving Music Increases Psychological Transportation and Behavioral Intentions." *Journal of Experimental Psychology: Applied* 21, no. 1: 57–72.

Striedter, Jurij. 1989. *Literary Structure, Evolution, and Value: Russian Formalism and Czech Structuralism Reconsidered.* Cambridge, MA: Harvard University Press.
Suddendorf, Thomas, Donna Rose Addis, and Michael C. Corballis. 2009. "Mental Time Travel and the Shaping of the Human Mind." *Philosophical Transactions of the Royal Society B: Biological Sciences* 364: 1317–1324.
Suddendorf, Thomas, and Michael C. Corballis. 1997. "Mental Time Travel and the Evolution of the Human Mind." *Genetic, Social, and General Psychology Monographs* 123: 133–167.
Sullivan, Paul. 2017. "Towards a Literary Account of Mental Health From James' *Principles of Psychology.*" *New Ideas in Psychology* 46: 31–38.
Sumpf, Maria, Sebastian Jentschke, and Stefan Koelsch. 2015. "Effects of Aesthetic Chills on a Cardiac Signature of Emotionality." *PLoS One* 10, no. 6: e0130117.
Sundararajan, Louise. 2002. "Religious Awe: Potential Contributions of Negative Theology to Psychology, "Positive" or Otherwise." *Journal of Theoretical and Philosophical Psychology* 22, no. 2: 174–197.
Sunstein, Cass R. 2017. "How Star Wars Illuminates Constitutional Law." *Revista De Estudos Institucionais* 2, no. 2: 562–580.
Sutherland, Graham. 1953. "Notes by the Artist' for the *Exhibition Paintings and Drawings by Graham Sutherland*, Tate Gallery. 14 March–30 April 1953." https://www.tate.org.uk/whats-on/tate-britain/exhibition/paintings-and-drawings-graham-sutherland.
Sutherland, Peter. 1992. *Cognitive Development Today: Piaget and His Critics.* London: SAGE Publications Ltd.
Swift, Benjamin. 1898. *The Destroyer.* London: T. Fisher Unwin.
Symons, Arthur. 1958. *The Symbolist Movement in Literature.* New York: Dutton.
Tal-Or, Nurit, and Jonathan Cohen. 2010. "Understanding Audience Involvement: Conceptualizing and Manipulating Identification and Transportation." *Poetics* 38, no. 4: 402–418.
Talarico, Jennifer M., and David D. Rubin. 2007. "Flashbulb Memories Are Special After All; in Phenomenology, Not Accuracy." *Applied Cognitive Psychology* 21: 557–578.
Tangerås, Thor Magnus. 2020. *Literature and Transformation: A Narrative Study of Life-Changing Reading Experiences.* London: Anthem Press.
Taruffi, Liila, and Stefan Koelsch. 2014. "The Paradox of Music-Evoked Sadness: An Online Survey." *PLoS One* 9, no. 10: E110490.
Taylor Shelley E., Laura Cousino Klein, Brian P. Lewis, Tara L. Gruenewald, Regan A. R. Gurung, and John A. Updegraff. 2000. "Biobehavioural Responses to Stress in Females: Tend-And-Befriend, Not Fight-Or-Flight." *Psychological Review* 107, no. 3: 411–429.
Teive, Hélio A. G., Renato P. Munhoz, and Francisco Cardoso. 2014. "Proust, Neurology and Stendhal's Syndrome." *European Neurology* 71: 296–298.
Temperley, David. 2018. *The Musical Language of Rock.* New York: Oxford University Press.
Thrale, Hester Lynch. 1942. *Thraliana. The Diary of Mrs. Hester Lynch Thrale 1776–1809. Volume 1*, edited by Katharine C. Balderston. Oxford: Oxford University Press.
Tigges, Wim. 1999. "The Significance of Trivial Things: Towards a Typology of Literary Epiphanies." In *Moments of Moment: Aspects of the Literary Epiphany*, edited by Wim Tigges, 11–35. Amsterdam: Rodopi.
Tinti, Carla, Susanna Schmidt, Silvia Testa, and Linda J. Levine. 2014. "Distinct Processes Shape Flashbulb and Event Memories." *Memory and Cognition* 42, no. 4: 539–551.

Tobin, Vera. 2009. "Cognitive Bias and the Poetics of Surprise." *Language and Literature* 18, no. 2: 155–172.
Tolstoy, Leo. 2010. *War and Peace*. Translated by Louise and Aylmer Maude. Revised by Amy Mandelker. Oxford: Oxford University Press.
Tomashevsky, Boris. 1965. "Thematics." In *Russian Formalist Criticism: Four Essays*, edited by Lee T. Lemon and Marion J. Reis, 65–95. Lincoln, NB: University of Nebraska Press.
Topolinski, Sascha, and Fritz Strack. 2009. "Scanning the "Fringe" of Consciousness: What is Felt and What is Not Felt in Intuitions About Semantic Coherence." *Consciousness and Cognition* 18, no. 3: 608–618.
Treloyn, Sally. 2009. "Half Way: Appreciating the Poetics of Northern Kimberley Song." *Musicology Australia* 31, no. 1: 41–62.
Trentini, Bruno. 2014. "The Meta as an Aesthetic Category." *Journal of Aesthetics and Culture* 6: 1–9.
Tulving, Endel. 1972. "Episodic and Semantic Memory." In *Organization of Memory*, edited by Endel Tulving and Wayne Donaldson, 381–403. New York: Academic Press.
———. 1983. *Elements of Episodic Memory*. Oxford: Oxford University Press.
———. 1985. "Memory and Consciousness." *Canadian Psychology/Psychologie Canadienne* 26, no. 1: 1–12.
Turner, Victor W. 1964. "Betwixt and Between: The Liminal Period." In *Rites De Passage: The Proceedings of the American Ethnological Society. Symposium on New Approaches to the Study of Religion*, 4–20. Seattle, WA: American Ethnological Society.
Turpin, Myfany, and Nigel Fabb. 2017. "Brilliance as Cognitive Complexity in Aboriginal Australia." *Oceania* 87, no. 2: 209–230.
Usher, M. D. 2007. "Theomachy, Creation, and the Poetics of Quotation in Longinus Chapter 9." *Classical Philology* 102, no. 3: 292–303.
Van Der Henst, Jean-Baptiste, and Dan Sperber. 2004. "Testing the Cognitive and Communicative Principles of Relevance." In *Experimental Pragmatics*, edited by Ira Noveck and Dan Sperber, 141–171. London: Palgrave Macmillan.
Van Eck, Caroline. 2010. "Living Statues: Alfred Gell's Art and Agency, Living Presence Response and the Sublime." *Art History* 33, no. 4: 642–659.
Van Gennep, Arnold. 1909. *Les Rites De Passage; Étude Systématique Des Rites De La Porte Et Du Seuil, De L'hospitalité, De L'adoption, De La Grossesse Et De L'accouchement, De La Naissance, De L'enfance, De La Puberté, De L'initiation, De L'ordination, Du Couronnement Des Fiançailles Et Du Mariage, Des Funérailles, Des Saisons, Etc*. Paris: E. Nourry.
Van Kesteren, Marlieke T. R., Dirk J. Ruiter, Guillén Fernández, and Richard N. Henson. 2012. "How Schema and Novelty Augment Memory Formation." *Trends in Neurosciences* 35, no. 4: 211–219.
Vingerhoets, Ad J. J. M., Randolph R. Cornelius, Guus L. Van Heck, and Marleen C. Becht. 2000. "Adult Crying: A Model and Review of the Literature." *Review of General Psychology* 4, no. 4: 354–377.
Visch, Valentijn T., Ed S. Tan, and Dylan Molenaar. 2010. "The Emotional and Cognitive Effect of Immersion in Film Viewing." *Cognition and Emotion* 24, no. 8: 1439–1445.
Von Hoffmansthal, Hugo. 2005. *The Lord Chandos Letter and Other Writings*. Translated by Joel Rotenberg. New York: NYRB.
Wassiliwizky, Eugen, Stefan Koelsch, Valentin Wagner, Thomas Jacobsen, and Winfried Menninghaus. 2017a. "The Emotional Power of Poetry: Neural Circuitry, Psychophysiology and Compositional Principles." *Social Cognitive and Affective Neuroscience* 12, no. 8: 1229–1240.

Wassiliwizky, Eugen, Thomas Jacobsen, Jan Heinrich, Manuel Schneiderbauer, and Winfried Menninghaus. 2017b. "Tears Falling on Goosebumps: Co-Occurrence of Emotional Lacrimation and Emotional Piloerection Indicates a Psychophysiological Climax in Emotional Arousal." *Frontiers in Psychology* 8, no. 41: 1–15.

Wassiliwizky, Eugen, Valentin Wagner, Thomas Jacobsen, and Winfried Menninghaus. 2015. "Art-Elicited Chills Indicate States of Being Moved." *Psychology of Aesthetics, Creativity, and the Arts* 9, no. 4: 405–416.

Weiskel, Thomas. 1976. *The Romantic Sublime: Studies in the Structure and Psychology of Transcendence*. Baltimore and London: Johns Hopkins University Press.

Whaley, John, John Sloboda, and Alf Gabrielsson. 2009. "Peak Experiences in Music?" In *The Oxford Handbook of Music Psychology*, edited by Susan Hallam, Ian Cross, and Michael Thaut, 452–461. Oxford: Oxford University Press.

Whitehouse, Harvey. 2004. "Toward a Comparative Anthropology of Religion." In *Ritual and Memory: Toward a Comparative Anthropology of Religion*, edited by Harvey Whitehouse and James Laidlaw, 187–205. Walnut Creek, CA: Altamira Press.

Whittier-Ferguson, John. 2011. "Repetition, Remembering, Repetition: Virginia Woolf's Late Fiction and the Return of War." *Modern Fiction Studies* 57, no. 2: 230–253.

Whittlesea, Bruce W. A., and Lisa D. Williams. 1998. "Why Do Strangers Feel Familiar, But Friends Don't? A Discrepancy-Attribution Account of Feelings of Familiarity." *Acta Psychologica* 98, no. 2: 141–165.

Wildman, Wesley J., and Patrick McNamara. 2010. "Evaluating Reliance on Narratives in the Psychological Study of Religious Experiences." *International Journal for the Psychology of Religion* 20, no. 4: 223–254.

Williams, D. G., and Gabrielle H. Morris. 1996. "Crying, Weeping or Tearfulness in British and Israeli Adults." *British Journal of Psychology* 87, no. 3: 479–505.

Williams, Helen Maria. 1996. "A Tour in Switzerland." In *The Sublime: A Reader in British Eighteenth-Century Aesthetic Theory*, edited by Andrew Ashfield and Peter De Bolla, 300–302. Cambridge: Cambridge University Press.

Wilson, Deirdre, and Dan Sperber. 2004. "Relevance Theory." In *The Handbook of Pragmatics*, edited by Laurence R. Horn and Gregory Ward, 607–632. Oxford: Blackwell.

Wilson, Deirdre, and Robyn Carston. 2006. "Metaphor, Relevance and the 'Emergent Property' Issue."*Mind and Language* 21, no. 3: 404–433.

Wilson, Stephen M., Istvan Molnar-Szakacs, and Marco Iacoboni. 2008. "Beyond Superior Temporal Cortex: Intersubject Correlations in Narrative Speech Comprehension." *Cerebral Cortex* 18, no. 1: 230–242.

Wilson, Timothy D., David B. Centerbar, Deborah A. Kermer, and Daniel T. Gilbert. 2005. "The Pleasures of Uncertainty: Prolonging Positive Moods in Ways People Do Not Anticipate." *Journal of Personality and Social Psychology* 88, no. 1: 5–21.

Windsor, Mark. 2019. "What is the Uncanny?" *The British Journal of Aesthetics* 59, no. 1: 51–65.

Wolf, Philipp. 1999. "'The Lightning Flash': Visionary Epiphanies, Suddenness, and History in the Later Work of W B Yeats." In *Moments of Moment: Aspects of the Literary Epiphany*, edited by Wim Tigges, 177–193. Amsterdam: Rodopi.

Woolf, Virginia. 1917. "Lord Jim." In *The Essays of Virginia Woolf*, edited by Andrew McNeillie. 1987. Volume II. 1912–1918, 140–142. London: The Hogarth Press.

———. 1918. "Moments of Vision." In *The Essays of Virginia Woolf*, edited by Andrew McNeillie. 1987. Volume II. 1912–1918, 250–252. London: The Hogarth Press.

———. 1928. "Moments of Being; "Slater's Pins Have No Points."" In *The Complete Shorter Fiction of Virginia Woolf*, edited by Susan Dick. 1985, 209–214. London: The Hogarth Press.
———. 1969. *Mrs Dalloway*. London: Penguin.
———. 2006. *To the Lighthouse*. Oxford: Oxford University Press.
Wordsworth, William. 1807. *Poems, in Two Volumes*. London: Printed for Longman, Hurst, Rees, and Orme.
Wu, Kaidi, and David Landau Dunning. 2018. "Hypocognition: Making Sense of the Landscape Beyond One's Conceptual Reach." *Review of General Psychology* 22, no. 1: 25–35.
Wundt, Wilhelm. 1874. *Grundzüge Der Physiologischen Psychologie*. Leipzig, Germany: Verlag von Wilhelm Engelmann.
Yandell, Keith E. 1993. *The Epistemology of Religious Experience*. Cambridge: Cambridge University Press.
Zacks, Jeffrey M., and Barbara Tversky. 2001. "Event Structure in Perception and Conception." *Psychological Bulletin* 127, no. 1: 3–21.
Zacks, Jeffrey M., Nicole K. Speer, and Jeremy R. Reynolds. 2009. "Segmentation in Reading and Film Comprehension." *Journal of Experimental Psychology: General* 138, no. 2: 307–327.
Zacks, Jeffrey M., Nicole K. Speer, Khena M. Swallow, Todd S. Braver, and Jeremy R. Reynolds. 2007. "Event Perception: A Mind-Brain Perspective." *Psychological Bulletin* 133, no. 2: 273–293.
Zajonc, Robert B. 1968. "Attitudinal Effects of Mere Exposure." *Journal of Personality and Social Psychology Monographs* 9, no. 2: 224–228.
Zak, Paul J. 2015. "Why Inspiring Stories Make Us React: The Neuroscience of Narrative." *Cerebrum: The Dana forum on Brain Science* 2015: 2.
Zakay, Dan, and Richard A. Block. 1996. "The Role of Attention in Time Estimation Processes." *Advances in Psychology* 115: 143–164.
Zemka, Sue. 2012. *Time and the Moment in Victorian Literature and Society*. Cambridge: Cambridge University Press.
Zentall, Thomas R. 2005. "Animals May Not Be Stuck in Time." *Learning and Motivation* 36, no. 2: 208–225.
Zhang, Dora. 2014. "Naming the Indescribable: Woolf, Russell, James and the Limits of Description." *New Literary History* 45, no. 1: 51–70.
Zickfeld, Janis H., Patrícia Arriaga, Sara Vilar Santos, Thomas W. Schubert, and Beate Seibt. 2020. "Tears of Joy, Aesthetic Chills and Heartwarming Feelings: Physiological Correlates of Kama Muta." *Psychophysiology* 57, no. 12: 2–26.
Ziolkowski, Theodore. 2014. "'Tolle Lege': Epiphanies of the Book." *Modern Language Review* 109, no. 1: 1–14.
Žižek, Slavoj. 1989. *The Sublime Object of Ideology*. London: Verso.
Zwaan, Rolf A., Joseph P. Magliano, and Arthur C. Graesser. 1995. "Dimensions of Situation Model Construction in Narrative Comprehension." *Journal of Experimental Psychology: Learning, Memory, and Cognition* 21: 386–397.
Zwaan, Rolf A., Mark C. Langston, and Arthur C. Graesser. 1995. "The Construction of Situation Models in Narrative Comprehension: An Event-Indexing Model." *Psychological Science* 6, no. 5: 292–297.
Zyngier, Sonia, Willie Van Peer, and Jémeljan Hakemulder. 2007. "Complexity and Foregrounding: In the Eye of the Beholder?" *Poetics Today* 28, no. 4: 653–682.

INDEX

Abraham, Anna 84, 143
Addison, Joseph 21, 57, 100
aesthetic emotion 16, 83, 84
affordance 37, 125
aha experience 37, 38, 68, 96, 117
Akiba, Fuminori 36, 166
Albertus Magnus 139
Alfieri, Vittorio 26
amygdala 82, 104–6, 134
Appel, Markus 134, 150
Armstrong, Thomas 36
arousal 4, 10, 13, 15–17, 22, 24, 28, 30, 34, 37, 55, 64, 79–97, 100, 103, 105, 107, 110, 112, 119, 120, 129, 131, 132, 134, 137–39, 149, 151, 174, 179
attention 17, 34, 46, 102, 105, 110, 111, 113, 116–20, 124, 130, 133, 150, 155, 158, 161, 168, 170, 173, 175
Auerbach, Erich 156
Augustine 173
Austen, Jane 61
autonoetic quality 47, 53, 101, 124
awe 4, 24, 25, 29, 30, 35, 85, 89, 95

Baddeley, Alan D. 111
Baillie, John 99
Barfoot, C. C. 40
Barraza, Jorge A. 95, 96, 129
Barthes, Roland 174, 178
Bartlett, Frederick C. 47, 137
Barwick, Linda 156, 160
Bauman, Richard 144, 147
Beja, Morris 3, 29, 39, 65, 75, 119, 142, 154, 156–58, 164
Bell, Claudia 70, 87, 164
Benedek, Mathias 88–90, 95
Benjamin, Walter 124, 130, 157, 167, 177

Bergson, Henri 123
Berlyne, Daniel E. 107, 109, 110, 113, 118, 144
Bezdek, Matthew A. 128
Bharucha, Jamshed J. 108
Biddle, Jennifer L. 55
Bidney, Martin 35, 40
Biederman, Irving 91
Bindra, Dalbir 92
Bishop, Jonathan 160
Blair, Hugh 148, 170
Blood, Anne J. 91, 133
Blood, Benjamin 122
Bloom, Harold 26
Bohrer, Karl Heinz 15, 119
Bohrn, Isabel C. 107, 114, 117, 167
Bortolussi, Marisa 132
Botterill, Steven 71, 73
Boyer, Pascal 11, 13, 50, 108
Brady, Emily 22
breathing 31, 88, 95, 96
Brecht, Bertolt 157, 167, 178
Brewer, William F. 150
Brontë, Charlotte 56, 154
Brown, Alan S. 126
Browning, Robert 55, 119, 147
Bruya, Brian 111, 117
Bühler, Karl 38
Bullot, Nicholas J. 113
Bunyan, John 40, 172
Burke, Edmund 22, 25, 82, 88, 89, 99, 100, 106, 129, 137, 157, 159, 169

Carston, Robyn 165
Chard, Chloe 154, 164
Chater, Nick 27, 110

chills 1, 4, 17, 27, 38, 80, 82, 85, 88–92, 96, 107, 133, 134, 145, 179
Chopin, Kate 141
Chun, Marvin M. 117, 118
Clark, Kenneth 2, 130
Cleary, Anne M. 14, 126
Clore, Gerald L. 60, 67, 137
closure 18, 35, 110, 116, 143, 145–47, 158
Cohen, Gillian 133
Coldstream, Nicola 160
Coleridge, Samuel Taylor 146, 159
Collingwood, R. G. 96
complexity 17, 51, 112, 118, 144, 145, 149
confirmation bias 113, 135, 136
Conrad, Joseph 41
Conway, Martin A. 135
Cook, Guy 48
Coplan, Amy 65
Corlett, Philip R. 122
Cosmides, Leda 84
Craik, Fergus I. M. 112
Crotch, William 59
crying: *see* tears
Csikszentmihalyi, Mihaly 118
Čukić, Iva 133
Culross ecstasy 120, 176
Cupchik, Gerald C. 107, 113, 115, 117
curiosity 109–10, 117, 134

Dalton, Douglas M. 27
Darwin, Charles 81, 92
Davy, Humphry 91
de Baca, Janet C' 34, 71
de Chirico, Giorgio 123
de Clerq, Raphael 76
de Saussure, Ferdinand 178
Decety, Jean 127
defamiliarization 26, 110, 113, 117, 126, 151, 168, 181
default mode network 84, 112, 117, 118
déjà vu 4, 7, 14, 46, 47, 125–27
Deleuze, Gilles 164
delusion 121–22, 124, 125
Dennis, John 22, 59
Detweiler-Bedell, Brian 36
Dick, Philip K. 156
Dickinson, Emily 141
difficulty of processing 23, 112, 113, 115, 145

Dixon, Peter 132
Donne, John 40, 149
dopamine 104, 121–22, 124, 125, 133
Dorter, Kenneth 169
double 11, 15, 30, 50, 61, 144, 168, 170, 171, 174
Douglas, Mary 51
Douglas, Shawn 69, 128, 166
Dutton, Donald G. 138

ecstasy 3, 5, 30–32, 34, 70, 72, 75, 88, 92, 95, 100, 118, 120, 122, 132, 159, 176
Efran, Jay S. 93, 96
Einstein, Albert 37, 38
Eliot, George 39
Eliot, T. S. 31, 55, 129
Elkins, James 29, 59, 92, 95, 97
Ellis, Catherine 156
Emerson, Ralph Waldo 138
Emmott, Catherine 155, 175
emotion 4, 10, 15–16, 22, 25, 26, 33, 34, 36, 50, 54, 59, 69, 80–86, 89, 91, 92, 94, 104–7, 118, 127–30, 136, 137, 151
emotional contagion 64
empathy 10, 17, 29, 32, 36, 42, 65, 67, 76, 85, 92, 122, 127–30, 135, 146, 151, 152, 156, 166
Enfield, Nick 7, 126
epiphany 1, 2, 6, 34, 35, 37–39, 48, 54, 66, 74, 100, 113, 118, 123–26, 130–32,138, 147–48, 156–59, 161–62, 164, 171–72, 179
episodic memory 52, 55, 101, 124, 164
epistemic feeling 5, 16, 17, 21, 30, 33, 37, 45–47, 58, 67, 70, 80, 114, 121, 122, 132, 166, 174, 179
Ernst, Max 170
Eskine, Kendall J. 82
Etlyn, Richard A. 159
event structure 48, 116, 149, 151–57
expectation 13, 15, 50, 101, 105, 106, 108, 121, 128, 145, 150, 152, 179, 181

Fabb, Nigel 52, 111, 116, 132, 142, 146, 168
feeling of knowing 67–69
Ferri, Sabrina 26, 87
fight-flight-freeze 13, 21, 85, 92, 95, 103, 129, 134

INDEX 213

flashbulb memory 54, 56, 124, 148
Fletcher, Paul C. 121, 124
flow 118, 150
fluency of processing 47, 100, 110, 114–15, 126, 145
Fodor, Jerry 9, 45, 46, 74
Folk, Charles L. 118
Ford, John 155
Foster, Meadhbh I. 66, 70, 103, 114, 152
fragment 15, 24, 34, 54–55, 148, 172–76
Freedberg, David 97, 130
Freud, Sigmund 4, 13, 30, 108, 126
Frey, William H. 93
Friedrich, Paul 148, 171
fringe experience 46, 53, 114, 116
Frith, Chris 62, 117, 121, 124, 125
Frye, Northrop 161

Gabrielsson, Alf 1, 5, 8, 64, 71, 144
Garry, Maryanne 115
Gell, Alfred 129
gender 134
Gerrig, Richard 83, 109, 127, 150
Gibbon, John 119
Gibbs, Raymond W. 167
Gibson, James J. 37, 118, 125
Gil, Sandrine 119, 120
Glucksberg, Sam 167
Goethe, Johann Wolfgang von 59
Goldstein, Avram 90, 91
goosebumps 4, 22, 34, 36, 64, 80, 86, 88–90
goosetears 88
Graesser, Arthur C. 113, 151
granularity 48, 124, 133, 153, 172
Green, Melanie C. 150
Grewe, Oliver 89, 90, 95, 96, 134
Griffiths, Thomas L. 150
Gross, James J. 93

Haidt, Jonathan 3, 4, 30, 35–37
Halle, Morris 146, 149
Hanauer, David 133
Hart, Joseph 67
Heaney, Seamus 39, 42, 57, 67
heart rate 31, 88, 89, 96, 102–3, 133, 139, 144
Heilman, Kenneth M. 122
Hein, Grit 128

Henke, Suzette 157
Hernandez, Ivan 113
Herrington, Tony 38
Hoeken, Hans 150
Hogan, Patrick 50, 145
Holmes, Emily A. 55
Homer 23, 143, 177
Hopkins, Gerard Manley 123, 132
Housman, A. E. 32, 79, 92, 96, 138, 172
Huron, David 4, 13, 16, 36, 85, 88, 93, 95, 96, 101–4, 109, 115, 138, 150
Hymes, Dell 156, 157
hypercognition 7, 16, 43, 136
hypocognition 7, 16, 43, 127, 131, 136, 180

Illich, Ivan 177
Inbody, Joel 89
ineffability 5, 10, 21, 27, 34, 41, 46, 48, 55, 56, 63, 67, 71–77, 80, 100, 116, 128
infectiousness 5, 15, 61, 64, 142, 147
intertextuality 53–54, 57, 67, 136
introspection 135–39
Iser, Wolfgang 60
Ishizu, Tomohiro 22, 82

Jakobson, Roman 144, 148, 168
James, William 2, 6, 25, 27–29, 46–47, 67, 71, 72, 81, 92, 116, 122, 125, 136, 172
Jaspers, Karl 121
Jeffries, Lesley 49
Jensen, Jakob 134, 150, 151
Jentsch, Ernst 30, 108
Johnson, Marcia K. 150
Joyce, James 2, 13, 35, 39, 57, 65, 123, 131, 143, 158, 162, 172, 177
Juslin, Patrik 59

Kaeppler, Adrienne L. 166
Kahneman, Daniel 112, 117
Kames, Lord 95, 170
Kang, Yul H.R. 68, 125
Kant, Immanuel 2, 21, 25–27, 47, 60, 100, 103, 128, 159, 165, 177, 180
Keane, Mark T. 66, 70, 103, 114, 152
Keats, John 32, 59, 79
Keltner, Dacher 3, 4, 30, 35–37
ketamine 122
Keyser, Samuel Jay 149

Kim, Sharon 3
Kirk, Ulrich 133
Kirwan, James 22
Köhler, Wolfgang 38
Konečni, Vladimir J. 90, 91
Konijn, Ellya 83
Koopman, Eva Maria 127
Kreilkamp, Ivan 148
Kuiken, Don 27, 37, 69, 113, 128, 165

Labov, William 145, 158
Lamb, Jonathan 57
Langbaum, Robert 3, 40, 158
Lanz, Henry 149
Laski, Marghanita 3, 5, 8, 30–32, 34, 59, 63, 70, 72, 88, 91, 95, 96, 120, 132, 134, 136, 159, 176, 177
Laub, Doris 38
laughter 24, 85, 86, 96, 106
Leder, Helmut 114
LeDoux, Joseph 104
Lessing, Gotthold Ephraim 166
Levy, Robert 7, 16, 30, 43, 127, 131, 136
Leypoldt, Günther 146
liminality 25, 32, 35, 41, 65, 132, 148, 154–56, 158, 160–65, 173, 177
literary epiphany 3, 35, 39–43, 75, 100, 119, 138, 156
Loewenstein, George 27, 109
Longinus 7, 22–24, 59, 113, 148, 165, 169, 170, 177
looming 21, 24, 26, 71, 105
López-Sintas, Jordi 118
Losey, Jay 42, 142
Lowth, Robert 22
Luhrmann, Tanya M. 62
Lyotard, Jean-François 26

Magherini, Graziella 4, 96
Magliano, Joseph P. 127, 152
Maltby, Paul 40, 42
Mandler, George 107
Mangan, Bruce 46, 67
Mar, Raymond A. 134, 151
Margulis, Elizabeth H. 88, 95, 170
Maruskin, Laura A. 87, 90, 134
Marvell, Andrew 40, 149
Maslow, Abraham 29, 32–35, 71

Massey, Doreen 164
McCrae, Robert R. 134
McGlone, Matthew S. 115
McGregor, Ronald 77
McNamara, Patrick 6, 29, 56, 71, 125, 133, 135
Mendelssohn, Moses 15, 24, 89, 96, 99, 171
Menninghaus, Winfried 106
mental representation 9, 45–46, 48, 52, 57, 74
metacognition 10, 14, 25, 31, 37, 43, 46, 47, 52, 54, 60, 62, 70, 84, 100, 113, 127, 131, 138, 170, 172, 177, 180
metacognitive surprise 13–15, 42, 61, 66, 77, 172, 180–82
metaphor 23, 54, 58, 63–64, 66, 76, 128, 155, 165–68, 171
metarepresentation 9–10, 46, 60, 61, 66, 127, 131
metre 24, 114–16, 142, 146–49
Meyer, Leonard B. 105
Meyer, Wulf-Uwe 12, 49, 101, 102, 152
Miall, David 26, 113
Miceli, Maria 22
Michaelis, Christian Friedrich 50
Miller, Christopher R. 14
Miller, William 3, 4, 34, 71
Mishara, Aaron L. 121, 122
moment of being 3, 55
moment of vision 2, 3, 13, 40, 42
Monk, Samuel H. 25
mood 65, 81, 121, 142
Moore, Thomas 21
Mori, Kazuma 93, 133
Morley, Simon 26, 95, 129
Morphy, Howard 132
motif 35, 176–78
multiple 11, 15, 50, 61, 144, 168, 170, 171, 177
music 1, 2, 4–6, 13, 18, 27, 32, 34, 38, 45–46, 50, 59, 69, 71, 74, 76, 83, 86, 88–92, 95–97, 101, 107–9, 131, 133, 138, 141, 144, 148, 156, 158, 161, 170
mystical experience 1–5, 27–30, 33, 34, 71, 72, 122, 126, 159

INDEX

Nabokov, Vladimir 138
narrative 2, 42, 54, 55, 71, 83, 105, 107, 109, 112, 115, 127, 128, 143, 145, 149–59, 166, 181
Nelson, Lowry 76
Neppe, Vernon M. 125
Newman, Barnett 69
Nichols, Ashton 39, 42, 67, 147, 162, 176
Nickerson, Raymond S. 135
Nielsen, F. V. 149
Nisbett, Richard E. 135
noetic quality 27, 33, 47, 67
nonshivering thermogenesis 94
Noordewier, Marret K. 16, 85

Oatley, Keith 107, 109, 113, 129
Öhman, Arne 71, 95, 102
openness to experience 35, 133, 134
orienting response 102
Ortony, Anthony 16, 48, 49, 165
Otto, Rudolf 29, 30, 34
Owen, G. 121
Owen, Stephen 77
oxytocin 90, 91, 97, 128

Panksepp, Jaak 27, 80, 89–91, 97, 134
Panzarella, Robert 34, 118, 174
parallelism 23, 114, 144, 157, 168–71
Pater, Walter N. 119
peak experience 3, 32–34, 37, 135, 174
Pelowski, Matthew J. 36, 92, 166
Pennebaker, James W. 60
Piaget, Jean 27, 35, 36
Piff, Paul K. 36
piloerection: *see* goosebumps
poetic effects 58, 70, 76, 166
Polito, Vince 132
Potter, Sally 143
prediction error 104, 121–22, 124–28, 152
prediction error, false 121, 124–25
processing effort 17, 110–16, 117, 128, 145, 147, 149, 151, 152, 155, 158, 167, 168, 170, 171, 175
prolactin 85, 90, 91, 93, 97
Proust, Joëlle 47
Proust, Marcel 39, 73, 88, 119, 174

quantum change 4, 34

Radvansky, Gabriel A. 127, 151
Raffman, Diana 46, 74, 76
Ramachandran, V. S. 50
Ramey, Peter 158
Rapp, Alexander M. 167
Reber, Rolf 17, 47, 113, 114
Recanati, François 63
Reisenzein, Rainer 12, 49, 101, 152
relevance theory 57–59, 70, 114, 165, 168
religion 3, 10, 11, 13, 27, 29, 31, 33, 34, 39, 55–6, 59, 63, 108, 125, 133, 136
Renbourn, Edward 94
Reynolds, Joshua 99
Richards, I. A. 135
Richardson, Alan 22, 26, 60
Rickard, Nikki S. 83, 87, 88, 95
Ricoeur, Paul 54, 155, 156, 159, 166
ritual 64, 130, 132, 160, 166
Robinson, Michael D. 137
Rubin, David C. 53, 54
Rumelhart, David E. 48, 49, 101, 165

Sachs, Matthew E. 134
Salimpoor, Valorie N. 88, 89, 91, 95, 96
Santayana, George 100
Scharfstein, Ben-Ami 76
schema 10–15, 17, 23–30, 36–37, 41–42, 45, 47–52, 61, 66, 75, 92–93, 99–109, 111, 113, 124, 128, 137, 142–44, 149, 151, 161, 165, 179–82
Scherer, Klaus R. 76, 81–83, 104, 107, 132
Schmidt, Gwenda L. 112
Schoeller, Félix 38, 146
Schooler, Jonathan W. 38
Schopenhauer, Arthur 123, 177
Schurtz, David R. 89
Schwan, Stephan 116
Schwitzgebel, Eric 135
self 29, 34, 36, 37, 53, 65, 67, 71, 82, 87, 128, 133, 135, 139, 157, 166
Semino, Elena 48
semi-propositional representation 10, 52, 62, 66, 76
serotonin 133
Shaftesbury, Earl of 165
Shaw, Philip 165, 171

Sheller, Mimi 164
Shurtz, David R. 36
significance 2–4, 27, 42, 46, 47, 58, 66, 69–71, 102, 123, 131, 157, 160, 166, 172–74, 181
Sikora, Shelley S. 113
Silvia, Paul J. 107, 118
Sircello, Guy 22
skin conductance level 85, 93, 95, 133
Skolnick, Deena 84
Sloboda, John 1, 5, 33, 86, 92, 96, 144, 150, 158
Smallwood, Jonathan 117
Smith, Alison 29, 159
Smith, Barbara Herrnstein 18, 110, 116, 147, 158
Smith, Logan Pearsall 40
Spangler, Timothy J. 93, 96
Speidel, Suzanne 155
Sperber, Dan 9, 51, 57, 59, 62, 70, 111, 114, 135, 166
spine, shiver down 42, 79, 90, 138
Stange, Ken 29, 33
Stearns, Carol Z. 16
Stearns, Peter N. 16
Stendhal's syndrome 4, 96, 164, 175
Stetson, Chess 120
Stevenson, Robert Louis 166
stomach 64, 80, 86, 96
strong experience 1–5, 179–82
sublime 1, 2, 13, 15, 17, 21–27, 29, 35–37, 47, 50, 57, 59, 60, 69–71, 82, 87, 89, 95, 99–100, 103, 108, 113, 128–31, 148, 154, 157, 159, 164–66, 169–71, 179
Suddendorf, Thomas 52, 53
Sullivan, Paul 75
Sumpf, Maria 88, 96, 135
Sundararajan, Louise 29
surprise 1, 4, 6–16, 23, 24, 32–34, 49–50, 61, 66, 70, 74, 85, 93, 95–97, 99–109, 113–15, 121–22, 124, 126, 128, 138, 142–3, 146, 149–50, 152, 163, 167, 179
surprise discourse organization 150
Sutherland, Graham 2, 13, 130
sweating 85, 86, 94
Symons, Arthur 119

Tang, Yi-Yuan 111, 117
Tangerås, Thor Magnus 37, 39, 60, 64, 127
Taruffi, Liila 83, 90
tears 1, 2, 4, 22, 37, 59, 64, 79, 80, 83, 85, 88, 92–94, 142, 144, 158, 173, 179
Tennyson, Alfred 176
tension 25, 77, 105, 111, 146, 148, 161
Thrale, Hester 99
thrill 1, 5, 17, 28, 33, 49, 61, 64, 69, 80, 82, 86, 87, 89, 91, 104–6, 116, 131, 141, 144, 179
thrill, catching a: *see* infectiousness
Tigges, Wim 39, 40, 158
Tinti, Carla 53
Tobin, Vera 150
transportation 134, 150
trauma 38, 55, 56
Treloyn, Sally 161
trembling 24, 86, 89, 142
trigger 4, 5, 13–17, 31, 34, 35, 53, 61, 66, 70, 81, 82, 84, 86, 89, 91, 107–08, 126, 131–32, 137, 141–78
Tulving, Endel 47, 52, 53, 55, 112
Turner, Victor 160
Turpin, Myfany 132
Tversky, Barbara 151–53, 155

uncanny 4, 13, 17, 30, 50, 108, 121, 126, 144, 166, 171, 174

valence 10, 16, 81, 82, 84, 90, 95, 106, 115
Van Eck, Caroline 129, 165
van Gennep, Arnold 160
vasoconstriction 85, 88–90
Vermeer, Johannes 175
Vingerhoets, Ad 92–94
Visch, Valentijn T. 151
von Hoffmansthal, Hugo 15
von Meysenbug, Malwida 28

Wassiliwizky, Eugen 17, 88, 89, 92, 116
Weiskel, Thomas 129
Wesley, John 94
Whitehouse, Harvey 55, 64
Whittier-Ferguson, John 57
Whittlesea, Bruce W. A. 68, 100
Williams, Helen Maria 139
Wilson, Deirdre 58, 70, 114, 165

Wilson, Stephen M. 112
Wilson, Timothy D. 59, 135
Woolf, Virginia 3, 39, 40, 55, 57, 75, 145, 154, 161, 172
Wordsworth, William 14, 39, 57, 65–67, 71–2, 87, 95, 100, 123, 134, 146, 160, 162, 171
working memory 102, 110–11, 116–17
Wundt, Wilhelm 113, 144, 148

Yandell, Keith E. 29

Zacks, Jeffrey 116, 127, 151–53, 155
Zak, Paul J. 129
Zatorre, Robert J. 91, 133
Zeki, Semir 22, 82
Zemka, Sue 42, 55, 119, 157
Zentall, Thomas R. 53
Zhang, Dora 75
Zickfeld, Janis H. 86, 92
Ziolkowski, Theodore 39, 161, 174
Žižek, Slavoj 26
Zwaan, Rolf A. 107, 151

www.ingramcontent.com/pod-product-compliance
Lightning Source LLC
Chambersburg PA
CBHW021141230426
43667CB00005B/206